4/6/01 highlighter pps 198

MASS MEDIA

OPPOSING VIEWPOINTS®

Other Books of Related Interest in the Opposing Viewpoints Series:

MASS MEDIA
OPPOSING VIEWPOINTS®

David Bender & Bruno Leone, *Series Editors*

William Barbour, *Book Editor*

OPPOSING
VIEWPOINTS
SERIES®

Greenhaven Press, Inc.   PO Box 289009   San Diego, CA 92198-9009

Cover photo: © Owen McGoldrick/CNN News

Library of Congress Cataloging-in-Publication Data

Mass media : opposing viewpoints / William Barbour, book editor.
    p.   cm. — (Opposing viewpoints series)
    Includes bibliographical references and index.
    ISBN 1-56510-107-3 (lib. bdg. : alk. paper) — ISBN 1-56510-106-5 (pbk. : alk. paper)
    1. Mass media. I. Barbour, William, 1963–   II. Series: Opposing viewpoints series (Unnumbered)
P91.25.M27 1994
302.23—dc20   93-30960
                                                  CIP
                                                    AC

"Congress shall make no law . . .
abridging the freedom of speech,
or of the press."

First Amendment to the U.S. Constitution

The basic foundation of our democracy is the first amendment guarantee of freedom of expression. The Opposing Viewpoints Series is dedicated to the concept of this basic freedom and the idea that it is more important to practice it than to enshrine it.

Contents

Why Consider Opposing Viewpoints?

"The only way in which a human being can make some approach to knowing the whole of a subject is by hearing what can be said about it by persons of every variety of opinion and studying all modes in which it can be looked at by every character of mind. No wise man ever acquired his wisdom in any mode but this."

John Stuart Mill

In our media-intensive culture it is not difficult to find differing opinions. Thousands of newspapers and magazines and dozens of radio and television talk shows resound with differing points of view. The difficulty lies in deciding which opinion to agree with and which "experts" seem the most credible. The more inundated we become with differing opinions and claims, the more essential it is to hone critical reading and thinking skills to evaluate these ideas. Opposing Viewpoints books address this problem directly by presenting stimulating debates that can be used to enhance and teach these skills. The varied opinions contained in each book examine many different aspects of a single issue. While examining these conveniently edited opposing views, readers can develop critical thinking skills such as the ability to compare and contrast authors' credibility, facts, argumentation styles, use of persuasive techniques, and other stylistic tools. In short, the Opposing Viewpoints Series is an ideal way to attain the higher-level thinking and reading skills so essential in a culture of diverse and contradictory opinions.

In addition to providing a tool for critical thinking, Opposing Viewpoints books challenge readers to question their own strongly held opinions and assumptions. Most people form their opinions on the basis of upbringing, peer pressure, and personal, cultural, or professional bias. By reading carefully balanced opposing views, readers must directly confront new ideas as well as the opinions of those with whom they disagree. This is not to simplistically argue that everyone who reads opposing views will—or should—change his or her opinion. Instead, the series enhances readers' depth of understanding of their own views by encouraging confrontation with opposing ideas. Careful examination of others' views can lead to the readers' understanding of the logical inconsistencies in their own opinions, perspective on why they hold an opinion, and the consideration of the possibility that their opinion requires further evaluation.

Evaluating Other Opinions

To ensure that this type of examination occurs, Opposing Viewpoints books present all types of opinions. Prominent spokespeople on different sides of each issue as well as well-known professionals from many disciplines challenge the reader. An additional goal of the series is to provide a forum for other, less known, or even unpopular viewpoints. The opinion of an ordinary person who has had to make the decision to cut off life support from a terminally ill relative, for example, may be just as valuable and provide just as much insight as a medical ethicist's professional opinion. The editors have two additional purposes in including these less known views. One, the editors encourage readers to respect others' opinions—even when not enhanced by professional credibility. It is only by reading or listening to and objectively evaluating others' ideas that one can determine whether they are worthy of consideration. Two, the inclusion of such viewpoints encourages the important critical thinking skill of objectively evaluating an author's credentials and bias. This evaluation will illuminate an author's reasons for taking a particular stance on an issue and will aid in readers' evaluation of the author's ideas.

As series editors of the Opposing Viewpoints Series, it is our hope that these books will give readers a deeper understanding of the issues debated and an appreciation of the complexity of even seemingly simple issues when good and honest people disagree. This awareness is particularly important in a democratic society such as ours in which people enter into public debate to determine the common good. Those with whom one disagrees should not be regarded as enemies but rather as people whose views deserve careful examination and may shed light on one's own.

Thomas Jefferson once said that "difference of opinion leads to inquiry, and inquiry to truth." Jefferson, a broadly educated man, argued that "if a nation expects to be ignorant and free . . . it expects what never was and never will be." As individuals and as a nation, it is imperative that we consider the opinions of others and examine them with skill and discernment. The Opposing Viewpoints Series is intended to help readers achieve this goal.

David L. Bender & Bruno Leone,
Series Editors

Introduction

"The prospect of multiplying today's TV listings has launched a furious debate over what . . . society will do with 100—or 500—offerings. Will scores of narrowcast channels . . . fracture whatever remains of a mass culture, leaving Americans with little common ground for discourse?"

Philip Elmer-Dewitt, Time, April 12, 1993

A rarity at the end of World War II, the television set now occupies a central place in most American homes. Its importance in American life is indicated by the fact that, according to writer Andrew L. Shapiro, "Americans spend almost thirty hours a week watching television, the most of any nation for which data is available." In the near future, new technological advancements are expected to revolutionize the medium. It is predicted that the fusion of telephone, computer, and television technologies will transform the ordinary television set into an interactive multimedia device that will offer news, movies, sports, books, magazines, video games, shopping, and other services on demand. Experts anticipate that all this information will travel on an "electronic superhighway" composed of state-of-the-art coaxial and fiber-optic cables that will be able to transmit as many as five hundred television channels simultaneously.

Many people worry that the availability of five hundred channels will fragment American society. They credit early television's limited number of channels and limited variety of programming with helping to create and sustain a "mass culture"— a shared sense of the nation's identity and values. According to Matt James, communications director of the Kaiser Family Foundation in Menlo Park, California, "For the past 40 years, television has helped America share experiences." James and others fear that because producers of the future will target small audiences—a practice referred to as "narrowcasting"—society will no longer be united by the experience of watching the same television programming. Instead, they argue, channels aimed exclusively at women, blacks, youth, gays, and other specific groups may divide society into separate subcultures. According to James, "The cross-pollination of cultures, ideas and opinions may actually be eroded by a megachannel system. The system that many hope will ensure diversity may instead ensure that individual groups will tune out others' opinions and experiences."

Other commentators believe that a diversity of television channels will help unify society. They contend that rather than uniting the nation in a mass culture, the television programming of the 1950s and 1960s divided the country by perpetuating, in the words of professor of government Frederick R. Lynch, "an overly sanitized, homogenized, middle-class, white world-view" that excluded minorities and working-class citizens. Many people hope that the coming diversification of programming will incorporate the groups and interests previously excluded from the media and expose the populace to the reality of a heterogeneous American society. Moreover, Joshua Meyrowitz, a professor of communication, and John Maguire, a freelance science journalist, suggest that narrowcasting will not fragment society into "subcultural enclaves" because everyone will have access to the same channels. They write, "Though the media may be fragmenting, we are all experiencing this fragmentation together. So we remain unified." Charles Oliver, a writer for *Investor's Business Daily*, agrees: "In the future, Americans will not be united by a bland, one-size-fits-all culture. But they will not be divided into multitudes of tiny subcultures either. They will be united by a common cultural bazaar."

Whether the new television technology will fragment America into subcultures or encourage diversity, experts agree that the role of television and other media in American society is shifting dramatically. These changes are reflected in the various arguments included in *Mass Media: Opposing Viewpoints*, which contains the following chapters: Are the Media Biased? Do the Media Accurately Reflect American Society? How Do the Media Influence Society? Should the Media Be Regulated? How Do the Media Affect Politics? and Is Advertising Harmful to Society? The varying opinions expressed here reveal and explore the important place the mass media occupy in American society and culture.

Are the Media Biased?

Chapter Preface

Many people believe that the media should provide the public with an objective representation of facts and events. According to columnist William Murchison, the media "exist for the purpose of developing and transmitting the information a democratic society uses to make decisions." Murchison and others argue that journalists should be neutral observers, keeping their opinions and partisan loyalties out of their reports. "Information," says Murchison, "like meat, should arrive untainted."

While most commentators agree that objective reporting is the ideal, few believe it is possible in practice. Because journalists are human beings, not cameras and tape recorders, they are, in the words of Heritage Foundation scholar Ted J. Smith III, "prisoners of their own subjective views."

The news profession has developed guidelines to guard against biased reporting. According to journalism professor Robert Miraldi, journalistic conventions dictate that reporters must strive for "balance" in each story by presenting various points of view. Furthermore, good policy mandates that all facts and explanations must be supported by evidence and attributed to sources other than the reporter.

However, some commentators argue that the very conventions of objective reporting enable journalists to slant their reporting to express their own biased views. For example, even while following the "rules," journalists are able to convey their own opinions by attributing them to outside sources. Jack Nelson of the *Los Angeles Times* describes the process of shopping for the right source: "When you are going to make an opinionated kind of statement, particularly in the news columns, editors insist you attribute it to someone other than yourself—so you go shopping." Even while claiming to be objective, according to Lawrence C. Soley, "journalists simply 'marshal facts or quotes' that are consistent with their presumptions. Information that is inconsistent with the slant of their stories is discarded."

Whether the guidelines for objective reporting guard against or encourage biased reporting, the debate over bias in the media is fervent. Some believe the media promote a liberal bias, others see the media as the champions of corporate America, and still others contend the media are mechanisms of government propaganda. The viewpoints in the following chapter reflect these conflicting perceptions of bias in the media.

"Journalists as a group are very liberal—more liberal than the general public and more liberal than others with similar backgrounds."

The News Media Reflect a Liberal Bias

Steven Allen

In the following viewpoint, Steven Allen argues that America's limited primary media sources present a slanted picture of the world that emphasizes liberal ideology and downplays conservative views. The media's liberal bias, he argues, can be gleaned from the beliefs, affiliations, and statements of journalists, and has been demonstrated by studies of their word choices, their policy recommendations, and their tendency to stress the liberal agenda over conservative interests. Allen believes that the biased media shape public opinion to favor liberal ideology and reject conservative opinion. Allen is a Washington, D.C., writer who specializes in policy issues.

As you read, consider the following questions:

1. According to Allen, why did media bias matter less in the past?
2. Why is the public so often surprised by the course of events, according to the author?
3. How do the news media control the nation's agenda, according to Allen?

Writers, editors, and producers of the national news media claim to be objective. They contend that they "just report the truth," arguing that a person's personal political philosophy has no more effect on the work of journalists than on the work of scientists and engineers.

But to report on abortion or taxes or national defense is not like counting the clicks on a Geiger counter or calculating the distance to the moon. Journalism is inherently subjective; a journalist's approach to a story invariably reflects his opinions.

No one would accept the statement of a Ku Klux Klansman, in line for a judgeship, that he was capable of applying the civil rights laws objectively, without regard to his personal opinions. Yet the argument is advanced by members of the media that a reporter can cover George Bush fairly even if he believes that Bush is a tool of fascist warmongers and racist plutocrats.

"Big Media"

In days past, the biases of individual journalists mattered less because the journalistic profession allowed for a greater diversity of views.

Though the first two television networks with news, CBS and NBC, offered little variety in the 1950s, then and earlier most towns had at least two newspapers that served to act as a check on each other. If there were a strike at the local steel mill, the *Daily Democrat* would blame it on money-grubbing capitalists and the *Daily Republican* would blame it on radical out-of-town labor agitators. A reader could pick the paper that reflected his philosophy—or he could read both papers and figure out what was *really* happening.

Today, most cities have only one daily newspaper. Few radio stations cover local news other than car wrecks and shootings, and most local TV stations hire news personnel more for their looks than for their reporting ability. . . .

Most coverage of national news comes from a few sources, referred to [here] as "Big Media"—*The New York Times, The Washington Post* (which also publishes *Newsweek*), *The Wall Street Journal*, Gannett (which publishes *USA Today* and other papers), *Time*, AP and UPI, ABC, NBC, CBS, PBS, and the Cable News Network (CNN). Roughly the same political attitudes are held by reporters, editors, and producers for the national news media. Exceptions are rare. Virtually every newspaper gets national news stories off the AP and UPI wire machines. In addition, both *The New York Times* and *The Washington Post* own news services that distribute their stories across the country. . . .

However a national news story is credited, wherever it appears, it almost certainly originated at one of a handful of news organizations based in Washington and New York.

As a result, the American people get a slanted picture of their country and the world. That's why we are so often surprised by the course of events—for example, by Jimmy Carter's failures, Ronald Reagan's successes, and the crisis in world communism. In each case, the media told us to expect the opposite.

Conservatives, of course, foresaw Carter's failures, Reagan's successes and communism's decline, as well as the evil of the Ayatollah Khomeini, the drug-running dictatorship of Manuel Noriega, the malignant growth of the welfare state, the ethical lapses of [House Speaker] Jim Wright and his cronies—all of which took the national news media by surprise. But conservatives weren't selecting the stories to cover; they weren't picking the experts to quote; they weren't even present in the newsrooms when those decisions were made. The events seemed to come with no warning. Continuing befuddlement is the price we pay for the absence of conservatives in most of the major national media.

Asay, by permission of the *Colorado Springs Gazette Telegraph*.

But though bias in the media exists, it is rarely a conscious attempt to distort the news. It stems from the fact that most members of the media elite have little contact with conservatives and make little effort to understand the conservative viewpoint. Their friends are liberals, their sources are liberals, what they read and hear is written by liberals. This helps explain why policies considered "liberal" by the public are seen as "mainstream" by reporters and editors.

Conservatives are as rare in the nation's newsrooms as blacks and women once were (and, in some cases, still are). They're rare for much the same reason: Editors and producers, like all bosses, tend to hire people like themselves.

For decades, the media denied that they discriminated against blacks and women. When they finally recognized the problem, they began slowly to solve it. Likewise, if media bias is to be corrected, the first step is to acknowledge that the problem exists. . . .

No Smoking Gun

It should be noted that, in the case of media bias, there is no "smoking gun"—no single piece of evidence so incriminating that the defendant breaks down on the witness stand and confesses. Over the years, however, the Media Research Center and other organizations have developed methods of demonstrating media bias. Some methods are objective, like fingerprints on a murder weapon. Others are subjective, like eyewitness testimony. . . . The following methods quantify the media's bias:

1) Surveys of the political attitudes of journalists, particularly members of the media elite, and of journalism students.

These are conducted in the same way as opinion surveys of any group. A random sample is selected from the members of the group being studied. They are asked to respond to a series of questions regarding their attitudes about various political leaders and ideas. They are asked, for example, how they voted in recent elections, whether they consider themselves liberal or conservative, and which "experts" (liberal or conservative) they turn to for reliable information.

The results of the surveys . . . show that journalists as a group are very liberal—more liberal than the general public and more liberal than others with similar backgrounds. They are more likely to vote liberal, more likely to consider themselves liberals, and more likely to select a liberal instead of a conservative as a credible expert on a given subject. Journalism students, the future members of the media elite, are even more liberal than their elders.

2) Studies of journalists' previous professional connections.

Studies demonstrate that when members of the media elite engage in politics, their candidates or causes are usually liberal or Democratic. Conversely, the vast majority of former political activists currently working in the media have had professional ties to liberals and Democrats. In fact, every major national media outlet has reporters and executives who were previously professionally associated with liberals, e.g., Gary Hart's press secretary [became] the Political Editor for CBS News, a Jimmy Carter speechwriter [became] an Associate Editor of *U.S. News & World Report*, and an aide to Mario Cuomo [became] Washington Bureau Chief for NBC News. A relatively small number of journalists have had associations with conservatives or Republicans.

3) Collections of quotations in which prominent journalists reveal their beliefs about politics and/or about the proper role of their profession.

In unguarded moments—as when they grant interviews to friendly publications or speak to friendly audiences—prominent journalists often admit that they are liberals, or hold liberal views, or even promote a liberal political agenda. Walter Cronkite, for example, once declared, "I think most newspapermen by definition have to be liberal. If they're not liberal, by my definition of it, then they can hardly be good newspapermen."

Bias Through Labeling

One of the most subtle and effective ways to bias the news is through the use of labeling. Reporters tinker with the credibility of political groups by regularly identifying conservative groups as conservative but refusing to do the same for liberal organizations.

We surveyed every news story on 14 liberal groups and seven conservative ones from 1988, 1989 and 1990 in the Los Angeles *Times*, the New York *Times*, and the Washington *Post*. Our study documented that conservative groups were labeled more than liberal groups by a ratio of 14 to one. . . .

Readers don't have time to research the ideological perspective of every group they see quoted in news stories. They rely on the media, but reporters are not only failing to describe liberal groups as liberal; they're burnishing their credentials, making them more compassionate or more scientific than their conservative opponents.

The media's failure risks leaving readers uninformed about the intentions and agendas behind those commenting on public policy.

L. Brent Bozell III and Tim Graham, *Human Events*, July 27, 1991.

---

4) Word-use analysis.

Using the Nexis® computer system, researchers can isolate newspaper and magazine articles based on particular words or combinations of words. A researcher seeking articles in which Jesse Jackson was called anti-Semitic could ask the computer for all articles in which Reverend Jackson's name appeared within fifty words of the words "anti-Semitic," "anti-Semitism," "Farrakhan," "Hymietown," "Israel," or "Koch."

With this method, it was possible to determine, for example, how often in a given period *The Washington Post* called Senator Jesse Helms "ultraconservative" and Ted Kennedy "ultraliberal," or how often *The New York Times* mentioned "Reaganomics" in good economic times versus bad.

As it turned out, conservatives were far more likely than liberals to be painted as ideologues and extremists. Moreover, when derogatory labels ceased to be derogatory the media stopped using them. For instance, the media used the term "Reaganomics" to describe President Reagan's supply-side economic policies during the 1982 recession, but gave it up when the economy improved.

This type of word and topic analysis also allows researchers to determine how much coverage the media gave a particular subject. . . . News contradicting liberal ideology, such as the murder of millions of people in communist Cambodia, was often ignored, sometimes for years or decades. And when and if such news was reported, the role of the perpetrator—communism in the case of Cambodia—was usually played down or ignored. In another instance, charges made by conservatives that Jim Wright was corrupt were initially written off as the product of paranoia. Specifically, when conservative Congressman Newt Gingrich suggested in 1987 that the House ethics committee investigate the Speaker's financial dealings, Big Media ignored him. But when Common Cause, a liberal lobbying group, questioned Wright's ethics, the national news outlets decided to make it a big story.

Policy Recommendations of the Left

5) Studies of policies recommended in news stories.

Studies show that when reporters list possible solutions to society's problems, the solutions are almost always those of the Left—"raise taxes," "cut defense," "have taxpayers pay for abortions."

In the past, most news stories were content to relate a sequence of events, but recently an increasing number mix reporting with specific recommendations for government policy. *Time* magazine's "Planet of the Year" story at the end of 1988 included, as examples of the actions government "must" take to avoid ecological catastrophe, a wish list of liberal and ultraliberal ideas. "Raising the federal gasoline tax by 50 cents per gallon, from 9 cents to 59 cents, over the next 5 years would renew drivers' interest in fuel conservation" was one solution *Time* proposed.

By compiling lists of policy recommendations, we can determine how often the media endorsed conservative or liberal proposals. . . . Studies demonstrate the media consistently see higher taxes as the answer to federal budget problems. If spending must be cut, journalists prefer to trim defense rather than social programs. Moreover, when conservative economic policies are successful, they will track down any available hardship case to dampen the impact.

6) Comparisons of the agenda of the news media with the agendas of political candidates or organizations.

In this method, researchers count the number of seconds or lines given to controversial issues to determine which ones are given the greatest play. The issues are ranked, then the list is compared with the agendas of, say, the opposing parties in a political campaign. For example, Reagan's age was an issue on the agenda of the Democrats in 1984, and Geraldine Ferraro's finances were an issue on the Republican agenda. Which issue got more coverage?

Studies . . . reveal a pattern of playing up items on the liberal/Democratic agenda and playing down items on the conservative/Republican agenda.

7) Positive/negative coverage analysis.

This method involves two steps: first, classifying news stories and/or comments within news stories in respect to the subject as follows: "favorable," "unfavorable," "neutral," or "ambiguous." Second, analysts measure the relative number of stories, comments, or words that fall in each category. Most such studies simply count the number of transcribed lines or seconds of reporting that fall into each classification.

This is one of the more subjective techniques for measuring bias. Some stories are obviously negative or positive; a story about Richard Nixon that mentions Watergate in every line would unquestionably be negative toward Nixon, while a story about Jimmy Carter that concentrates on the Camp David Accord would just as clearly be positive toward Carter. In other cases, however, reasonable people could differ about whether some statements are favorable or unfavorable. This at times depends on the context: "Senator Phogbound admits he's homosexual" might be an unfavorable story in the *Moral Majority Report* but a favorable report in the *Gay Community News*.

But . . . in most cases the ratio of positive-to-negative stories, comments, and total words favors the Left beyond reasonable doubt. One study . . . finds, for instance, that during one period President Reagan's coverage in the national media was negative by a ratio of 20-to-1. Even if the researchers had an error rate of 10 to 20 percent, the ratio would still be overwhelming.

Why Does Media Bias Matter?

What difference does it make if the media are biased? After all, the media attacked Ronald Reagan constantly from the moment he entered politics and they couldn't stop him from being elected and reelected Governor of California and President of the United States.

No, they don't win every time, but they *do* win most of the time. As a wise man once said, the battle goes not always to the strong nor the race to the swift, but that's the way to bet.

By exercising control over the nation's agenda—picking and choosing which issues are fit for public debate, which news is "fit to print"—the news media can greatly influence the political direction of the country. They can ignore or ridicule some ideas and promote others. They can wreck a politician's career by taking a quote or two out of context or by spotlighting a weakness in his background. They can make winners look like losers and vice versa, knowing that, in the political world, appearance easily supplants reality.

The Left Sets the Agenda

Consider what happens in a political campaign. An able candidate will concentrate on gaining control of the agenda. If he has a pleasing personality and his opponent is a jerk, he will try to have the election decided on the basis of personality. If he is philosophically in tune with the district and his opponent is not, he will attempt to see that the election is decided on philosophical terms. The key factor may be race, religion, geography, economic class, party affiliation, or something else, but whichever, the winning candidate is typically the one who sets the agenda—picks the correct key factor—and puts his opponent on the defensive.

Now, envision American politics as a sort of permanent campaign in which one side almost always gets to set the agenda. That's the power the media give to the Left. For example:

• The media charge that conservatives are out of the political mainstream, that they can't get elected except in unusual circumstances or in backwater districts. As a result, some conservatives are discouraged from running for office. Some adopt more liberal positions to satisfy what the media present as the proper and popular view. Others run as conservatives anyway but can't raise sufficient funds because potential contributors think they "can't win," and then, of course, they don't. How many potential Ronald Reagans never got to first base in politics because of media bias?

• The media want greater government regulation and less individual choice, higher taxes and less take-home pay. A newspaper can win a Pulitzer Prize for advocating tax hikes and the Robert F. Kennedy Prize for advocating an expansion of the bureaucracy. There are no prizes for seeking to restore power to neighborhoods and to families. What price have working people and small business people paid for the massive expansion of government power fueled by this particular bias of the media?

• The media generally ignore atrocities in communist countries (unless, as in the Tienanmen Square Massacre, the atrocities occur within camera range). For forty years, the media depicted communism as the wave of the future in the Third World. They characterized anticommunists as threats to world peace. During the Vietnam War, they pictured the communists as nationalist reformers, valiant underdogs struggling against the imperialist United States. How long did the media prolong the Cold War, and how many people died as a result?

• The media treat technology as a fearsome thing. They aggravate people's natural fear of nuclear power, never pointing out its safety compared to power derived from fossil fuels. They publicize the adverse side effects of drugs, but, except in the cases of AIDS treatment, they ignore the suffering and death that result from unnecessary delays in the approval of new drugs. They mockingly label space-based defense "Star Wars" in an effort to kill it, never mentioning the alternative—Mutual Assured Destruction, a suicide pact with the Soviets. How successful have the media been in their efforts to impede the technological progress that would improve our standard of living, make us healthier, and help prevent war?

We All Pay

We all pay a price for media bias. As long as an autocratic orthodoxy rules the major national news organizations, the media will continue to defend the political status quo and turn a blind eye to corruption, even as they pride themselves on their independence and incorruptibility.

News people, being human, judge the virtue of ideas by the degree to which those ideas match their own beliefs and prejudices. Until conservatives are given fair access to the newsrooms of this country, and until the American people demand to see and hear both sides of the argument on the major issues of the day, the news media will continue to serve less as a referee than as a cheerleader for one side.

"The right influences the mass media by generating rightist themes . . . and then working these into the communication mainstream."

The News Media Reflect a Conservative Bias

Michael Parenti

In the following viewpoint, Michael Parenti contends that the views of the left are given limited media exposure relative to those of conservatives, who are often funded by large corporations and millionaires. Parenti analyzes media accounts of antigovernment, antiwar, and pro-labor demonstrations that, he says, ridiculed protesters, trivialized issues, and undercounted crowds in order to discredit left-wing opinions. Parenti holds a Ph.D. in political science from Yale University. His books include *Make-Believe Media: The Politics of Entertainment*, *Democracy for the Few*, and *Inventing Reality: The Politics of News Media*, from which this viewpoint is excerpted.

As you read, consider the following questions:

1. According to Parenti, why does the right have less popular support than the left for its political agenda?
2. Parenti says that political talk shows and newspaper columns present "a display of false balancing." In what ways are they unbalanced, according to Parenti?
3. According to the author, how do the news media scant the content of demonstrations?

From *Inventing Reality: The Politics of the News Media* by Michael Parenti, 2nd edition, © 1993 by St. Martin's Press, Inc., New York.

There exists not only public opinion but media opinions about public opinion. What the people think is one thing; what is *publicized* about what they think can be something else. The media cannot mold every political feeling we have, but they can fill the air with pronouncements about what our feelings allegedly are. The press may not be able to create a conservative mood within us but it can repeatedly announce that a conservative mood exists, thereby doing much to create the impression of such a mood and encouraging conservative forces to come to the fore. The press cannot stop protests, but it can discredit and ignore them, thereby discouraging popular political actions. In short, even more than manipulating actual opinions, the media have a great deal of power in controlling *opinion visibility*. They create a media image of public opinion that often plays a more crucial role in setting the issue agenda than does actual public opinion and which has a feedback effect on actual opinion. . . .

Both the left and right try to extend their influence into the political mainstream. The left, by mobilizing large numbers of people, hopes to gain greater visibility, win more adherents, and create a ground swell for social change. The right usually does not have that kind of popular support for its political agenda, there being no mass of people out on the streets demanding still more funds for the Pentagon, still more favorable banking laws for Chase Manhattan or wider tax loopholes for Exxon, no elderly agitating for cuts in medical care, no workers demonstrating for higher corporate profits and wage slashes. So the right attempts to channel popular grievances into noneconomic issues such as busing, school prayers, pornography, and abortion, issues that might cut into the support of progressive causes and candidates while strengthening conservative ones.

The right is not seeking changes of a kind that burden or threaten the interests of the dominant corporate class. If anything, it advocates a view of the world that wealthy media owners look upon with genuine sympathy, unlike the view offered by left protesters. The centrist media is, in a word, more receptive to the right than to the left because its owners and corporate heads share the right's basic feelings about free enterprise, capitalism, communism, labor unions, popular protest, and US global supremacy, even if not always seeing eye-to-eye with it on specific policies and certain cultural issues. In addition, the right has the money to buy media exposure and the left usually does not.

The Right Feeds the Center

The right influences the mass media by generating rightist themes in its ultra-conservative publications and then working these into the communication mainstream. The rise of the "KGB menace" in America provides an example of how the right feeds into the center. The first time I heard of this updated version of the Red Menace was when the conservative columnist M. Stanton-Evans, whom I happened to be debating at a college campus in 1980, announced that "KGB agents had infiltrated our American institutions" and were "walking the streets of our nation's capital." The claim brought skeptical smiles to faces in the audience, so outlandish did it sound. First germinating on the far-right fringe, then repeated again and again by right-wing propagandists like Robert Moss, Arnaud de Borchgrave, Claire Sterling, and Michael Ledeen, the KGB charge began to slowly seep into the center. Through the process of repetition and dissemination it began to sound less outlandish. William Preston and Ellen Ray provide a good summary of how a determined right feeds a receptive center:

> A theme which is floated on one level—a feature item on VOA [Voice of America] about Cuba for example—will appear within record time as a lead article in *Reader's Digest*, or a feature in a Heritage Foundation report, or a series of "exposés" by Robert Moss and Arnaud de Borchgrave or Daniel James in some reactionary tabloid like *Human Events* or the *Washington Times* or *Inquirer*. Then they will all be called to testify by Senator Jeremiah Denton's Subcommittee on Security and Terrorism, repeating one another's allegations as "expert witnesses." After that they are given credibility by the "respectable" Cold War publications like the *National Review*, *Commentary*, and the *New Republic*. And finally, since they have repeated the theme so many times it must be true, they are given the opportunity to write Op-Ed pieces for the *New York Times* or the *Washington Post*.

Not only are they given the opportunity to write guest pieces, but as we have already observed in the case of the KGB bogey, regular mainstream columnists like Flora Lewis begin referring to the KGB's "vast masterful network to spread disinformation among us.". . .

Pundits to the Right

[A] growing number of conservative editorialists, columnists, TV commentators, and radio talk-show hosts tell us what to think about the news. A rightist perspective dominates TV political talk shows like NBC's "McLaughlin Group," PBS's "One on One" (with McLaughlin as host), CNBC's "McLaughlin Show" (with guess who), William Buckley's "Firing Line," CNN's "Evans and Novak" and "Capital Gang" (both featuring conservative newspaper columnist Robert Novak as host), ABC's "This Week with David Brinkley," and PBS's "American Interests."

The range of opinion on these shows and in the opinion columns of newspapers varies from far right to moderate centrist. In a display of false balancing, the right as represented by Robert Novak, William Buckley, John McLaughlin, George Will, and Pat Buchanan is pitted against the "left" as dubiously represented by Michael Kinsley, Sam Donaldson, and Mark Shields. The trouble is, these latter are mostly centrists with no real linkage to left causes and no left analysis, in contrast to the militant, right-wing ideologues they face. The "left-liberal" Kinsley has even written columns praising Britain's former prime minister Margaret Thatcher and defending the South African government's resistance to one person, one vote. Donaldson has asserted that "Mikhail Gorbachev and the Soviet system is a terrorist system," and has described Daniel Ortega as "the Nicaraguan dictator." A genuinely left progressive analysis of US foreign and domestic policy is not to be found in mainstream commentary.

Often the "debate" is between two conservative positions, as when, on CNN's "Op-Ed Commentary," conservative Morton Kondracke praised the Bush administration's foreign policy

Tom Tomorrow © 1991. Reprinted with permission.

while conservative Fred Barnes attacked the White House for not being tough enough, or as on "American Interests," when a Reagan cabinet member, Caspar Weinberger, was paired with a Bush cabinet member, Robert Mossbacher.

The Right Gets Exposure

Despite all this, conservative media-watch groups like Accuracy in Media (AIM) continue to attack the press for being too liberal: that is, for not being as completely right-wing as AIM would want. AIM's Reed Irvine has a weekly column that circulates in some hundred newspapers and a daily radio commentary that plays on seventy stations. Leftist and other progressives cannot hope for anything resembling that kind of exposure. Yet Irvine continues to charge that left views are heavily favored in the media.

Scores of other right-wingers dominate the talk-radio circuits, including such political Neanderthals as Rush Limbaugh who reaches 1.3 million listeners on more than 340 affiliated radio stations. Limbaugh attacks "commie-libs," "femiNazis," "liberal Democrats," "gays," and other unpatriotic traitors who might utter a good word about labor unions or gun control or a critical word about the socio-economic status quo. Then there is Bob Grant whose right-wing and anti-ethnic comments, coming out of the greater New York area on WABC radio, reach late-night audiences across most of the land east of the Mississippi.

Right-wing organizations and media-watch groups like AIM are able to draw from affluent sources like the multimillionaire Richard Mellon Scaife (who has donated over $100 million to conservative causes in recent years), New York investment banker Shelby Cullom Davis, Richard Nixon, Bebe Rebozo, and multimillionaire Walter Annenberg. The John Olin Foundation gives over $5 million a year to right-wing causes. Big corporations like Du Pont and GE give millions more.

The conservative Christian Broadcast Network brings in an annual $22 million from members around the country. Right-wing fundamentalist broadcasting is a $2-billion-a-year industry, controlling more than 1,000 full-time radio stations and more than 200 full-time TV stations, or about 10 percent of all radio and 14 percent of all television in the nation. There is also a Christian left in the United States composed of persons who advocate social reform at home, aid to the poor and homeless, and an end to US militarism and armed interventions in the Third World. But they lack the financial backing needed to give them any substantial access to media.

On those infrequent occasions the national media report popular protests, the coverage is usually scant and slighting. The *Washington Post* coverage of the May 1981 "March on the

Pentagon" can serve as a case study of how the supposedly liberal press treats protests on the left. Buried in Section C along with local news and obituaries, the story, written by Mike Sager, seems more concerned with trivializing the protesters than with telling us anything about the content of their protests, about why they were out there in the first place:

> They marched carrying banners for their causes while licking ice-cream bars and taking pictures of each other with complicated camera gear. . . . Yesterday's minions carried a few placards and repeated a few chants, but some also took time to eat picnic lunches, smoke marijuana, drink beer and work on their tans.

(A "minion," according to *Webster's Unabridged Dictionary*, is "a term of contempt" describing "a servile follower.")

Two fairly large photographs accompanying the story show no one sunbathing or consuming picnic lunches, marijuana, beer, or ice cream. And the photos reveal not "a few placards" but what must be hundreds of placards and banners. To be sure, some of the participants may well have paused to refresh themselves—in a demonstration that continued for some seven hours under the hot sun. What might be questioned is why the *Post* writer treated these minor activities as central to the event, thereby suggesting a frivolous atmosphere that denies the protesters the seriousness of their concerns.

We read that the demonstrators varied "from long-haired hippie hold-outs with painted faces to L.L. Bean-clad outdoorsmen to health-conscious joggers who had stopped by to witness the spectacle. . . . The demonstration took on a flea market atmosphere—something for everyone." It was a "hodge-podge collection." Even the headline proclaimed: "25,000 PROTESTERS MARCH FOR MIXED CAUSES." The *Post* story assumed there was an incongruous mix of issues, when in fact the demonstration sought to link a range of domestic and foreign policies and make common cause against the government. Such linkage is easily misunderstood by a press that treats political issues as isolated, unrelated events. . . .

Ignoring and Undercounting

The press makes a regular practice of undercounting the size of demonstrations; "disparagement by numbers" is what one media critic calls it. The press regularly ignores the estimates offered by rally organizers and fails to make an independent estimate from the number of chartered buses, trains, and auto flow or from "grid" counting. Instead, reporters treat as accurate the "official" figures provided by generally unsympathetic police, while seldom raising a question about how they arrive at their estimates. However, on those rare occasions when a police count proves too favorable, the press is capable of conjuring a lower figure. Thus when the police reported that organized labor's September 1981 protest march on Washington numbered 400,000, the *Washington Post* reported 260,000 and the *New York Times* put it at 240,000.

The Media Favor Business

The U.S. press is often accused of being politically liberal and adversarial to those in power. . . .

Complaints about the "liberal media" ring especially hollow given the soft treatment accorded to Big Business on leading editorial pages. During the first six months of 1991, for example, there were more editorials in the *New York Times* that focused on the weather or the change in seasons than editorials that were explicitly critical of a major U.S. corporation.

FAIR [Fairness and Accuracy in Reporting, a national media watch group] surveyed the *New York Times* editorial page (edited by Jack Rosenthal, a former State Department official) during the first half of 1991, reviewing a total of 690 editorials. When business was mentioned at all, it was usually in a favorable context, conveying the impression that corporations are essentially upstanding, benevolent institutions. . . .

Far from being too liberal or adversarial, U.S. mass media are too close to power—governmental and corporate power. But don't expect to read that assessment on the editorial page of your newspaper.

EXTRA!, October 1991.

In 1991, hours before President Bush began his all-out air attack against Iraq, ABC did a brief report on domestic opposition to the impending war. All ABC's Ted Koppel could find was a "small group" (his words) of people in Iowa and another in Berkeley, California, engaged in candlelight vigils. ABC ignored the large and dramatic demonstrations occurring that same day in the San Francisco Bay area in which 10,000 people shut down the federal building and 2,000 shut down the Bay Bridge, the latter action resulting in hundreds of arrests.

A peace march in San Francisco on January 19, 1991, stretching from Dolores Park along the full width of Market Street all the way to Van Ness—about the length of ten or twelve football fields, easily 150,000 people—was reported by KRON-TV and CNN as 25,000.

On January 26, 1991, peace advocates launched a massive march on Washington to protest President Bush's Gulf war.

Over a thousand buses filled to capacity with demonstrators from all over the Northeast, South, and Midwest rolled into the city. Tens of thousands of people came by car, Amtrak, and the Washington Metro. During the event itself, marchers tightly packed in broad uneven lines about sixty to seventy across, moving at a brisk pace, took about four hours to pass any given point. Organizers claimed 250,000. But the figure widely reported in the news was 75,000, provided by the unsympathetic Park Police. (It never would have taken four hours for 75,000 to march by.) Even worse were the early CNN reports, which noted that "organizers were hoping for 50,000 but they appear to be well short of that goal.". . .

Scanting of Content

Almost never do the media give us the arguments and motives behind a protest demonstration, the reasons why so many thousands feel impelled to travel long distances to march for hours in the streets. The signs and slogans projected by the demonstrators are regularly ignored as are the speeches that deal with the grievances at hand. The event is depicted as something of a spectacle connected to little more than its own surface appearances and not as part of a democratic struggle over vital issues. Viewers might easily come away with the notion that the crowd is just a noisy bunch of malcontent or unpatriotic people, especially viewers who have been fed nothing but the official view of things.

In fact, far from being an inchoate, mindless mass, antiwar demonstrations through their signs, slogans, chants, and speeches often reflect the passion and critical intelligence of informed people who care about what is happening in the world and in their own country. The media always seem to miss this story about the strength and vitality of democracy in the streets.

Content is also scanted through single-issue reductionism. The indictments made against the policies that help foster poverty, racism, sexism, economic exploitation, environmental devastation, capitalism, and imperialism are reduced to just one or two specific complaints by the press—for example, "end the war." While the demonstrators are sometimes branded as extremists intent upon disrupting orderly society, the press reduces the truly radical content of their message to a minimal reformist demand.

This dilution of the protest message can extend to characterizations about popular leaders. Thus the national media repeatedly tell us that Martin Luther King, Jr., was an outstanding civil rights leader but they fail to mention that he was also a strong critic of the American economic system, US foreign policy, and US militarism. King not only had a dream about racial brotherhood, he had something more dangerous than that—an *analysis* linking racism and poverty to class and power policies at home and abroad. So with Malcolm X, who is portrayed as a militant Black separatist but whose anti-imperialist ideas seem to have been forgotten. Not long after King and Malcolm began to link racial issues to class and economic conditions, they were assassinated.

As noted earlier in the discussion of the *Washington Post*'s account of the May 1981 "March on the Pentagon," the press regularly directs our attention to surface appearances and ignores the substance of the protest. In doing so, it is free to ascribe irrational and frivolous motives to the demonstrators, using selective details to make light of their dress, age, language, presumed lack of seriousness, and self-indulgent activities. The demonstrators are depicted as a deviant and unrepresentative sample of the American people, lacking in credible life-styles and therefore credible politics. "Social problem" or "crisis" no longer describes the wrongful conditions that provoke popular response. The popular response itself is now the crisis or the problem.

Another way to marginalize a group is to portray it as violent and irrational, or linked to groups thought to be violent or in some way threatening. One TV announcer on January 18, 1991, dismissed the massive antiwar outpouring in San Francisco by saying "it has been discredited because of its violence." The screen showed a police car burning and protesters throwing rocks at a building, then a woman who said she was very upset by the "violence." As during the Vietnam War, so with the Gulf war, the media made no distinction between the massive violence perpetrated by US forces against an entire people and the relatively minor violence against property—except to treat the latter as a far more serious problem.

In sum, the mass media are owned by large corporate conglomerates whose financial dominance gives them the means to control news content and limit the range of acceptable media opinion, injecting a bias against organized labor, antiwar protesters, socialists, environmentalists, feminists, ethnic minorities, Third World liberation struggles, and all progressive causes.

"African-Americans . . . and other minorities will be needed to cover one of the biggest stories in modern history: the changing face of America."

The News Profession Needs More Diversity

Angela Dodson

In 1968, the Kerner Commission (formed by President Lyndon B. Johnson to investigate the causes of racial violence) chastised the journalistic profession for its failure to employ blacks. Since then, reports Angela Dodson, minorities have entered the nation's newsrooms in increasing numbers. According to Dodson, however, the 1992 riots in Los Angeles renewed concerns highlighted by the Kerner Commission's findings. Minorities continue to be excluded from managerial positions, she argues, so they have limited control over major decisions. She concludes that the news profession needs greater diversity in order to reflect the nation's shifting ethnic makeup. Dodson is senior editor for administration of the *New York Times*, a New York City daily newspaper.

As you read, consider the following questions:

1. What was surprising about the Kerner Commission report, according to Dodson?
2. According to the author, what did the commission identify as the "sins of the media" during riot coverage?
3. Why has the "business side" of the news industry begun to advocate diversity, according to Dodson?

From "Twenty-Five Years After Kerner" by Angela Dodson. A longer version of this article first appeared in the April 1993 *Quill* magazine, published by the Society of Professional Journalists, and is reprinted here with permission. Copyright © 1993 by *Quill*.

What goes around, comes around.

In my culture that saying seems to convey two concepts: that one reaps what one sows and that those who forget history are doomed to repeat it. For many journalists who watched the coverage of the rebellion in Los Angeles in 1992, it appeared that 1967 had come 'round again and that little had been learned from the violence that poured into the streets, the authoritative investigation of it, or the quarter century of journalism that had transpired since.

In between, nearly two generations of people of color had been sought out for service in America's newsrooms and stood at the ready. Many reporters and editors were to express dismay or even outrage later that they were little used or ill used and that the story suffered as a result.

In 1992 in Los Angeles, according to a National Association of Black Journalists [NABJ] task force on the coverage there, newspapers failed to take advantage of what they already had. While it said black journalists "played pivotal roles," they were virtually shut out of the decision making and there was "little brainstorming" about the coverage.

"There is simmering frustration among many black journalists—about how they were utilized, about how they are regarded, about the slow pace of racial change in newsrooms," the report said. "In relatively few cases did black journalists direct coverage or participate in front-page decisions."

To understand the bewilderment, it is useful to review the history.

The Media and the Riots

In the summer of 1967, 150 American cities had reported racial disturbances, ranging from minor skirmishes between police and ghetto residents to the deadly riots that struck Newark and Detroit.

On July 27, 1968, with the Detroit riot barely quenched, President Lyndon B. Johnson issued a proclamation establishing a commission to find out why America was burning and what could be done about it. Among the things he wanted to know was: "What effect do the mass media have on the riots?"

It was a simple question, plainly stated.

Contained in it were the seeds of a controversy that had brewed throughout the civil rights movement of the 1950s and '60s: Were the media merely bystanders, or were they instigators?

At the time, many Northerners had blamed the media for much of the rioting, in the way some Southerners blamed Communist sympathizers for stirring up the coloreds before.

"What effect do the mass media have on the riots?"

Those were the only words pertaining to the media in the long proclamation empowering the commission to look at the root causes of violence. President Johnson created the National Advisory Commission on Civil Disorders, headed by Governor Otto Kerner, an Illinois Democrat, to "find the truth and express it."

It was a query that barely stood out among all the other questions about our society. It set in motion seven months of study by the Kerner Commission and 25 years of outside scrutiny and self-examination by the media.

White Males Are in Charge

Why can't the media get it right [about urban problems]? Scholarly reports and seminars have debated this question for years, but one answer is so obvious that it is often overlooked: Who is in charge?

The 1968 Kerner Commission on civil disorders decided that the nearly all-white media was part of the problem, and recommended that the professional staff of news operations should be integrated. But at the top of most news organizations in 1992, at least 95 percent of decisions are made by white males. . . .

It is tragic that 51 percent of newspapers—mostly the smaller ones—don't have a single non-white journalist on staff. The American Society of Newspaper Editors has a laudable goal of achieving parity between the newsroom and the African-American population by the year 2000, which would mean about 13 percent. But in 1992, a headcount shows about 2,600 African-American journalists at U.S. newspapers—less than 5 percent of all newspaper reporters. (It's advanced from 4.1 percent in 1990 to 4.8 percent in 1992—at that rate, they'll be at 8 percent by the year 2000.)

Barbara Reynolds, *EXTRA!*, July/August 1992.

The commission answered the question in a most surprising way: it nearly absolved the media of guilt in how they covered the story on deadline, but found them, along with other parts of the Establishment, accessories to a greater crime: being blind to the conditions that led up to the rebellion and distorting the picture of America long before the urban riots.

The thundering resonance of the report had not been anticipated. The commission itself epitomized moderation in an era of sweeping passions. Kerner, a 33-year veteran of the National Guard credited with integrating it and supporting fairness in housing and jobs, had little national standing to speak of. While his fellow commissioners were considered good and decent

Americans, few could be counted in the forefront of any of the great movements of their day.

The result was expected to be a whitewash.

One Nation, Divided

In an introduction to a 1968 instant paperback version of the committee's report, published by Bantam Books, *The New York Times'* Tom Wicker took note of what ordinary mortals these were. "This report is a picture of one nation, divided," he wrote. "It is a picture that derives its most devastating validity from the fact that it was drawn by representatives of the moderate and 'responsible' Establishment.

"But just as it sometimes takes a hawk to settle a war . . . so did it take bona fide moderates to validate the case that had to be made. A commission made up of militants, or even influenced by them, could not conceivably have spoken with a voice so effective, so sure to be heard in white, moderate, responsible America. And the importance of this report is that it makes plain that white, moderate, responsible America is where the trouble lies."

In its efforts to find the truth, the commission looked under every rock—commissioning studies, visiting cities, and hearing testimony—and came back on March 2, 1968, with a 1,485 page warning, eloquent but brutal, that if America wanted to avoid "urban apartheid" it had a lot of work to do to integrate society, to improve slum conditions, and to police itself better and more humanely.

The words were front-page news across the country, and they were heard. Within 11 days the Bantam version had sold out of all 740,000 copies of the first printing. About 2 million copies eventually were sold.

In those pages were some 10,000 well-chosen words that had been drafted by a media task force headed by Abram Chayes, a Harvard law professor, and by the commission to answer Johnson's one-sentence directive on the media. *Editor & Publisher*, the industry weekly, reprinted most of the media chapter the following week, words that have been heard ringing in many journalists' ears figuratively and literally ever since:

> *"The journalistic profession has been shockingly backward in seeking out, hiring, training, and promoting Negroes."*

Its conclusions were based on far more than opinion. The commission sent out survey teams to ask about attitudes and reactions to the coverage, it interviewed people in the media and people in the ghetto, it commissioned a quantitative analysis of newspaper and television content in 15 cities. It also convened a conference of people from all levels of the media in Poughkeepsie, New York, November 10-12, 1967. . . .

In the final report, the commission presented a picture of the media that perhaps surprised the leaders of the Fourth Estate and exposed a streak of myopia. Black Americans were probably not surprised, except by the notion that someone in the Establishment was helping to give voice to their complaints.

Distortions Crept In

Examining the riot coverage, the report said Commissioners found "a significant imbalance" between what happened and what the local media outlets said happened.

It found that while the media had tried "to give a balanced, factual account" of the disorders, distortions had crept in resulting in "an exaggeration of both mood and event."

"We found that the disorders, as serious as they were, were less destructive, less widespread, and less a black-white confrontation than most people believed," the report said.

The sins of the media in the heat of battle included using scare headlines over relatively mild stories, staging events like rock throwing, reporting rumors, broadcasting live from a riot site without the benefit of editing, speculating about potential violence, unskeptical reliance on official sources, displaying "a startling lack of common sense" in personal conduct, and playing up riots in distant cities while one's own was burning.

Interestingly, it did not find that the media played up emotional voices to the exclusion of calm ones, nor that reporting on the riot fanned the flames—if for no other reason than people in the ghettos believed little on television and almost none of what they read in the papers.

The most far-reaching conclusion was that "the media have thus far failed to report adequately on the causes and consequences of civil disorders and the underlying problems of race relations."

Thus the Kerner Commission found the media were among the many guilty parties in bringing America to the violence.

Quick Action Generated

It is not that nothing happened between then and now. Far from it. "In fact the media did more to implement its recommendations than many other segments of society singled out in the report," said Lena Williams, a 20-year veteran of *The New York Times* who was preparing to enter journalism school at Howard University when the report was issued.

The commission urged the media to set guidelines for covering disturbances, establish better rapport with the police, monitor coverage for bias, and form an Institute for Urban Communications. That institute was to offer training, recruitment, and placement of blacks, improve relations with police, monitor performance and dispense news through an urban affairs service, and conduct research.

Within a few short years, the work had at least begun to address the concerns, and many black journalists, followed by more Hispanic, Asian, and Native American journalists, began entering newspapers, television studios, and radio stations. There were to be many more conferences, reports, special programs, organizations, seminars, fellowships, mentoring programs, task forces, retrospectives on the meaning of Kerner, and stories filed from the urban beat. Early on, a program was started at Columbia University to train the new journalists, and a separate effort was made to start an urban news service.

Skewed News

Inside journalism, on a systematic basis, white people retain a disproportionate share of the power. That imbalance affects how the news gets reported every day. "Even when stories dealt with baldfaced injustices and black-community disenchantment," Kirk Johnson concluded in his study of Boston's mass media, "most reporters failed to acknowledge racism as an underlying mechanism. Indeed, the very word 'racism' was rarely uttered in the major media; when racism *was* mentioned, it was treated not as a continuing tradition, but as a mere historical footnote. Euphemisms such as 'the disadvantaged' and 'the underprivileged' suggested a reluctance to acknowledge the persons or institutions responsible for causing the 'disadvantage.'" Victims without victimizers—a common theme in media coverage of domestic issues. . . .

Chicago's news, Mayor Harold Washington contended, "never quite came out the way things actually happened. It came out in a skewed fashion because we didn't have Hispanics, women, blacks and other minorities to winnow out, interpret and help make the news more meaningful to the majority of people in our city." Shortly before his death, he predicted that news coverage "shall forever be biased in Chicago, until people get fed up and start demanding that something be done about it. We need to reevaluate the whole structure of the news industry—the owners, editors, anchorpersons, producers, journalists on the street."

Martin A. Lee and Norman Solomon, *Unreliable Sources: A Guide to Detecting Bias in News Media*, 1990.

Chayes, still at Harvard, thinks the report generated quick action. "Within a year or so you have blacks on every news show, so there must have been some qualified people available," he said. "And once you got people in visible positions, you changed attitudes."

In 1968 the Kerner report speculated that about 5 percent of the media work force was black, almost all of that in the black press. By 1992, according to the American Society of Newspaper Editors [ASNE], there were 5,100 people of color working in daily newspapers, 9.4 percent of the work force.

A Call to Arms

The report had been "a call to arms," said Brenda Lane Richardson, who was about to transfer from a seminary in Virginia to college in North Carolina in 1968 when a friend's mother persuaded her that her writing and speaking skills would be useful in journalism. "She said, 'You know, there's this report out—that they're looking for black people to go into journalism,'" Richardson said. "From that moment on I decided I wanted to be a journalist. Once we heard that, 'Yes, we want them here' and I wouldn't have to fight my way in the door, I and a lot of other people wanted to work in journalism."

Richardson, now a West Coast author, majored in English, won a fellowship in journalism, and later talked her way into an internship in the Washington bureau of *The New York Times* before going on to a career in newspapers and television.

All over the country similar conversions were taking place and doors were being opened. At 16 in West Virginia I was oblivious to the report but became editor of the school paper in a rural school that was 97 percent white. I got my first full-time reporting job at the *Huntington Advertiser* while a journalism major at Marshall University. I went to Washington in 1974 as a correspondent for Gannett News Service at the ripe old age of 23 before going on to graduate school and other newspapers. In Washington I found dozens of other black journalists who had been similarly pressed into service in the capital's bureaus and the local newspapers.

At that time, Columbia University's program was destined to close a few years later because officials felt the problem of integrating the media was being solved. Bob Maynard and others led a move to keep it going. In 1974 the program found a home at the University of California at Berkeley and became known as the Institute for Journalism Education [IJE]. Its purpose, said Dorothy Gilliam, a *Washington Post* columnist who is chairman of IJE, was to put to rest "that phrase we all hope we never hear again: 'We can't find anyone qualified.'"

Meanwhile black journalists had been talking about the need for a national membership organization to assist those already in the business and to help bring in more. Forty-three people attending a news event at a Washington hotel founded NABJ on December 12, 1975. Its first convention was held the next year. (Membership is now 2,400. In the meantime Hispanic, Asian, and Native American journalists have organized. So have women, minority managers, gay and lesbian journalists, and the industry's disabled.) NABJ began pressuring the industry as well as offering mutual aid to its members. It grew as the numbers of people in the industry grew.

Still a Long Way To Go

When the Kerner report's 10th anniversary rolled around in 1978, there was a sense that still not enough was being done. IJE sponsored a conference in Washington to push the ASNE to take a stand. The ASNE set a goal that by the year 2000 the number of minority people in newspapers would reach parity with their representation in the population, then 17 percent. Some people "were outraged" that the timetable was so long, said Gilliam, a vice president of NABJ.

Would news executives have to lower standards to find enough people? Maynard countered: "It is not an issue of supply. It is an issue of demand."

That year was the first that ASNE compiled figures, and it found that 4 percent of the reporters and editors on daily newspapers were members of minority groups. Only 11 minority people were high-level managers.

Progress would prove to be reasonably steady but slow. The overall industry numbers inched up, to 6.56 percent representation by 1987. Parity was a moving target and there was still a long way to go. As the 20th anniversary loomed, IJE held another conference in Washington in 1987 to press for new initiatives.

The Importance of Diversity

Sometime after 1987 the dialogue became less one-sided. Minority journalists were no longer alone on the outside demanding to be let in. It had to do with shifting demographics and money. Publishers and others on the business side were pulling people aside and explaining that diversity was good for the bottom line and that the cause was urgent, especially in large urban centers where people of color were already the majority.

"Are we going to go out of business tomorrow if we do not diversify our staff and our management? No," said Arthur Sulzberger Jr., publisher of The New York Times in a Fall 1992 interview with Lena Williams for the company's journal. "But will we at some point? The answer, I believe, is 'Absolutely, yes.'"

So, too, believes Betty Anne Williams of USA Today, who wrote in the Freedom Forum's Media Studies Journal: "For the media, turning a blind eye to diversity and gender issues could be a costly mistake in a nation where, census projections show, 87 percent of population growth between now and 2010 will be in minority communities, and where women already make up 51 percent of the population and 45 percent of the work force."

At a media industry diversity summit December 3, 1992, several participants complained that even if top management was sincere, middle managers were thwarting their efforts. When it came to managing diversity, said Sidmel Estes-Sumpter, an Atlanta television news manager who is president of the NABJ, "You just don't get it—that it's not an affirmative action thing, not a quota thing."

Rather, the struggle is to find ways to speak to new customers as the demographics change. The issue is not merely inclusion, it is portrayal. African-Americans, Hispanics, Asians, Native Americans, and other minorities will be needed to cover one of the biggest stories in modern history: the changing face of America.

Goals Have Not Been Accomplished

For many journalists, Los Angeles provided a case study again in 1992. While some newspaper executives felt they were damned if they did send in minority reporters and damned if they didn't, the NABJ report said, "For black journalists, division of duties was part of a larger problem: influence over the final product." Some felt the final product again contained distortions and failed to reflect underlying tensions.

Kerner noted that few black editors were working in America's newsrooms. People of color now make up 1.9 percent of senior newsroom management, and that is not enough. In Los Angeles, the NABJ report found, the biggest problem was that few minority people were in a position to direct coverage of a story with so many ethnic nuances. Partly that was a function of success. They had fanned out to the editorial boards, business departments, features sections, and even foreign bureaus. And partly, journalists said, it was that the news media have focused on the numbers and little on where the numbers were deployed.

"We continue to bemoan the slow pace of the numbers, but the issue of coverage is very crucial," Gilliam said. "The reason for increasing the numbers is to improve portrayal." Few have made it to the top jobs on the city or national desks, and even fewer were managing editors, executive editors, or publishers.

While our industry deserves credit for answering the call of Kerner, it has not accomplished even the goals it set for itself. The lesson of Los Angeles is that we must look beyond numbers in colorizing the newsroom and install editors with clout—for what goes around, comes around.

"The press has too long basked in the white world, looking out of it, if at all, with white men's eyes and a white perspective," the commission said. "That is no longer good enough."

"Newsroom diversity [works] to suppress ideas and information."

Emphasis on Diversity Harms the News Profession

Daniel Seligman

In the following viewpoint, Daniel Seligman argues that an emphasis on proportional representation for minorities in the newsroom has resulted in a kind of self-censorship. He contends that reporters and editors, paralyzed by fear of offending the various factions represented by their fellow workers, have adopted the politically correct policy of avoiding language and stories that might possibly be interpreted as prejudicial. Therefore, rather than broadening the spectrum of information, says Seligman, diversity has led to a suppression of ideas. Seligman is a columnist and former senior editor at *Fortune* magazine.

As you read, consider the following questions:

1. According to Seligman, what are the "propositions" associated with the term "diversity"?
2. How did the events at the *Washington Post* in 1986 affect its subsequent reporting, according to the author?
3. According to Seligman, what is the *New York Times*'s position on gay-related issues?

From "PC Comes to the Newsroom" by Daniel Seligman, *National Review*, June 21, 1993, © 1993 by National Review, Inc., 150 E. 35th St., New York, NY 10016. Reprinted by permission.

Proposition: The mighty American media have begun moving down the politically correct road long trodden by the colleges, and are doing so for many of the same reasons. The tilt to PC [political correctness] in the press is a sickening phenomenon, and it needs to be distinguished from the merely maddening liberal bias often groaned about by conservatives. Indicia of this bias have been abundant for years. Polling data on reporters, editors, and anchormen have consistently shown such characters to be more liberal than the public as a whole. A carefully crafted survey done by the Center for Media and Public Policy showed that 81 per cent of high-level media folks had voted for George McGovern in 1972 (when he got only 38 per cent of the popular vote). . . .

"Diversity" Takes Over

Media liberalism doubtless provided an ideal environment for the nurturing of political correctness, but PC has in some ways transformed that environment. Now solidly based in scores of newsrooms, it still looks much like its progenitors on campus—a movement driven by truly totalitarian impulses. Its byword continues to be "diversity," a term of art now associated with several different propositions: We need a lot more affirmative action to forestall racism and sexism. We need to promote messages that tout the achievements and elevate the self-esteem of minorities, women, and gays. We need speech codes and sensitivity workshops to ensure suppression of ideas that might offend these groups. A lot of what the political-correctniks are selling just seems laughable, especially the never-ending discoveries of bias built into terms like "waitress" and "blackball." Not so laughable is the genuine pressure created by the movement to flee from the evidence when the conclusion—that minorities have higher crime rates than whites, for example, or that women on average have less mathematical ability than men—is judged politically incorrect.

One good reason for worrying about PC filtering into the media is the recent emergence of diversity as a major theme in numerous news organizations. A Nexis [computerized database] search asking for all 1992-93 articles mentioning "diversity" within thirty words of "media" or "newsroom" turned up 598 articles. One learns that the *New York Times*, Knight-Ridder, Hearst, Gannett, Chicago's Tribune Co., the *Boston Globe*, the *Seattle Times*, the *Los Angeles Times*, and others have made increased diversity of the workforce a major priority; many have established diversity committees of one kind or another in their newsrooms. The *Tribune* has told senior managers that their bonuses will be affected by their success in hiring and promoting minorities. *New York Times* advertising revenue has been in a long slide, but new boss Arthur Sulzberger Jr. says "the single most important issue this newspaper faces" is—diversity. Sulzberger gives every indication of being a true believer: the Diversity Task Force set up in 1992 by the *Times* has poked its nose into numerous corners of the enterprise, and the official ideology says that there is a News Case for Diversity: The more diverse staff will do a better job of reporting. Also a Business Case: The *Times* must reach out to the more multicultural markets of the next century. (The capital letters appear in the paper's own statements about diversity.) . . .

Diversity in the media seems to mean exactly what it has always meant on campus. Definition propounded by the *Times* task force: "Diversity is understood to include people of every sex [huh?], race, color, ethnicity, culture, lifestyle, sexual orientation, age, experience and all other characteristics that make individuals unique." As at Harvard, the word refers to differences just about everywhere except in the realm of ideas.

Conventions of editors and publishers these days feature endless chatter about diversity, along with box scores evidencing the degree of success attained by each of the fifty largest newspapers in bumping up its minority proportion. (*USA Today* is the leader, with 20.8 per cent.) The American Society of Newspaper Editors has formally embraced a goal of proportional representation by 2000: By that year, America's newsrooms are supposed to have a minority representation of about 25 per cent, in line with the over-all population percentages. ASNE is obviously not going to meet that goal (the figure today is around 10 per cent), so every year's meeting features expressions of rage and betrayal by groups of minority journalists and of contrite determination by the bosses to do better in the future. Inspiring diversity sentiment of outgoing ASNE president Seymour Topping of the *New York Times*, at the 1992 convention: "We must forge ahead even more strongly."

In a pattern recognizable from the campuses, management's affirmative-action efforts are guaranteed never to reduce the quantity of racism out there. At the December 1992 meeting of the Newspaper Association of America, the president of the National Association of Black Journalists said that newsrooms "are increasingly hostile to minorities," and black journalist Wanda Lloyd of *USA Today* said she regularly gets calls from all over the country complaining about racism and hostility in different organizations. "Go to any minority journalism association meeting," she said, "and you hear that."

Special Interest Movements in the Newsroom

Like students on campus, journalists are increasingly divided along racial/ethnic/sexual lines. In addition to the black journalists, there is a National Association of Hispanic Journalists, an Asian American Journalists Association, a Native American Journalists Association, American Women in Radio & Television, the National Federation of Press Women, and the National Lesbian and Gay Journalists Association, all panting to proclaim their victimhood. Lois Lauer Wolfe of the Press Women complains that the newspaper industry is concentrating hiring efforts on minorities, and "what has been left out of the equation is women." Naturally not organized are white males, but it seems that they too have their grievances. A Gannett News Service report recently described a seminar on diversity that took place at an American Press Institute meeting in Reston, Virginia, and turned into a gripe session by non-minority men telling stories about being passed over because of their skin color. Gannett's PC reporter made it clear he was not too sympathetic.

Sensitive Subjects Should Not Be Avoided

There was a time when American journalism thrived on controversy, the very essence of the news business. But in an era when an ill-chosen phrase can spark a nationwide backlash, the profession seems infused with a new skittishness, a growing fear that some group or faction or minority might be offended by industrial-strength opinions.

Is it still possible to explore candidly the treacherous terrain of race, crime, poverty, abortion or homosexuality without triggering a firestorm of protest? Or is the journalism of the 1990s destined to be a bland form of discourse that tiptoes around the sensitive subjects that people are thrashing out in private?

This is not to say that people shouldn't complain, and loudly, about opinions they find objectionable. And sure, some comments are so hateful that they are beyond the pale of acceptable discourse. But any difficult subject—say, the withholding of medical care from the hopelessly ill—has an extreme position at the end of its slippery slope. That doesn't mean it should be *verboten* for the news columns and airwaves, any more than academics should let themselves be terrorized by campus demands for "politically correct" views.

Howard Kurtz, *The Washington Post National Weekly Edition*, January 28-February 3, 1991.

The media's PC problems obviously reflect increased fears in editors' offices that something might be published that would offend the various movements represented in the newsroom. This does seem odd. One might suppose the movements' members would be fearful of jeopardizing the positions they hold, and disinclined to make waves; after all, good jobs in journalism have been scarce for quite a few years. But it doesn't seem to work that way. News stories about rumbles in the newsroom generally leave you with the impression that the disgruntled or furious staff feels it has the moral high ground, while the senior editors nominally in charge look nervous and defensive.

Astonishing Humiliations

Senior journalists deemed responsible for offending ethnic or sex-related sensibilities have suffered astonishing humiliations in recent years:

• In December 1990, the *Philadelphia Inquirer* ran an editorial suggesting that young welfare mothers, unable to care for more children, be offered incentives to use Norplant (the contraceptive implant). The proposal was termed "slow genocide" by Vanessa Williams, an instantly enraged *Inquirer* reporter who also happened to be president of the local chapter of the black journalists' association. One *Inquirer* columnist got into print comparing editorial-page editor Dave Boldt to David Duke. In the ensuing row, the paper's senior editors repudiated the editorial; in addition, they expanded the editorial board to include three blacks. Deputy editorial-page editor Donald Kimelman has been quoted as affirming that "in practice . . . we won't write anything on race that doesn't have the support of the board's three black members."

Several weeks later, still stung by the outcries of some of its employees, the *Inquirer* introduced a hiring program explicitly identified as "quotas." The new rule was that henceforth half of all newsroom hires would be minority-group members; in addition, half had to be women. At the same time, the paper introduced training sessions in which all editorial employees were required to be introduced to sensitivity. To be sure, the sessions may have been less mandatory than advertised, as some news stories described rebellious white male employees boycotting them.

• The *Boston Globe*, which has instituted what it calls "race and gender workshops" for its staff, has been [forced to deal] with a towering problem presented by veteran columnist David Nyhan. It seems that Nyhan humorously disparaged another chap on the staff, applying to him a vulgar, if not obscene, synonym for "henpecked." He was immediately assailed by a female colleague who happened to hear the remark, assailed again in a memo to the staff by editor Matthew Storin ("Remarks that are racially or sexually offensive to co-workers will not be tolerated here"), and fined $1,250 (which the *Globe* said it would contribute to a women's organization). The *Globe* later relented on the fine but Nyhan, by all accounts, is crushed and apologetic.

• The *Los Angeles Times* has made a huge investment in expanding minority editorial employment (now 17.2 per cent of newsroom staff). It has an active diversity committee, charged with reducing racial tensions; it also has a Unity Caucus—an ad-hoc group of minority employees who use the in-house electronic bulletin boards to conduct a running "consciousness-raising" critique of the paper's editorials, landing with thuds on anything judged offensive, and plenty is. The critiques get widely circulated, and I found myself reading one of them in the *Washington Post*. The bulletin-board entry was responding to a *Times* article that said Ghanaian leader Jerry Rawlings had a "reputation for personal probity that sets him apart from the rest of the continent's leaders." The in-house response: This was "besmirching the entire continent." A subsidiary row on the *L.A. Times*, or possibly it is the main point, involved minority staffers who protested when asked to abandon their usual beats and pitch in to cover the May 1992 riots. After much back-and-forth without agreement on the fairness of such assignments, the *Times*, like the *Inquirer*, reached for the quota button: It proclaimed that 50 per cent of all new editorial hires would be minority-group members or women.

Pounding the *Post*

• In 1986, the *Washington Post* introduced and proudly promoted a redesigned Sunday magazine section. Unfortunately for the grand opening, the first issue contained two problematic features. One was a cover story about a black rap star accused of murder. The second and larger controversy swirled around a column by Richard Cohen noting that many crime-ridden jewelry stores in the District routinely declined to buzz in young black males, and suggesting a certain amount of sympathy for the store managers. The new magazine brought down an avalanche of abuse on Cohen and the *Post*. A Washington Post Magazine Recall Committee (which wanted the magazine abolished) gained the support of the Washington Urban League, the Archdiocese of Washington, numerous local unions, and District Delegate Walter E. Fauntroy. Executive editor Ben Bradlee wrote a formal apology "for the offense that [the articles] inadvertently gave to certain segments of our audience," and (responding to a subsidiary grievance that surfaced when the recall committee got going) also promised that more black models would henceforth appear in the magazine's advertisements. Protestors nevertheless continued dumping thousands of copies of the Sunday magazine on the steps of the *Post* building for several months.

The *Post* itself reported that these shattering events had had an impact on coverage. Signaling that cheerleading time had come, Bradlee said the paper was now searching aggressively for stories "that would reflect the strengths of the community." Magazine editor Jay Lovinger was quoted in the *Post* as saying that his story decisions were now being second-guessed, and it was obvious that the protests were poisoning the atmosphere in which journalistic decisions are made. When the magazine did a feature story on Jeffrey Levitt, an S&L [savings and loan] operator who had stolen money, Jewish readers wrote in to complain that the *Post* was now dumping on Jews just to show blacks the paper was impartial.

Okay, all this was in 1986. But you had better believe memories of those events still haunt the *Post* editors. A 1991 article by its media correspondent, Howard Kurtz, observed with remarkable candor that "creeping self-censorship," especially on racial issues, was a problem at the *Post* (and a lot of other places). He quoted offending columnist Richard Cohen as opining that "there are issues the media just can't discuss."

Actually, that's not quite right. The press is free to discuss any problem under the sun. It gets into trouble only when it serves up politically incorrect solutions.

The Patricia Bowman Legend

• *New York Times* in-house legends feature numerous attacks on senior management by the troops, but the 1991 row over Patricia Bowman is hard to top. Miss Bowman is the woman who famously accused young William Kennedy Smith of raping her when she returned with him to the family compound after some late-hour bar-hopping in Palm Beach. Like most papers, the *Times* protects the privacy rights of rape victims and does not use their names in news stories. But after Miss Bowman was named first by a supermarket tabloid and then by NBC, the *Times* decided that the privacy issue was moot: it identified her and in the process told its readers quite a lot about her, including several marginally discreditable details (e.g., the suspension of her driver's license after numerous tickets and unpaid fines).

Willie Smith ultimately was acquitted of raping Miss Bowman, but in the *Times* newsroom he was guilty as Bluebeard at the time her name was disclosed, and the violation of her already vanished privacy was a high crime. When executive editor Max Frankel showed up for work the next morning, he immediately discerned Sunday Book Review editor Rebecca Sinkler shouting that the paper's behavior was a disgrace. Contemplating petitions and other signs of hysterics, Frankel called a staff meeting in the paper's auditorium with every seat occupied, he then had to endure prolonged abuse from journalists of every gender; he also had to sit still for an Anna Quindlen column denouncing the *Times* coverage. The logic of the column was bizarre, arguing that the name had been disclosed because the Kennedys are well connected whereas Miss Bowman belonged to the less privileged classes. But *Times* columnists report directly to the publisher, and in this case he was on the rebels' side. Sulzberger turned up in the newsroom and gave Anna a conspicuous kiss. Owing to its progressive etiology, the buss [kiss] triggered no charges of sexual harassment.

The standard argument for diversity in journalism is that it expands the organization's reportorial range. Hispanic reporters will be more knowledgeable about what's happening in the barrios, and women in the media will have unique insights into female-related issues. It is a facially plausible story line; in practice, however, one has difficulty pointing to examples. What you see instead are proliferating versions of the Bowman case: of newsroom diversity working to *suppress* ideas and information. The racial/ethnic/sexual "movements" represented in the newsroom are inflexibly PC, and as hinted by the catalogue of humiliations recited above, senior editors do well not to cross them.

My own sense of the matter is that on many issues the press seems entirely capable of overriding its familiar liberal biases. It can surprise you with a series favorable to Dan Quayle (which the *Washington Post* produced in 1992) or articles suddenly registering skepticism about global warming. Conservatives cannot fairly complain nowadays that the press is giving a free ride to the Clintonites. Still, it has this large problem in the newsroom. What it is increasingly unable to do is offend the movements represented there or even deal with their interests in a reasonably professional manner. . . . When movement interests are involved, cheerleading is the new norm.

Pro-Gay Media

Conspicuously so when gay rights are concerned. Polling data show the American people deeply divided over Clinton's proposal to let acknowledged homosexuals serve in the military: A CNN-*USA Today*-Gallup survey in late April 1993 showed 50 per cent opposed to the idea, 44 per cent in favor, 6 per cent undecided. No such divisions are discernible in the media, where you see a landslide in favor of Clinton's proposal. A Nexis search turned up 47 editorial-page endorsements of the proposal, with only one paper (the *Washington Times*) opposed.

Media coverage of gay-related issues insistently reminds one that much of it is being done by the movement's partisans. The April 1993 march in Washington was clearly being covered by reporters on the team. The *Seattle Times* reportage was performed by Lily Eng, a leader of the National Lesbian and Gay Journalists Association [NLGJA], whose dispatch noted a mysterious distinction: "As a journalist, I don't consider myself an activist, but as a lesbian." The *Minneapolis Star Tribune* was represented by Jennifer Juarez Robles, who is also active in NLGJA and was one of many gay journalists certifying that the authorities had undercounted participants in the march. The *New York Times* interviewed a sizable number of news executives and reported that virtually all of them said they wouldn't take a reporter's sexual orientation into account in deciding whom to assign to the parade. That seems a bit disingenuous. Anyone wading through many newspaper reports on the march would surely conclude that the issue facing many newsroom assignment editors was whether they *had to* assign a gay or lesbian to the parade. The *Times* itself assigned gay reporter Jeffrey Schmalz, whose hurrahs were unabashed ("the feeling of brotherhood . . . seemed pervasive") and whose report concluded with a judgment at variance with that reached by numerous goggle-eyed C-SPAN viewers: "We're just like everybody else in America."

The view from the top at the *Times* is that the paper's new perspective on gay-related issues represents another victory for diversity and more inclusive coverage. In a videotaped message to the NLGJA in 1992, Sulzberger promised that the *Times* would get itself some openly gay senior editors or top managers, and added, clunkily: "I'm convinced that if newspapers are to survive, they can no longer be exclusionary bastions of a single view of the world." In fact, the *Times* now has a single view of gay-related issues: the view of gay partisans themselves. Its reports on these issues have been one long exercise in cheerleading. "Chancellor Fernandez Stands Tall" was the heading over the *Times* editorial when Joe Fernandez suspended a Queens school board that had rebelled against orders to teach acceptance of gays to young children. On this issue, on gays in the military, on the moral right of a gay contingent to march in New York's St. Patrick's Day parade, on the total wonderfulness of the April 1993 demonstration in Washington, the paper's coverage has been relentlessly one-sided.

It is unclear how far the media will travel down the PC road. Some of the follies perpetrated by academic groups like, say, the Modern Language Association will almost surely meet more resistance in the media than at Stanford, if only because the media's handiwork is more exposed to public view. One somehow doubts that "womyn" will ever become acceptable usage at the *New York Times*.

But the new diversity-based pressures are real and powerful. David Boldt, editorial-page editor of the *Philadelphia Inquirer* and a conspicuous victim of the pressures, may have had it about right when he grieved in a 1991 interview: "I have this vision of America, with all 250 million of us standing up to our chins in sewage and everyone's saying, 'Don't make waves.'"

> *"The mission [of PBS] . . . provides a rationale under which extreme Left viewpoints have a presumptive claim on public air time."*

Public Television Promotes a Left-Wing Political Agenda

David Horowitz

In the 1960s, David Horowitz was editor of Ramparts, *a magazine of radical politics. More recently, however, in* Destructive Generation *(1989), he and coauthor Peter Collier rejected the protest culture of the 1960s and chronicled their conversion to conservative politics. In the following viewpoint, Horowitz argues that a pro-communist political bias pervades the programs aired by the Public Broadcasting Service (PBS)—especially its television documentaries. He concludes that public television has twisted its mandate to provide balanced programming into a rationale to promote left-wing political opinions.*

As you read, consider the following questions:

1. According to Horowitz, why were radicals easily integrated into the "PBS community"?
2. In what way was the CIA documentary *On Company Business* misleading, according to the author?
3. According to Horowitz, why has PBS positioned itself "even more firmly on the Left" in recent years?

Created by the Public Broadcasting Act of 1967, the present system of public television is by now one of the last El Dorados of the Great Society. From relatively modest beginnings it has grown into a $1.2-billion leviathan which is virtually free of accountability to the taxpayers who shell out an annual $250 million to pay for the system while also enabling it to get matching grants from private individuals, foundations, and corporations. . . .

Centralized Power Dominates

Executives of the Public Broadcasting Service (PBS) portray their network as if it were a decentralized service to diverse publics, the very incarnation of America's democratic spirit. A typical statement reads:

> PBS is owned and directed by its member public television stations, which in turn are accountable to their local communities. This grassroots network is comprised of stations operated by colleges, universities, state and municipal authorities, school boards, and community organizations across the nation.

Yet notwithstanding organizational complexities of Rube Goldberg dimensions, and the lack of a single programming authority, the truth is that centralized power dominates public television and creates its characteristic voice. Of the 44 million taxpayer dollars annually available for programs to the 341 separately owned PBS stations across the nation, fully half the total—$22 million—goes to just two: WGBH in Boston and WNET in New York. (Another $10 million goes to a group of producers affiliated with WNET, to three other stations, and to PBS itself, which brings the centralized total to 77 percent of the funds.) This money is then leveraged against grants from private foundations and other sources by a factor as great as two, three, or even five times the original amount.

The result is that most major public-television series— *MacNeil/Lehrer, American Playhouse, Frontline, NOVA, Sesame Street, Great Performances, Masterpiece Theater,* and Bill Moyers's ubiquitous offerings—are produced or "presented" by WNET and WGBH. Others are produced by a group of stations known as the "G-7" (after the tag given to the major industrial powers), often with WNET and WGBH as the dominant partners. [The other five G-7 stations are WETA (Washington, D.C.), WTTW (Chicago), WQED (Pittsburgh), KCET (Los Angeles), and KQED (San Francisco).]

In creating the new system in the late 60's, its architects attempted to square the circle of a government-funded institution that would be independent of political influence. The result was a solution in the form of a problem: a private body—the Corporation for Public Broadcasting (CPB)—that would distribute the government funds. Compromise was the order of the day. The Carnegie Commission (whose report had led to the 1967 Act) wanted the governing board of CPB to be composed of eminent cultural figures; Lyndon Johnson wanted (and got) political appointees. Carnegie wanted a permanent funding base in the form of an excise tax on television sets; Congress said no. But as a sop to the broadcasters, emphasis was placed on the private nature of CPB as a "heat shield" to insulate the system from governmental influence.

Congress also limited CPB's mandate, insisting that it be established on the "bedrock of localism." (The idea of an elite network financed by the taxpayer would have been political anathema.) To prevent CPB from creating a centralized "fourth network," Congress barred it from producing programs, operating stations, or managing the "interconnection" between them. In addition to insisting on the safeguards of a decentralized system, Congress inserted a clause requiring "fairness, objectivity, and balance" in all programming of a controversial nature. . . .

A New Base of Radical Operations

Vietnam and Watergate: public television's birth by fire in the crucible of these events created its political culture, which today often seems frozen in 60's amber. . . . In fact, the protest culture, which everywhere else had withered at the end of the 60's when its fantasies of revolution collapsed, discovered a new base of operations in public television. A cottage industry of activist documentarians had sprung up during the 60's to make promotional films for the Black Panther party, the Weather Underground, and other domestic radical groups, and for Communist countries like Cuba and Vietnam. This group now began its own "long march through the institutions" by taking its political enthusiasms, its film-making skills, and its network of sympathetic left-wing foundations into the PBS orbit.

The integration of these radicals into the liberal PBS community was made easier by the convergence of political agendas at the end of the Vietnam war, when supporters of the Communist conquerors were able to celebrate victory over a common domestic foe with liberals who had only desired an American withdrawal. Another convergence occurred around the post-60's romance between New Left survivors and the "Old Left" Communists, whom cold warriors like Richard Nixon had made their targets. Most liberals shared the radicals' antipathy for the anti-Communist Right, along with their sense that any political target of the anti-Communists was by definition an innocent victim of persecution.

A prime expression of this liberal-Left convergence was *The Unquiet Death of Julius and Ethel Rosenberg* (1974), a two-hour special which attempted to exonerate the most famous "martyrs" of the anti-Communist 50's, and which PBS described as "the kind of programming that we enjoy presenting [and] hope to continue to present."

Asay, by permission of the *Colorado Springs Gazette Telegraph*.

What was striking about the film was not just that it cast doubt on the verdict of the Rosenbergs' trial; or that it did so even as massive FBI files released under the new Freedom of Information Act were confirming their guilt; or even that it went beyond the airing of questions about the case to imply that there had been a government frame-up and that the verdict represented an indictment of American justice. What was most disturbing (and prophetic in terms of future PBS productions) was that the film also amounted to a political brief for the Communist Left to which the Rosenbergs had belonged.

Thus, the narration introduced the Rosenbergs:

> With millions of others they question an economic and political system that lays waste to human lives. Capitalism has failed. A new system might be better. Socialism is its name.
> For many the vehicle for change is the Communist party.

The film then cut to an authority explaining that Communists were people who "believed that you couldn't have political democracy without economic democracy. . . . Being a Communist meant simply to fight for the rights of the people. . . ." The authority was the longtime Stalinist Carl Marzani, a fact that the program neglected to mention. . . .

Far from being an isolated example, the PBS treatment of the Rosenbergs proved typical. Individual Communists who were later admiringly profiled on PBS specials included Paul Robeson, Angela Davis, Dashiell Hammett, Bertolt Brecht, and Anna Louise Strong. These were amplified by the collective portrait *Seeing Red* (1986), a 90-minute celebration of American Communists as progressive idealists, and *The Good Fight* (1988), a nostalgic tribute to the Communists who volunteered to fight in the Spanish Civil War.

In a clear violation of PBS's enabling legislation, this opening to the discredited pro-Soviet Left was never balanced by any reasonably truthful portrait of American Communism; nor was it matched by any provision of equal time to anti-Communists, whether of the Left or Right. Thus, although there were specials on the personal trials of American radicals who had devoted their lives to a political illusion and enemy power, there was nothing on the tribulations of those former radicals who had changed their minds in order to defend their country and its freedom—Max Eastman, Jay Lovestone, James Burnham, Whittaker Chambers, Bayard Rustin, Sidney Hook.

Bashing the CIA

While PBS searched for silver linings in the dark clouds of the Communist Left, it found mainly negative forces at work in those American institutions charged with fighting the Communist threat, in particular the Central Intelligence Agency (CIA), which became a PBS symbol of American evil. In 1980, PBS aired a three-hour series called *On Company Business*, which its producers described as "the story of 30 years of CIA subversion, murder, bribery, and torture as told by an insider and documented with newsreel film of actual events."

The CIA "insider" on whom the PBS film relied for editorial guidance was Philip Agee, who in a 1975 *Esquire* article had written: "I aspire to be a Communist and a revolutionary." The same year a Swiss magazine asked Agee's opinion of U.S. and Soviet intelligence agencies. He replied:

> The CIA is plainly on the wrong side, that is the capitalistic side. I approve KGB activities, Communist activities in general, when they are to the advantage of the oppressed. In fact, the KGB is not doing enough in this regard because the USSR depends upon the people to free themselves. Between the overdone activities that the CIA initiates and the more modest activities of the KGB there is absolutely no comparison.

Agee had been expelled from the Netherlands, France, and England because of his contacts with Soviet and Cuban intelligence agents, but the PBS special identified him only by the caption "CIA: 1959-1969." When Reed Irvine of Accuracy in Media (AIM) and other critics objected to the program's "disinformation," they were dismissed out of hand by Barry Chase, the PBS vice president for News and Public Affairs. Chase even sent a memo to all PBS stations describing *On Company Business* as "a highly responsible overview of the CIA's history and a major contribution to the ongoing debate on the CIA's past, present, and future."

PBS's next summary view of American intelligence was a Bill Moyers special called *The Secret Government* (1987), which insinuated what no congressional investigation had ever established: that the CIA was a rogue institution subverting American policy. The wilder shores of this kind of conspiracy thesis were subsequently explored in two *Frontline* programs, *Murder on the Rio San Juan* (1988) and *Guns, Drugs, and the CIA* (1988), which leaned heavily on the fantasies of the far-Left Christic Institute. *The Secret Government* was followed by a four-part series called *Secret Intelligence* (1988), which, like all three of its predecessors, rehearsed the standard litany of left-wing complaints—Iran, Guatemala, the Bay of Pigs, Chile—and culminated in a one-sided view of the Iran-*contra* affair as an anti-constitutional plot.

An Editorial Position

All these programs judged the CIA to be more of a threat to American institutions than a guardian of American security. And while PBS officials continued to pay lip service to the idea of "balance," no sympathetic portrait of the CIA's cold-war activities was ever aired, no equally partisan account of its role in supporting the anti-Communist rebels in Afghanistan or Angola.

In the absence of countervailing portrayals of American cold-war policies and institutions, the indictments presented in PBS documentaries amounted to an editorial position. In the PBS perspective, the United States emerged as an imperialist, counterrevolutionary power whose national-security apparatus was directed not at containing an expansionist empire but (in the words of the producers of *On Company Business*) at suppressing "people who have dared struggle for a better life.". . .

The "Mission" of PBS

In trying to understand . . . the generally leftist bias of PBS, it is necessary to recognize that the entire public-television community (and that includes its friends in Congress) operates out of loyalty to what insiders refer to as the "mission." Simply put, the mission is a mandate to give the public what commercial television, because it is "constrained by the commercial necessity of delivering mass audiences to advertisers," allegedly cannot provide. The words belong to the president of PBS, Bruce Christensen, and are contemporary. But they could as well have been taken from the Carnegie Commission report of 25 years ago. The mission is what makes public television "public." It is its life principle and *raison d'être*. It is what justifies the hundreds of millions of government and privately contributed dollars necessary to keep the system going.

But the mission is also what provides a rationale under which extreme Left viewpoints have a presumptive claim on public air time. This is the rationale that justifies the indefensible propaganda of programs like *Days of Rage* [a 1989 anti-Israel documentary on the Palestinian *intifada*] and the promos for Communist guerrillas in Central America [such as *Fire from the Mountain* (1988) and *Nicaragua: Report from the Front* (1984)]. It is the rationale under which a partisan journalist like Nina Totenberg, who was involved in the leak that nearly destroyed Clarence Thomas, could be assigned by PBS as its principal reporter and commentator on the hearings triggered by that very leak.

Redefining "Balance"

Just how much a part of the ethos of public television this attitude has become can be seen in a controversy involving Bill Moyers, who has been praised as a "national treasure" by the PBS programming chief, Jennifer Lawson. Moyers had come under fire as the author of PBS's only two full-length documentaries on the Iran-*contra* affair, *The Secret Government* (1987) and *High Crimes and Misdemeanors* (1990). Critics (of whom I was one) questioned whether these programs met the standards of fairness and balance that public television was legally supposed to honor. Moyers's response was a tortured invocation of public television's mission:

> What deeper understanding of our role in the world could we have come to by praising Oliver North yet again, when we had already gotten five full days before Congress, with wall-to-wall coverage on network, cable, and public airwaves, to tell his side of the story? *In fact, it hardly seems consistent with "objectivity, balance, and fairness" that the other side of his story got only two 90-minute documentaries on public television.* [Emphasis added.]

For anyone not steeped in Moyers's own political mythology this was an eccentric view of what had taken place. North, of course, had not produced his own network documentary. He had been hauled before a congressional committee largely made up of political enemies who were bent on exposing him as a malefactor and on discrediting the administration in which he had served. Yet because he had turned the tables on them and emerged from his ordeal with a positive approval rating, Moyers blithely and blandly assumed that the commercial networks had been telling only North's "side of the story." Therefore the mission of public television was not to present a balance of views within its own schedule, as its enabling legislation required, but to attack North more successfully than the stagers of the hearings had managed to do.

Quite apart from its absurdity, Moyers's position reveals how out of date is the concept that originally inspired public television. For the fact that the Iran-*contra* hearings, which attempted to impugn the integrity and even the legitimacy of the Reagan presidency, were aired on all three networks, not to mention C-Span and CNN, means just the opposite of what Moyers seems to think it means. It means that public television can no longer position itself as the only channel on which anti-establishment views can be broadcast. Recognizing this occupation of its point on the spectrum, public television has sought a new space by positioning itself even more firmly on the Left.

There is also, perhaps, another factor at work here—bad conscience. This bad conscience stems, first, from PBS's increasing reliance on big corporations in its search for funds. Thus, between 1973 and 1978, corporate "underwriting" of public television went up nearly 500 percent. By the 1980's, corporate sponsorship accounted for almost as much of the public-television budget as its entire federal subsidy. Worse yet for the liberal conscience, the leaders in this trend, contributing more than half the total support, were big bad oil companies like Mobil, Exxon, and Gulf.

But even more significant is the degree to which, with the advent of cable, commercial stations have begun to compete directly with PBS. The Arts & Entertainment network (A&E) was started by the head of PBS's cultural programming, and its schedule—whether showing European movies, or serious drama, or biographies of historical figures—is comparable to anything PBS can offer. Another cable channel, Bravo, features drama from Aeschylus to Eugene O'Neill, film from Laurence Olivier to Luis Buñuel, and music from Claudio Monteverdi to Olivier Messiaen. The Discovery channel now repeats the nature shows that made PBS's early career, while C-Span provides 'round-the-clock political interviews and discussions at the most serious level, including live sessions of Congress, and political conventions and meetings. The one PBS feature that these channels do not offer is the monotonous diet of left-wing politics.

"By underwriting public TV, corporate entities can go beyond hawking products to espousing the economic models a corporation . . . favors. "

Public Television Promotes Corporate Interests

Eric Konigsberg

The programming of the Public Broadcasting System (PBS) is increasingly being funded by corporations, Eric Konigsberg points out in the following viewpoint. Consequently, says Konigsberg, PBS's numerous business programs support tax, trade, and regulatory policies consistent with corporate interests, while the concerns of workers are virtually ignored. Konigsberg contends that this intrusion of private, commercial interests into public television should be countered by a new funding policy. Konigsberg is a writer based in Washington, D.C.

As you read, consider the following questions:

1. Why did IBM back away from funding the Audubon Society series on environmental hazards, according to Konigsberg?
2. Why does the author find it excessive for public television to air three investment programs?
3. What has PBS gained by promoting itself as having a high-income audience, according to Konigsberg?

"Stocks, Bonds, and Barney" by Eric Konigsberg, *The Washington Monthly*, September 1993. Reprinted with permission from *The Washington Monthly*. Copyright by The Washington Monthly Company, 1611 Connecticut Ave. NW, Washington, DC 20009. (202) 462-0128.

In the spring of 1992, as Congress reconsidered the funding of public broadcasting, Bob Dole shared a few choice words. "The liberals love it," he snapped on the floor of the Senate. "They have their own network. . . . I have never been more turned off and more fed up with the increasing lack of balance and the unrelenting liberal cheerleading I see and hear on the public airwaves."

An Un-Liberal Trend

Hard to tell which PBS Dole has been watching. The network's handful of headline-grabbing episodes in the early 1990s has indeed been about documentaries deemed by conservatives too liberal to run. But as with "Tongues Untied," a treatment of black homosexuals, the result in dozens of cases was a speedy retreat in the face of right-wing pressure. (Over 200 of PBS's 351 stations declined to run "Tongues Untied.") Meanwhile, gradually and with less fanfare, a decidedly un-liberal trend has developed: Corporations are underwriting more and more public programming. The results are a proliferation of the kinds of shows that a Republican Minority Leader, and, more frequently, anyone playing the stock market, might just stay home to watch.

PBS has been using its sizable viewership—a 2 to 5 percent share of the Nielsen ratings—to lure companies into sponsoring programs. The network is too poor to fund any shows in toto, but corporate underwriting—up 22 percent from 1991—comes with a variety of built-in catches. In 1992, for instance, Texaco pulled its funding from the "Great Performances" series the week before it was to air "The Lost Language of Cranes," a drama about gays. IBM had a near-valiant go at corporate conscientiousness a few years ago and agreed to put up $2 million for a series the Audubon Society had developed on environmental hazards, but Big Blue backed away before any episodes could be filmed. Why? Although IBM had a clean enough pollution record, the same could not be said of dozens of its clients. "The Machine That Changed the World," on the other hand, a series about computers, was paid for in part with $1.9 million from Unisys. Turns out Unisys evolved from the company profiled in the series's first episode.

Espousing Corporate Interests

By underwriting public TV, corporate entities can go beyond hawking products to espousing the economic models a corporation, by nature, favors. Corporate interests are more likely to promote management over labor, free manufacturing over regulatory laws, and certain tax policies like investment tax credits and a capital gains tax cut. The business programming on PBS—shows like "Wall $treet Week with Louis Rukeyser,"

"Adam Smith's Money World," and "The Nightly Business Report"—is subtly anti-labor and anti-tax, undoubtedly due in no small part to the fact that all three of PBS's regular business shows are heavily financed by corporations.

In a single week's worth of watching "The Nightly Business Report" early in the summer of 1993, you would have seen, to list but a few examples: guest analyst Beryl Sprinkel suggesting how the rejection of President Bill Clinton's stimulus package would achieve Clinton's economic goals of promoting growth and cutting the deficit; Nikko Securities economist Robert Brusca dismissing Clintonomics as "detrimental and in fact hostile to job growth"; and a spot on how government efforts to crack down on money laundering have only served to over-regulate the banking and auto industries.

But over that time, not one defense of Clinton's proposal to raise taxes was given by anyone other than a Clinton official or a congressional Democrat. One program skipped the pros and cons of the issue altogether and was instead devoted entirely to illuminating the loopholes in existing estate tax.

PBS, a few weeks earlier, had aired Adam Smith's lament for the over-regulated drug industry, which Smith sympathetically described as "punch-drunk" before intoning: "Pharmaceuticals—this is a high-tech, high-wage industry. It's creating jobs in America. But the drug companies are under attack. Their stocks have nosedived. Where's the attack coming from? No, not from the Japanese or the Germans, but Washington."

Emphasis on Investment

"Wall $treet Week's" host, Louis Rukeyser, peppers his investment advice with watch-your-wallet quips throughout the program. In the same weeks during which the above episodes ran, you could have tuned in to catch references to "our tax-hungry politicians," and "Washington. . . [where] the folks apparently have a thirst for taxing everything from income to output." A reference to *Jurassic Park* led to the jibe that "we have creatures in unions and management who haven't had an original thought in at least 65 million years."

And on June 18, 1993, came a 5-minute address to Clinton, pretending to advise the President on how to succeed in the private sector:

> Mr. President . . . even though you were, in fact, a hard-working, relatively low earner all the years up to now, the minute you started bringing in the bigger bucks in the private sector, some crazy politician would probably start talking about you as if you had been a permanent member of that hated class, the rich. . . . Why, some nutty guy is even likely to start taking potshots at you as one of those who had some kind of obscene party in the eighties when the rest of the country sup-

posedly suffered and who therefore needs to be hit with every kind of punitive new tax they can think of. Plus 10 percent.

Of course, nobody watching a show on how to invest money wants to be told to pay more taxes. Still, public television evidences a less than populist conceit by running three such programs, what with only 2 percent of the country's population trading a stock more than five times a year, according to a 1986 Federal Reserve Board study. In fact, only 4 percent of American families own bonds, a mere 3 percent have trusts, and well over half don't even have a savings account. For the 43 percent that do, the average worth is only $1,500.

An Absence of Labor

Public television is such a willing host to business TV, of course, because the business shows are cheap; they receive near-total corporate funding, usually from financial firms. But what about programs geared toward the work force? There's nothing at the national level right now, save one show, "We Do the Work," a magazine series about laborers, and it airs on only 40 stations nationwide. A City University of New York study completed in 1989 found that nine times the amount of PBS programming focused on the upper classes as "addressed the lives and concerns of workers as workers."

Business as Usual

In programming on the economy, it's business as usual. PBS stations offer regular coverage of corporate news and agendas: "Adam Smith's Money World," "Wall $treet Week" hosted by conservative Louis Rukeyser, and the "Nightly Business Report." PBS does not offer a single weekly news/talk show presenting the agendas of groups often in conflict with big business, such as consumers, labor or environmentalists.

Jeff Cohen and Norman Solomon, *Seattle Times*, March 28, 1992.

It's not because labor's allies aren't trying. In 1980, when labor unions offered to provide seed money for "Made in USA," a series about working people's history—not about labor unions—PBS told union representatives their sponsorship constituted a conflict of interest and would be grounds for not airing the shows. Asked how the situation differed from that of "Wall $treet Week"—funded at the time by Prudential-Bache—PBS's then-president Larry Grossman told the *New York Times*: "There's a difference between an underwriter with a general interest in the program's subject and one with a specific interest in it." In other

64

words, a financial company has a general interest in finance, but a labor union has a specific interest in labor. Hmmmm.

PBS eventually conceded to the union, but not without limiting labor contributions to *.3 percent* of the series's projected budget. So where to go for the money? "It's pretty near impossible to get a corporation to underwrite a labor program," says Gordon Quinn, an award-winning producer who has peddled several ideas for labor-oriented shows, "and going straight to PBS for money is sort of a hopeless cause. The answer you usually get is, 'We already did something on labor this year.'"

Perhaps PBS doesn't see any value in pumping money into something so downmarket as labor unions. "Our demographic is higher-income than any of the commercial networks," boasts PBS corporate spokesman Stu Kantor.

"Petroleum Broadcasting Service"

Not by much, it turns out—22.2 percent of public-TV households earned $60,000 a year or more, compared to the 19.3 percent of the overall-TV market. Still, it's an image PBS is intent on cultivating. Jan Wilson, director of corporate support for PBS, wrote an article in *The Advertiser*, a trade magazine put out by the Association of National Advertisers, entitled "Public Television: How It Can Fit into Your Marketing Plan." She wrote that she was able to convince Lexus to underwrite the series "Travels" because "it knew its principal market would be people who are affluent, sophisticated, and active." "Masterpiece Theater" was actually the brainchild of the Mobil p.r. chief Herb Schmerz, who set out to create the series as an advertising forum for his company. It was underwriting like this that earned PBS the tag "Petroleum Broadcasting Service." The Schmerz legacy lives on in the form of those 30-second "underwriter-ID spots" which made an end run around PBS's "no advertising" rule and now punctuate most programs.

PBS isn't entirely to blame for this corporate invasion. "It was a matter of survival," admits John Wicklein, a former administrator of the Corporation for Public Broadcasting. Indeed, when a public-sector organization gets less than one-fifth of its budget from Congress, the odds are strong that it'll have to cozy up to corporate America. So is complete congressional appropriation the answer? No, because that would leave PBS hostage to the very government good journalism is supposed to monitor. As it stands, public television has more than once been held to this constraint. Remember "The Lawmakers"? In 1982, the series profiling members of Congress was nearly pulled from scheduling because of its slavishness. But the members themselves, particularly Tip O'Neill and Stephen Solarz, lobbied the Corporation for Public Broadcasting to keep the show on the air.

What's needed is a trust fund, untouchable by Congress or any presidential administration. The money could come from taxing American households for each television set in use (à la the British system), or charging local broadcasting stations for their use of the airwaves, in effect collecting the licensing fee that has forever been waived by Congress, but which could raise as much as $1 billion a year. Both ideas have been kicking around Washington for years, but to no avail. "There's not one member of Congress who sees public broadcasting as a cause within his or her own constituency," says Jack Willis, the station director of Minneapolis's public station, KTCA, and a former PBS executive. "So there's nobody on our side." But by counting more and more on big money, public television remains wedded to a remarkably narrow, upper-middle-class market. And there's nothing very "public" about that.

Periodical Bibliography

The following articles have been selected to supplement the diverse views presented in this chapter.

AIM Report	"The Blame-Whitey Media," January-B 1993. Available from Accuracy in Media, Inc., 1275 K St. NW, Washington, DC 20005.
Ellis Cose	"A City Room of Many Colors," *Newsweek*, October 4, 1993.
Gail Dines	"Capitalism's Pitchmen," *Dollars & Sense*, May 1992.
EXTRA!	"Focus on Racism in the Media," July/August 1992.
EXTRA!	"How to Read a Newspaper: A Reader's Guide," October 1991. Special issue on bias in the newspaper.
Patricia Hynds	"Balancing Bias in the News: Critical Questions Can Help Viewers," *Media & Values*, Fall 1992.
Jeremy Iggers	"What Price Objectivity?" *Utne Reader*, September/October 1991.
Barbara Kantrowitz	"No Cheering in the Press Box," *Newsweek*, July 19, 1993.
Michael Kinsley	"Bias and Baloney," *The New Republic*, December 14, 1992.
National Review	"The Decline of American Journalism," June 21, 1993.
Laurie Ouellette	"The Right Wing Targets Public TV," *Utne Reader*, May/June 1992.
Ted J. Smith III	"The Destructive Dialectic: The Decline of American Journalism and What to Do About It," *The Heritage Lectures*, September 22, 1992. Available from the Heritage Foundation, 214 Massachusetts Ave. NE, Washington, DC 20002-4999.
Laura Sydell	"How the Media Slants the Message—and Other Reportorial Sins," *On the Issues*, Summer 1992.
The World & I	"Public Broadcasting: Private Agenda?" February 1992.
Richard Zoglin	"Public TV Under Assault," *Time*, March 30, 1992.

Do the Media Accurately Reflect American Society?

Chapter Preface

In May 1992, Dan Quayle delivered a speech in which he blamed prime-time television for contributing to the disintegration of the American nuclear family. "It doesn't help matters," he said, "when prime-time TV has Murphy Brown . . . mocking the importance of fathers, by bearing a child alone, and calling it just another 'lifestyle choice.'" Underlying Quayle's comments was the belief that the entertainment media have the power to shape the values of American society.

Many people agree with Quayle that the entertainment media undermine America's traditional values. For example, Michael Medved, author of *Hollywood vs. America*, argues that Hollywood films consistently denigrate the institution of marriage. "There are very few movies about married people," he writes, and "those that are made tend to portray marriage as a disaster, as a dangerous situation, as a battleground. . . . The message [in Hollywood movies] is that marriage is outmoded, it is dangerous, oppressive, unhealthy." Medved believes this message has contributed to many people's reluctance to marry. He writes, "In this matter, as in so many others, by overstating the negative, the film industry leads viewers to feel terrified and/or insecure, and their behavior is adversely affected."

While critics like Medved argue that the entertainment media degrade America's traditional values, others contend that the media merely reflect social realities. For example, Douglas Davis, author of *The Five Myths of Television Power*, argues that the increasing number of single-parent families on television since the late 1950s is a reflection of—not the cause of—the fragmentation of the American nuclear family. In the sitcoms of the early 1990s, says Davis, "divorced or widowed fathers raise children, often daughters, on their own, precisely as I somehow managed two daughters as a bachelor father in the very same years." Davis contends that Murphy Brown's decision to have a child out of wedlock merely reflects the fact that "unmarried pregnancy is widespread." He maintains that "the pregnancy episode distressed the nation not at all" because "American life . . . had molded *Murphy Brown* and what she came to represent."

Thus, while some contend that the media harm society by undermining traditional values, others believe the media merely reflect American life accurately. In the following chapter, authors debate the extent to which the entertainment media offer a realistic portrayal of American society.

"Hollywood no longer reflects—or even respects—the values of most American families."

The Entertainment Media Do Not Accurately Reflect American Society

Michael Medved

The American public is increasingly dissatisfied with the products of the popular entertainment industry, according to Michael Medved. In the following viewpoint, Medved argues that while most Americans believe in marriage, religion, law and order, patriotism, and good manners, the entertainment media (television, film, and music) regularly contradict and undermine these values. Medved, a film critic, is the cohost of the Public Broadcasting System (PBS) show *Sneak Previews* and the author of several books, including *Hollywood vs. America: Popular Culture and the War on Traditional Values*, from which this viewpoint is excerpted.

As you read, consider the following questions:

1. According to the author, what does the common practice of "grazing" suggest about the quality of television?
2. The events surrounding Michael Jackson's video "Black or White" offer three lessons, according to Medved. What are they?

America's long-running romance with Hollywood is over.

As a nation, we no longer believe that popular culture enriches our lives. Few of us view the show business capital as a magical source of uplifting entertainment, romantic inspiration, or even harmless fun. Instead, tens of millions of Americans now see the entertainment industry as an all-powerful enemy, an alien force that assaults our most cherished values and corrupts our children. The dream factory has become the poison factory.

The leaders of the industry refuse to acknowledge this rising tide of alienation and hostility. They dismiss anyone who dares to question the impact of the entertainment they produce as a "right-wing extremist" or a "religious fanatic." They self-righteously assert their own right to unfettered free expression while condemning as "fringe groups" all organizations that plead for some sense of restraint or responsibility. In the process, Hollywood ignores the concerns of the overwhelming majority of the American people who worry over the destructive messages so frequently featured in today's movies, television, and popular music.

The Disenchanted Public

Dozens of recent studies demonstrate the public's deep disenchantment. In 1989, for instance, an Associated Press/Media General poll showed that 82 percent of a scientifically selected sample felt that movies contained too much violence; 80 percent found too much profanity; and 72 percent complained of too much nudity. By a ratio of more than three to one, the respondents believed that "overall quality" of movies had been "getting worse" as opposed to "getting better."

In 1990, a *Parents* magazine poll revealed similar attitudes toward television. Seventy-one percent of those surveyed rated today's TV as "fair, poor, or terrible." Seventy-two percent of this sample supported strict prohibitions against "ridiculing or making fun of religion" on the air, while 64 percent backed restrictions on "ridiculing or making fun of traditional values, such as marriage and motherhood.". . .

This widespread concern over the messages of the popular culture stems from an increasingly common conviction that mass entertainment exacerbates our most serious social problems. A *Time*/CNN survey in 1989 showed that 67 percent believe that violent images in movies are "*mainly* to blame" for the national epidemic of teenage violence; 70 percent endorse "greater restraints on the showing of sex and violence" in feature films. A *Los Angeles Times* survey of the same year reported 63 percent who assert that television "encourages crime," while a 1991 *Newsweek*/Gallup Poll showed 68 percent who hold that today's movies have a "considerable" or "very great" effect in causing real-life violence.

The Hollywood establishment chooses to ignore these public attitudes, or else to downplay their significance. Surveying the severe financial problems that currently plague every component of the entertainment industry, the top decision-makers see nothing more than a temporary slump in business. In one typical comment, John Neal, senior vice president for marketing for United Artists Entertainment, optimistically declared: "All it takes is one big hit movie and suddenly the whole picture changes."

Reprinted by permission: Tribune Media Services.

That "one big hit movie," however, will do nothing to end the alienation of an increasingly significant segment of the mainstream audience. The public's growing disillusionment with the content of the popular culture represents a long-term trend that won't suddenly disappear with the end of a recession, or the release of a new batch of lucky box-office blockbusters. The depth and breadth of the current crisis suggests fundamental flaws in the sort of entertainment that Hollywood, in all of its many manifestations, seeks to sell to the American people. That is why ventures as varied as home video and rock 'n' roll radio, feature films and prime-time television, are all suffering similar and simultaneous setbacks.

Consider, for example, the baleful situation with the three major television networks. In the last fifteen years they have lost a third of their nightly audience—some 30 million viewers. As a result, their cumulative profits have sunk from $800 million in 1984 to $400 million by 1988, to less than zero in 1991. Business analysts advance many theories for this disastrous falloff, but even television insiders consider that much of the public's disenchantment relates directly to the quality of the programs. "The networks have lost audiences because they've lost touch with the American viewer," according to Gene DeWitt, head of a prestigious New York media consulting firm interviewed by *Time* in November 1990. "They haven't delivered programs that viewers want to watch."

Syndicated columnist Mike Royko spoke for many Americans when he recently declared, "I enjoy TV trash as much as the next slob. But the quality of truly trashy trash has declined." He went on to explain that of the top seventy-one shows in the Nielsen Ratings, "there isn't even one that I now watch regularly." His fellow columnist Cal Thomas announced his resolution at the end of 1990 to give up watching the networks altogether. "They have not only abandoned my values," he wrote, "they now have sunk to the sewer level, dispensing the foulest of smells that resemble the garbage I take to the curb twice a week.". . .

One reflection of viewer restlessness is the tendency toward "grazing" in their nightly viewing—using remote controls to switch stations in the middle of a program. According to a major survey for *Channels* magazine in 1988, 48.5 percent of all viewers regularly change programs during a show—and nearly 60 percent of viewers in the crucial eighteen-to-thirty-four age group. "Grazing is by definition a sign of dissatisfaction," explained James Webster, professor of communications at Northwestern University. "Viewers know what is going to happen, and they wonder what they're missing on some other channel." According to the Gallup Poll, in 1974, 46 percent of Americans rated watching television as their favorite way of spending an evening; by 1990, that number had fallen to 24 percent. . . .

Artistic Lows

Even without the pronouncements of experts, ordinary Americans understand that Hollywood is in serious trouble. As a point of reference, ask yourself a simple question: When was the last time that you heard someone that you know say that movies—or TV, or popular music, for that matter—were better than ever? On the other hand, how recently have you listened to complaints about the dismal quality of the movies at the multiplex, the shows on the tube, or the songs on the radio?

In recent years, not even Jack Valenti, the well-paid cheer-leader for the Motion Picture Association, can claim with a straight face that the movie business is scaling new artistic heights. David Puttnam, Oscar-winning producer of *Chariots of Fire* and former chairman of Columbia Pictures, reports, "As you move around Hollywood in any reasonably sophisticated group, you'll find it quite difficult to come across people who are proud of the movies that are being made." In December 1991, industry journalist Grover Lewis went even further when he declared in the pages of the *Los Angeles Times*: "The movies, which many of us grew up regarding as the co-literature of the age, have sunk to an abysmal low unimaginable only a few years ago."

In fact, nearly everyone associated with the industry acknowl-edges the obvious collapse in the caliber of today's films, and at the same time manages to blame someone else for the disastrous situation. . . .

While searching for scapegoats, the entertainment industry ig-nores the obvious: that Hollywood's crisis is, at its very core, a crisis of values. It's not "mediocrity and escapism" that leave au-diences cold, but sleaze and self-indulgence. What troubles peo-ple about the popular culture isn't the competence with which it's shaped, but the messages it sends, the view of the world it transmits.

Not America's Values

Hollywood no longer reflects—or even respects—the values of most American families. On many of the important issues in contemporary life, popular entertainment seems to go out of its way to challenge conventional notions of decency. For example:

• Our fellow citizens cherish the institution of marriage and consider religion an important priority in life; but the entertain-ment industry promotes every form of sexual adventurism and regularly ridicules religious believers as crooks or crazies.

• In our private lives, most of us deplore violence and feel lit-tle sympathy for the criminals who perpetrate it; but movies, TV, and popular music all revel in graphic brutality, glorifying vicious and sadistic characters who treat killing as a joke.

• Americans are passionately patriotic, and consider them-selves enormously lucky to live here; but Hollywood conveys a view of the nation's history, future, and major institutions that is dark, cynical, and often nightmarish.

• Nearly all parents want to convey to their children the im-portance of self-discipline, hard work, and decent manners; but the entertainment media celebrate vulgar behavior, contempt for all authority, and obscene language—which is inserted even in "family fare" where it is least expected.

As a working film critic, I've watched this assault on traditional values for more than a decade. Not only have I endured six or seven movies every week, year after year, but I've also received a steady stream of letters from moviegoers who are upset by one or another of Hollywood's excesses. At times, they blame me for failing to warn them ardently enough about avoiding a particular film; in other cases they are writing to express their pent-up frustration with an industry that seems increasingly out of control and out of touch. My correspondents frequently use words such as "disgusting" or "pathetic" to describe the sorry state of today's films. In 1989 a young woman from Westport, Connecticut, expressed these sentiments with memorable clarity. "The problem is that whenever I take a chance and go against my better judgment and venture back into a movie theater," she wrote, "I always feel like a worse person when I come out. I'm embarrassed for the people who made this trash, and I'm embarrassed for myself. It's like watching the stuff that I've just watched has made me a smaller human being. Isn't that sad?"

Into a Moral Abyss

Today's traditional nuclear family is portrayed [on television] in the crudest terms imaginable: Dads belch at the dinner table, kids take pictures of their mothers shaving underarms, parents can do nothing right, and children are bratty, disrespectful and, worst of all, proud of it. . . .

"The Simpsons," "Married . . . With Children," and "Roseanne" may be successful and, at times, even amusing. But, in a very real way, they are helping to lead our nation into a moral abyss, a land where the worst kinds of values are uplifted and where goodness, achievement, and beauty are frowned upon.

Joseph Farah, *New Dimensions*, November 1990.

It *is* terribly sad, especially in view of the technical brilliance that turns up in so many of Hollywood's most recent productions. When people express their disappointment at the generally low level of contemporary films, they seldom indict the camera work, the editing, the set design, or even the acting. In fact, these components of moviemaking have reached a level of consistent competence—even artistry—that would be the envy of Hollywood's vaunted Golden Age. I regularly marvel at gorgeous and glowing visual images, captured on screen in the service of some pointless and heartless waste of celluloid, or sympathize with an ensemble of superbly talented performers, acting their hearts out, and trying to make the most of empty material that is in no way worthy of them. If Robert De Niro and Dustin

Hoffman have failed to inspire the sort of devoted and consistent following once enjoyed by Jimmy Stewart or John Wayne, it is not because they are less capable as actors. What ails today's films has nothing to do with the prowess or professionalism of the filmmakers. The true sickness is in the soul.

Dazzling Degradation

This heartbreaking combination of dazzling technique wedded to a puerile and degrading purpose shocked the country in one of the most heavily hyped entertainment "events" in history: the world premiere of the music video "Black or White," from Michael Jackson's album *Dangerous*.

On November 14, 1991, Fox Network, MTV, and Black Entertainment Television simultaneously broadcast the first showing of this eleven-minute extravaganza, which had been created by director John Landis at an unprecedented cost of $7.2 million. To prepare the public for the momentous occasion of the televised premiere, Epic records released the song (without the accompanying images) to radio stations just two days in advance. Within twenty-four hours, "Black or White," described by the record company as "a rock 'n' roll dance song about racial harmony," had been added to the playlists of 96 percent of America's 237 Top 40 radio stations. This broke the previous record for a first-day release—94 percent—which had been set by Madonna's "Like a Prayer" in 1989.

On the fateful Thursday night of the televised premiere, an estimated 40 million individuals tuned in—helping Fox Network score the highest ratings of any night in its five-year history. To insure maximum exposure to the children and preteens who make up such an important part of Michael Jackson's core audience, the video featured well-advertised cameo appearances by both TV favorite Bart Simpson and diminutive movie star Macaulay (*Home Alone*) Culkin.

The video begins, in fact, with a tender domestic scene between Culkin and George Wendt (of TV's "Cheers"), playing his irritable dad. Macaulay is upstairs in his room, happily listening to music, when his father orders him to turn it down, threatening the child with a wagging finger. In response, the adorable boy hauls some huge amplifiers and speakers downstairs, tells Dad to "Eat this!" and proceeds to blast the music at such an ear-shattering level that he literally blows his parent through the roof.

The video proceeds to a display of a dizzying succession of more or less random images, including dancing Cossacks in the Kremlin, whooping Native Americans in feathers and paint, and Michael and a partner hoofing their way through hundreds of speeding cars on a busy freeway. The most memorable sequence involves a series of fifteen magical transformations in the course of little more than a minute, using the costly computer-generated special effect called "morphing" and made popular by *Terminator 2*.

A Performance Piece

The most troublesome transformation comes near the end of this incoherent epic, as the song concludes and the soundtrack falls silent except for a selection of jungle growls, screeches, and roars. A stalking black panther turns miraculously into Michael Jackson as we've never seen him before—attempting a feeble impersonation of a sulky, menacing, inner-city tough guy, tap-dancing down a wet, deserted street. As if to prove his manliness, Michael grabs repeatedly at his crotch, with close-ups showing our hero pulling the zipper of his pants suggestively up and down. *Entertainment Weekly* magazine later counted thirteen instances in which the superstar touched his "private parts," and at one point he performs an exaggerated simulation of masturbation. Finally, this inane episode reaches its creepy climax, as Jackson picks up a garbage can to shatter a store window, and uses a crowbar to savagely bust up a parked car, for no apparent reason whatever. As director John Landis helpfully explained in an interview prior to the premiere broadcast: "The epilogue is really a performance piece by Michael Jackson that can stand totally on its own. It's essentially an improvisation of Michael's."

The national television audience failed to appreciate that improvisation. Immediately following the telecast, switchboards at MTV, Fox Network, and all the network affiliates lit up with outraged complaints. One Fox official commented: "In all my years of television, I never saw anything like it. We couldn't believe the volume, and we couldn't believe the intensity. It was like a tidal wave." A spokesman for Jackson's production company confirmed that negative feedback was coming at them "from all directions."

Within twenty-four hours, the chagrined superstar agreed to delete the controversial four-minute epilogue from all future versions of his video and issued an elaborate apology to his fans. "It upsets me to think that 'Black or White' could influence any child or adult to destructive behavior, either sexual or violent," his statement read. "I've always tried to be a good role model and therefore have made these changes to avoid any possibility of affecting any individual's behavior. I deeply regret any pain or hurt that the final segment of 'Black or White' has caused children, their parents, or any other viewers."

Fox Network issued a lame apology of its own, admitting that "based on calls we've received, the strong symbolism used in one sequence overshadowed the film's message about racial harmony. We apologize to anyone who interpreted that sequence as sexually suggestive or violent and was offended."

It is impossible to imagine how anyone could possibly interpret the sequence as anything *other* than "sexually suggestive or violent"—after all, toying with your fly in intense close-up and using a crowbar to shatter a parked car amount to the sort of "symbolism" that is hardly ambiguous.

The unanswerable question about this entire affair is how the experienced executives at the network, the record company, and Jackson's PR agency could seem to be so sincerely surprised by the public's outraged response. Did it never occur to them that people might find it more than a bit distasteful to use Macaulay Culkin and Bart Simpson to promote a video freak show that unequivocally encouraged vandalism and crotch-grabbing as forms of self-expression? With so many tens of millions of dollars riding on the outcome, with Michael's album setting all-time records for both its production and promotional costs, how could they afford to be so blind? . . .

Three Lessons

First, the Michael Jackson fiasco shows that some of the most powerful, highly paid, and widely respected titans in Hollywood are hopelessly out of touch with the public they are trying to reach. They don't begin to understand the values of the average American family, or the special concerns of the typical parents who worry about unwholesome influences on their children.

Second, the Jackson affair clearly demonstrates that the American people understand that media images influence real-life behavior. The entertainment industry may deny its own impact, but ordinary citizens know better. They know perfectly well that if tens of millions of kids watch repeatedly as Michael Jackson gleefully smashes a car with a crowbar, then their own car is that much more likely to get smashed someday—and their own kids are that much more likely to try some smashing. The logic of this assumption is so obvious and inescapable that only the most shameless entertainment executives and their hired academic experts would even attempt to argue against it.

Third, the outcome of the "Black or White" controversy proves that an outraged audience can force changes on even the most powerful figures in show business. As a result of the spontaneous public outcry, Michael Jackson and his associates agreed to the uncomfortable and expensive expedient of cutting four questionable minutes from their eleven-minute video. Similar pressure, applied in a sustained and coordinated manner on a range of issues in American entertainment, could alter the entire direction of the popular culture.

"Single-parent, working woman, fragmented family sitcoms . . . reflect real choices made in the real world."

The Entertainment Media Accurately Reflect American Society

Douglas Davis

In *The Five Myths of Television Power: Or Why the Medium Is Not the Message*, Douglas Davis refutes five commonly held assumptions about the power of television. In the following viewpoint, he contests "Myth Three"—that television dominates and dictates reality. Davis contends that television does not control society; rather, it reflects social trends. For example, the social conditions resulting from the maturation of the baby boom generation—relaxed marital and sexual codes, growing numbers of working women, and a greater degree of sophistication—are reflected in the shift from the stable television families of the 1950s to the fragmented television families of the 1990s, according to Davis. Davis has taught media theory at several universities.

As you read, consider the following questions:

1. According to Davis, why did the baby boom generation demand new types of television characters?
2. Why does Davis believe that the public would have accepted Murphy Brown's decision to have an abortion?

Though the power of print has been praised and feared since Gutenberg, the notion that any medium can effectively replace reality, enveloping us within itself, dates properly from the advent of television. Only then did the artificial, created world seem to overpower the real world. I vividly remember the appearance of TV in the neighborhood I grew up in, during the 1950s, in Washington, D.C. While each of the families on my block spent hours reading newspapers and listening to radio, no one warned me, on the street or in Sunday School, against the pernicious powers of word or of sound. But I recall uncles and aunts grumbling about the pervasive spread of Lucille Ball coiffures in offices, schools, and even church pews, as soon as the TV set became ubiquitous. Once I heard a sermon in which Satan and the new medium were clearly linked. Never had the Lone Ranger, who thundered through my living room radio every Sunday night, been so maligned, or feared.

For weeks thereafter, I kept my eye out for upswept batches of Lucy's red hair but couldn't detect a single strand. Her nonpresence on my block matched the invisibility of the loud Ranger, who couldn't be found around the corner, either, despite his ubiquity. As I grew up, I was constantly lectured to the contrary by journalists and authors like Marshall McLuhan (anticipating Frank Mankiewicz and Joel Swerdlow's *Remote Control*), who found Lucy, Desi, and Milton Berle in their morning cereal, dictating social trends, the news, and even the weather. . . . Many of us do now assume that for the vast majority of the TV audience, the screen, in effect, is a window. What we see on the other side of the window we believe, if not imitate, according to Myth Three [TV is (our) reality].

From a Stable to a Splintered Society

The historic roots of this credo reach back into my adolescence and early adulthood, that is, the late 1950s and early 1960s. These were the years when what is now known as the baby-boom generation emerged in nurseries everywhere, when neither the Vietnam War nor civil rights nor feminism was yet in full flower or full roar. The demographics of the nation, and of the mass-produced goods that served it, were stable: two parents, two children, a home, a garden, the suburbs. In his touching, slightly bewildered lament, *Whatever Happened to Madison Avenue?* Martin Mayer recalls the days when a giant corporation like Campbell's could market a soup with a logo and a visual concept (the plump and sprightly "Campbell's Kids") that lasted at least half a century, feeding a social structure that stayed in firm place.

It was the same family structure served by manicured network news, broadband comedians like Milton Berle, and primal sitcoms like *I Love Lucy, Father Knows Best, Leave It to Beaver, The Adventures of Ozzie & Harriet,* and, later, *Family Ties,* which somehow managed to adopt the counterculture, followed, finally, by *The Cosby Show* in the 1980s. I remember thinking in the early halcyon days that the audience was not outside looking in but the reverse, that Network TV had its nose pressed to the glass of the window, seeking to reproduce what it found on the other side, the *inside,* that is, the real world. In these early programs, the heart and soul of Myth Three, the nuclear family prevailed against all odds, centered, as Hal Himmelstein points out, in one of two classic personality types, either the "loser," the genial mom or pop who is half buffoon (Lucy, for example, Ozzie, for another), or the victor who is superior in mind and spirit, though trapped in the same mundane circumstances as the presumed viewer (cf. Robert Young, the father who knew best, and Harriet, the mother who occasionally knew).

But this imperturbable society, enforced at once by the dictates of fiction and of demographics, proved temporary. Sociologists tell us that the GI Bill generation, those who fled to the green suburbs in retreat from the vicissitudes of a world war, began to splinter as early as the late 1950s. The single-parent family multiplied as the divorce rate rose, empowered by rising incomes and mobility. If the networks moved slowly to recognize the perils of raising kids alone, this may account for the complaint by many viewers—when they were asked, occasionally, in polls—that the sitcoms, though beloved, ignored them. Meanwhile, the resident mother, TV's staple "market," began to leave the home in the late 1960s and throughout the next decade, for occupation, travel, friendship, and extra- as well as postmarital adventuring. Men and women in their mid-twenties and thirties returned to the campus in these years in droves, driving the average age of the college student way up.

TV Imitates Life

In *The Culture of Narcissism,* an august jeremiad against the dissolution of sober work-ethic values, Christopher Lasch, in company with those who accuse TV of dictating reality, rails against a culture bent on hedonistic dissolution. But surely these massive social shifts, finally acknowledged twenty years after the fact in single-parent, working woman, fragmented family sitcoms like *Mary Hartman, Mary Hartman, Kate & Allie, Who's the Boss?, Blossom, Davis Rules, Baby Talk, Full House,* and, in the 1990s, both *Roseanne* and *Married . . . with Children* reflect real choices made in the real world beyond the fictional frame. In *Blossom, Davis Rules, Full House,* and *Drexell's Class,* divorced or widowed fathers raise children, often daughters, on their own, precisely as I somehow managed two daughters as a bachelor father in these very same years. Which side of the TV screen is here impacting upon the other? When Marlo Thomas contrasted the worldliness of the heroine she played in a comedy special in 1986 with her demure Ann-Marie in *That Girl*, fifteen years before, she saw it as a maturation in the medium, not in the public, a sign that TV is imitating life ("It seems astonishing to me how TV has grown up"). . . .

Though it is rarely noted in the many articles and books written about the decisive shift that occurred in the content of prime-time network programming between the 1950s and the 1980s, the nature of the audience changed decisively first. By the time TV began gingerly to recognize single-parent households in shows like *My Three Sons* and *The Andy Griffith Show*, they were spreading rapidly in the land beyond, a consequence at once of education, the rising divorce rate, and the "liberation" of women from confinement in the suburban villa. The unprecedented increase in college graduates, caused first by the GI Bill, acted as a jump start in sophistication. In each of the decades beginning with the 1960s, Americans increasingly read more books, traveled more extensively, and attended more theater, live and film, than their grandparents and parents. The nouveau elite saw to it that their sons and daughters did the same. As for the "liberated" woman, she was now able to make a series of decisions all on her own, rather than waiting for Father/Husband to act first. According to anthropologist Helen Fisher of the American Museum of Natural History, this more than any other social change insured that the American divorce rate would reach the same level (approximately 50 percent) as that of virtually every other postindustrial nation. In her book *The Sex Contract: The Evolution of Human Behavior*, Fisher notes that historically women who have won economic independence have always preferred a series of husbands or lovers, that is, "serial" rather than pure monogamy.

A Libidinous Change

Given this fact, it is no wonder that television began to loosen its marital and sexual codes in the mid-1970s, in product commercials as well as sitcoms and even news documentaries. "Reality," or what appeared to be the real world, demanded this change, which lagged considerably behind events on the other side of the screen. Though *An American Family* [a 1970s PBS documentary that recorded six months in the lives of an average middle-class American family, including the parents' marital problems and the son's announcement of his homosexuality] seemed prurient to some reviewers and an affront to the nuclear family code to Christian fundamentalists, the mere incidence of divorce was hardly uncommon, anywhere in the United States.

"Gay rights" was not yet a political movement, but homosexuality was widely discussed, in private and in public, particularly by the generation emerging from the free-speech 1960s. By the mid-1970s, barely a few years after Lance Loud bared his soul [on *An American Family*], virtually every primetime "family" show had devoted itself to the subject of gay sex, nearly always in positive, understanding terms. *Soap*, a nighttime serial that appropriately satirized its own name, boasted a gay son in the heart of its "family." The few exceptions, like *My Three Sons*, were clearly holdovers from the stolid ethics of the 1950s.

The Consumer Determines the Product

There has been renewed discourse about Hollywood's moral obligations to the public and the extent to which the sex and violence of feature films does violence to existing social morés. . . . The renewed hand-wringing about movie morality has at its base a theory of communication enunciated more than 50 years ago by Harold Lasswell, who suggested a "hypodermic" notion of media, wherein communication processes are seen as something an individual or agency does to someone else. Like "impact" theories of art, this idea proceeds on the assumption that the public is a kind of *tabula rasa* (clean slate) upon which is inscribed all social, cultural, economic, political, and moral ideas. Such theories pay little attention to the role media have in reflecting ideas already circulating in society. . . .

If the show biz world is so out of step with American values and if, in fact, Hollywood is conspiring to rot our moral fiber, why do we keep buying? . . . The blame lies squarely and solely with the consumer. It is not in the interest of the commercial media to do anything but move product in the quickest and most efficient way possible.

Christopher Sharrett, *USA Today*, September 1993.

It is difficult to overestimate the functional importance of this libidinous change in the character of the medium's audience. To date, it has only been sensed—and critiqued—by writers like Lasch or Paul Hollander, in *Anti-Americanism: Critiques at Home and Abroad, 1965-1990*, who are engaged on differing levels in moral outrage. But in retrospect, the reversal seems inevitable. While Bob Hodge and David Tripp argue persuasively in *Children and Television* that economic class often determines viewing response, they and others overlook the power of what might be called "cultural class." Though the aging baby boomers gradually assumed economic power and respectability, they never entirely deserted the belief, rooted in the songs, literature, and politics of the decade in which they matured, that lovemaking was primarily to be indulged for pleasure. . . .

TV Is Not to Blame

TV is a tempting target for moralists and journalists. It is easier to use vivid examples of licentious behavior in prime time—teenagers losing their virginity, for example, on *Beverly Hills 90210* or *Doogie Howser, M.D.*—than to patiently pick apart mountains of often conflicting data, or quote the cross-cutting conclusions of psychologists, and therapists, to say nothing of progressive changes in religious practice: while the Moral Majority made headlines in the 1980s, many mainstream Christian and Jewish faiths revised their teachings on sexual behavior, within and without the bonds of marriage. Even so patient and skilled a writer as Joshua Meyrowitz in *No Sense of Place* invoked Myth Three to explain the dramatic shift in male-female role models in the 1970s and 1980s. Facing the complex truth about the economic and political transformation of what used to be called "the middle class," Meyrowitz concluded that TV, by lifting the veil that once covered the male and the female psyche, as well as their confidential discourse, had caused the merging of masculinity and femininity, that is, the long-predicted androgynous lifestyle.

But surely the epic shift in the means by which the "middle" of American society earned its living, cared for its children, and came into direct contact with a world it never visited before (through a quantum leap in international travel) dwarfed the influence of prime time. Not that TV ever fully commanded the allegiance of this "new class," which did not duplicate the settled habits of its parents. If it means anything, "middle class" denotes a certain sense of stability, of families living in state, in place, with roles clearly defined. Now, in an era when jobs, homes, and parenting responsibilities are evolving with the speed of light, the appeal of a "stability" that is rooted in a single place (or function) has disappeared, perhaps forever. Surely it is the fragmentation of the Middle, brought on by these deep-seated cultural, economic, and occupational changes, that provoked seismic change in the body politic, not the medium that reported and recycled them.

Education, Literacy, and Sophistication

Prime among these changes, charted in part by critical tracts like Daniel Bell's *The Coming of Post-Industrial Society* (1973), Peter Drucker's *The Age of Discontinuity* (1969, 1978), and Alvin Gouldner's *Intellectuals and the Rise of the New Class* (1979), is the proliferation of education and of literacy. During the very period when analysts like Meyrowitz and others saw *Dallas* and Calvin Klein *Obsession* commercials revising each sex's view of the other, the economy virtually demanded that change. As American dependence on industrial production changed to a need for software and services, for literacy, patience, and detail, trained, educated women became prime commodities in the work force, which is crucial to marketplace performance. It is no accident that the 1960s and the 1970s also saw a quantum leap in the number of women admitted to universities. By the mid-1980s, the sexes were virtually equal in their representation on campus, whereas before World War II, women made up less than 10 percent of the college and university student body. Men were similarly affected by these massive shifts in employment supply and demand. More and more they saw their livelihood dependent on knowledge, not brawn.

For the first time, perhaps, American men and women began to share equally in a culture based in print, in travel, and a multiplicity of professional contacts, as well as TV viewing. Chronologically, this change swept through the very generation weaned in the 1950s that suffered the slings and arrows of the civil rights struggle, the Vietnam War, and the assassinations of the Kennedys and Martin Luther King. This combination did not bode well for the simple monochromatic morality that attended early network TV. Producers and directors in the generation following hard upon *An American Family* had to deal with an audience packing a relatively sophisticated sense of how the world works. To say that this worldview was subtler, less given to the acceptance of stereotypical myths is an understatement. Many young adults felt themselves betrayed by a government that prosecuted what seemed an unwinnable, immoral war [Vietnam]; they did not believe in sheriffs with white cowboy hats and generals with braided visors. They demanded and instead received the very supply of ambiguous demi-heroes/villains that to this day continue to portend moral decline for TV preachers—lawyers and doctors who cheat, sadistic police officers, priests who are sex offenders. Once revered, authority figures became in these years suspect. *Watching America*, by Linda Lichter, Robert Lichter, and Stanley Rothman, documents, for example, a sharp rise in instances of workers ridiculing none other than the boss throughout the 1970s, without suffering any adverse consequences. . . .

Murphy Brown's Choice

With unprecedented access to disposable income, these New Class Americans, ranging from age thirty to fifty, have increasingly pursued multiple, often contradictory, directions in living, traveling, loving, eating, reading, voting, or viewing. Increasingly, these patterns daunted pollsters, marketing analysts, and evange-lists. They still do. But in fact, this evolution ought to be cele-brated, not excoriated. The informed freedom to think and to choose has been the central premise of mass education, not to say literacy, dating back to the eighteenth century and to the Enlightenment. Indeed, it is precisely this freedom of thought, ac-quisition and movement that attracted the citizens of repressive regimes in Eastern Europe and in Asia. Their pent-up desire ex-ploded in the late 1980s, leading to the fall of the Berlin Wall and the tragic drama of Tiananmen Square, in Peking. "Choice" on levels both mundane and high has become something approach-ing a sacred value at the end of this century, approaching the citi-zen's right to "elect" his own leaders in the eighteenth century. This conviction, which easily predates television, informs virtu-ally everything taught, written, filmed, or set to popular music in Western culture, though it rarely informs those who prefer to see our life choices guided by the nightly network serials.

Coincident with the rise in the economic and political power of women, "free choice"-as-ideal stoked the already heated con-troversy in the United States—and other countries—over the right to decide for or against abortion. When CBS decided in the fall of 1991 to allow its *Murphy Brown*/Candice Bergen to give birth out of holy wedlock (though the father turned out to be Murphy's ex-husband), we were once again warned by funda-mentalist pressure groups like Turn Off Television (who spon-sored "black-out" days in the state of North Carolina that year) and journalists committed to our myth that prime-time TV was subverting the morals of its audience. Diane English, the award-winning director and writer of *Murphy Brown,* defied critics in advance of the broadcast. Unmarried pregnancy is widespread, she pointed out to the press, quoting a female viewer who had written in asking "What's the big deal?" But Ms. English also confessed that Murphy had no choice but to give birth; if she aborted, *Murphy Brown* would be finished, bereft of sponsors surely frightened by right-to-life protesters.

Murphy Brown Representative

My own conviction is that *Murphy Brown* would have stayed the storm, just as then Governor Bill Clinton later survived those who predicted that his alleged extramarital affair would ruin his political career during the Democratic primary season of 1992. Ms. English underestimated both her fictional heroine and her "real-life" audience. A decision to abort would have seemed entirely logical for the aggressive, independent Murphy. Furthermore, she would follow, not trail-blaze, in the path worn by her audience. By the early 1990s, the advocates of choice outpolled their antiabortion opponents by margins ranging from

10 percent to 30 percent, depending on the state. When a male colleague attempted on the fall premiere to persuade Murphy Brown to abort with a crude joke, offering to accompany her "to some back alley," she replied, coolly:

> There is no back alley. Women in this country legally have a choice . . . at least I think they do. I haven't checked the papers today.

This is hardly radical doctrine. Though the press often portrayed Brown as a marginal, challenging figure, because of her wit and spectacular self-reliance (a TV news anchorwoman, she draws a hefty salary; further, she easily fields a cadre of attentive males), it is by now almost impossible to argue that she is unrepresentative, at least in attitude, if she ever was. In hindsight, it's clear that the pregnancy episode distressed the nation not at all. Rather, it pulled the highest rating the program had ever enjoyed to that point, and the follow-up mail was overwhelmingly favorable. By the time its heroine decided to speak out directly against the vice-president's dark lament (that she threatened oldstyle "family values"), Murphy had moved even more securely into the mainstream. On September 22, 1992, when Candice-as-Murphy-Brown-fictional-TV-anchorwoman rebuffed Quayle, she attracted 44 million people, a larger audience than had watched the Republican convention one month before. One of the viewers was Quayle himself, who began to speak reassuringly about his "respect" for single parents, perhaps because his aides had reminded him that more than one-third of American families, potential voters to the last, were commanded by single mothers and fathers. Who, in this exchange, represented fiction, who fact?

Certainly "Murphy" in the end spoke at least for the "fact" represented by her huge market. American life, in a sense, had molded *Murphy Brown* and what she came to represent. Granted, these forces made her into a complex figure, compared with the popular heroines who preceded her. Often, she seemed in these episodes neither male nor female, left nor right, yin nor yang. The decision she made earlier—to have the child in the face of all her misgivings ("What do I want with a baby?" she asks herself. "I'm living a highly complete life here.")—is precisely the kind of impossible choice often presented by postindustrial life to a new class that swims in a sea of options. In conditions of poverty, or of wealth, the options are simpler, if not softer. But the life now endured by most of us is neither. It offers an endless terrain of criss-crossed, cutting angles.

3

"In . . . films, only the woman who buries her intelligence . . . is granted a measure of professional success without having to forsake companionship."

American Films Reflect a Backlash Against Feminism

Susan Faludi

Susan Faludi is a reporter for the *Wall Street Journal*. In her book *Backlash: The Undeclared War Against American Women*, she argues that the 1980s witnessed a backlash against women's rights—"an attempt to retract the handful of small and hard-won victories that the feminist movement" won for women. This backlash is revealed, says Faludi, in the ways that women are portrayed in popular films. For example, female film characters who are independent and outspoken, and who pursue careers rather than families, are often depicted as unattractive, unhappy, and unfulfilled. According to Faludi, these films reflect American society's attempt to keep women in traditional roles as wives and mothers.

As you read, consider the following questions:

1. According to Faludi, why was Shirley Temple so popular among adult men?
2. Why does Faludi say that madness is a sign of sanity in women's films of the 1970s?
3. According to the author, what is the difference between children in the films of the 1970s and those of the 1980s?

The backlash [against the women's movement] shaped much of Hollywood's portrayal of women in the '80s. In typical themes, women were set against women; women's anger at their social circumstances was depoliticized and displayed as personal depression instead; and women's lives were framed as morality tales in which the "good mother" wins and the independent woman gets punished. And Hollywood restated and reinforced the backlash thesis: American women were unhappy because they were too free; their liberation had denied them marriage and motherhood. . . .

Hushed and Shrunk

Efforts to hush the female voice in American films have been a perennial feature of cinema in backlash periods. The words of one outspoken independent woman, Mae West, provoked the reactionary Production Code of Ethics in 1934. It was her caustic tongue, not her sexual behavior, that triggered these censorship regulations, which banned premarital sex and enforced marriage (but allowed rape scenes) on screen until the late '50s. West infuriated the guardians of the nation's morals—publisher William Randolph Hearst called her "a menace to the sacred institution of the American family"—because she talked back to men in her films and, worse yet, in her own words; she wrote her dialogue. "Speak up for yourself, or you'll end up a rug," West tells the lion she tames in *I'm No Angel*, summing up her own philosophy. In the '30s, she herself would wind up as carpeting, along with the other overly independent female stars of the era: Marlene Dietrich, Katharine Hepburn, Greta Garbo, Joan Crawford and West were all officially declared "box office poison" in a list published by the president of Independent Theater Owners of America. West's words were deemed so offensive that she was even banned from radio.

Having stopped the mouth of the forty-year-old West and the other grown-up actresses, the '30s studios brought in the quiet good girls. The biggest Depression female star, Shirley Temple, was not yet school age—and got the highest ratings from adult men. When she played "Marlene Sweetrick" in *War Babies*, she was playing a version of the autonomous Dietrich, shrunk now to a compliant tot. . . .

A Brief Infatuation with Feminism

For a while in the '70s, the film industry would have a brief infatuation with the feminist cause. Just as silent-era Hollywood gave the movement a short run—after a series of low-budget pro-suffrage films turned into big hits—movie studios in the late '70s finally woke up to the profit potential in the struggle for women's independence. In films like *Diary of a Mad Housewife*,

A Woman Under the Influence, An Unmarried Woman, Alice Doesn't Live Here Anymore, Up the Sandbox, Private Benjamin, and *The Turning Point,* housewives leave home, temporarily or permanently, to find their own voice. At the time, the female audience seemed to be on a similar quest. In New York movie theaters in 1975, women were not sitting placidly in their seats. They were booing the final scene of the newly released *Sheila Levine Is Dead and Living in New York,* because the script rewrote the bestseller's ending to marry off the single woman—to a doctor, of course, who would presumably cure her of her singles' sickness.

The *Fatal Attraction* Syndrome

It is no great revelation that women as movie characters have long been distorted and misinterpreted by Hollywood. This should come as no surprise in a society where men dominate leadership positions everywhere, and comprise over 90% of screenwriters. What we usually see on screen is not women as they are, but rather a male idea of women, how men perceive them and wish them to behave.

For the most part, these preconceptions have ranged from the belittling and insulting to the absurd, along the narrow spectrum of hooker to housewife. But these perceptions have taken a vicious turn, with women assigned to some of the most unbelievably depraved and pathological roles that ever stalked the screen.

This trend, which could be termed the *Fatal Attraction* syndrome, creates such caricatured female villains in order to then justify an inevitable brutal retaliation against them. . . .

Parallel to this villainization and attacks of women on screen are the assaults against their political and economic rights off screen. Witness the expanding feminization of poverty with comparatively lower wage scales for women and cutbacks in public assistance, a court system stacked against survivors of rape, sexual harassment, domestic violence and surrogate motherhood, and attacks against reproductive freedom regarding Roe vs. Wade and implementation of the abortion gag rule.

Prairie Miller, *Political Affairs*, February/March 1992.

Eventually, filmmakers came around to the boisterous audience's feminist point of view. The end of *Private Benjamin,* where the heroine rebuffs her domineering groom, is a case in point. "It was very important to me that she walk out of that church," recalls Nancy Meyers, who created the film with Charles Shyer. "It was important to write about women's identity, and how easily it could be lost in marriage. That sounds almost old-fashioned now, I guess. But I know it mattered to many, many women." After *Private Benjamin* came out, Meyers was inundated with letters from women "who saw themselves in her character." It was a liberating event for the film's leading actress, too: Goldie Hawn had been typed up until then as a blond bubblehead.

In *Private Benjamin*, Hawn plays the single Judy, whose "life's desire"—marriage comes crashing down when her husband dies on their wedding night. "If I'm not going to be married, I don't know what I'm supposed to do with myself," she says. She winds up enlisting in the army, where basic training serves as a metaphorical crash course in emotional and economic independence. Over thirty but not panicked about her single status, Judy goes to work and lives on her own in Europe. Eventually she meets a French doctor and they are engaged, but when she discovers his philanderings, she calls a halt to the wedding in midceremony, flees the church, and flings her bridal crown to the heavens. The scene recalls the famous ending of the 1967 *The Graduate*; but in the feminist version of this escape-from-the-altar scenario, it was no longer necessary for a man to be on hand as the agent of liberation.

Madness as Sanity

The women who go mad in the 1970s women's films are not over-thirty single women panicked by man shortages but suburban housewives driven batty by subordination, repression, drudgery, and neglect. In the most extreme statement of this theme, *The Stepford Wives*, the housewives are literally turned into robots created by their husbands. In *Diary of a Mad Housewife* and *A Woman Under the Influence*, the wives' pill-popping habits and nervous breakdowns are presented as not-so-unreasonable responses to their crippling domestic condition— madness as a sign of their underlying sanity. What the male characters label lunacy in these films usually turns out to be a form of feminist resistance.

Women in these '70s films do not turn to male "doctors" to cure them: in Private Benjamin, when her fiancé (who is, significantly, a gynecologist) offers to give Judy a shot to help her "calm down," she slaps his face. Instead, these heroines seek counsel from other women, who dispense the opposite advice of traditional male clinicians: take action and speak up, they urge. The housewife in Paul Mazursky's *An Unmarried Woman* seeks advice from an independent female therapist, who tells her to go out, enjoy sex, and "get into the stream of life." In Martin Scorsese's *Alice Doesn't Live Here Anymore*, the housewife turns to a wise-cracking and foul-mouthed waitress for wisdom. "Once you figure out what it is you want," the waitress advises, "you just jump in there with both feet and let the devil take the hindmost."

The American marriage, not the woman, is the patient under analysis in the '70s women's films, and the dialogue probes the economic and social inequities of traditional wedlock. "A woman like me works twice as hard and for what?" Barbra Streisand, the housewife Margaret in *Up the Sandbox*, demands of her husband, a history professor. "Stretch marks and varicose veins, that's what. You've got one job; I've got ninety-seven. Maybe I should be on the cover of *Time*. Dust Mop of the Year! Queen of the Laundry Room! Expert on Tinker Toys!" Margaret's mother offers the most succinct summation of what, in the opinion of these films, lies at the core of marital distress: "Remember, marriage is a 75-25 proposition. The woman gives 75."

In these films, the heroines are struggling to break out of the supporting-actress status that traditional marriage conferred on them; they are asking to be allowed, for once, to play a leading role in their own lives. "This story is going to be all about me," announces Judy Davis's Sybilla, in the first line of Gillian Armstrong's *My Brilliant Career*, an Australian film that became a hit in the United States in the late '70s. The youthful heroine turns down a marriage proposal not because she doesn't care for her suitor, but because marriage would mean that her own story would never have a chance to develop. "Maybe I'm ambitious, selfish," she says apologetically. "But I can't lose myself in somebody else's life when I haven't lived my own yet."

Of course, according to the conventional '80s analysis, these '70s film heroines *were* selfish, their pursuit of self-discovery just a euphemism for self-involvement. But that reading misses a critical aspect of the female quest in these movies. The heroines did not withdraw into themselves; they struggled toward active engagement in affairs beyond the domestic circle. They raised their voices not simply for personal improvement but for humanitarian and political causes—human rights in *Julia*, workers' rights in *Norma Rae*, equal pay in *9 to 5*, and nuclear safety in *The China Syndrome*. They wished to transform not only themselves but the world around them. They were loud, belligerently loud, because speaking up was a social, as well as a private, responsibility. "Are you still as angry as you used to be?" Julia, the World War II resistance fighter, asked Lillian Hellman in the biographical *Julia*. "I like your anger. . . . Don't you let anyone talk you out of it."

A Return to Housekeeping

If Vanessa Redgrave's Julia represented the kind of heroine that 1970s feminist cinema would single out for biographical study, then it fell to Redgrave's daughter, Natasha Richardson, to portray her counterpart for the late 1980s: Patty Hearst. As conceived in Paul Schrader's 1988 film, the bound and blind-folded heiress is all victim; her lack of identity is her leading personality trait. As Schrader explained: "[E]ssentially the performance is like a two-hour reaction shot."

The same might be said of the droves of passive and weary female characters filling the screen in the late 1980s. In so many of these movies, it is as if Hollywood has taken the feminist films and run the reels backward. The women now flee the office and hammer at the homestead door. Their new quest is to return to traditional marriage, not challenge its construction; they want to escape the workplace, not remake it. The female characters who do have professional lives take little pleasure from them. They find their careers taxing and tedious, "jobs" more than callings. While the liberated women of '70s films were writers, singers, performers, investigative reporters, and political activists who challenged the system, the women of the late '80s are management consultants, investment advisers, corporate lawyers, behind-the-scenes production and literary assistants. They are the system's support staff.

Most women in the real contemporary labor force are, of course, relegated to ancillary, unsatisfying or degrading work, but these films aren't meant to be critiques of sex discrimination on the job or indictments of a demoralizing marketplace. They simply propose that women had a better deal when they stayed home. The films stack the deck against working female characters: it's easier to rationalize a return to housekeeping when the job left behind is so lacking in rewards or meaning. It's hard to make the case that a woman misses out if she quits the typing pool—or that society suffers when an investment banker abandons Wall Street.

Unhappy Career Women

The career women of the late-'80s cinema are an unappealing lot. They rarely smile and their eyes are red-rimmed from overwork and exhaustion. "I don't know what I'm doing anymore," Cher, an attorney, complains to a co-worker in *Suspect*; he's single, too, but, being male, immune to burnout. She tells him:

> I don't have a life. The last time I went to the movies was like a year ago. The only time I listen to music is in my car. I don't date. I'd like to have a child but I don't even have a boyfriend so how can I have a child? . . . I don't think I can do it anymore. You know, I'm tired. I'm really tired.

In *Surrender*, Sally Field's Daisy is an "artist." But her artistry is performed at an assembly-line factory, where she mass-produces landscape art for hotels. Her one stab at a personal statement is to brush a tiny female figure into one of the canvases; it is a picture of herself drowning. All she wants to do, understandably, is quit and devote her life to marriage and motherhood. "If I'm not married again by the time I'm forty-one," she moans, "there's a twenty-seven percent chance I'll end up a lonely alcoholic." Her "biological clock" is practically a guest star in this film. She has a dream, she tells her enviably fertile friend, who is pregnant for the fourth time. "This dream has a husband and baby in it." The "bottom line," says Daisy, is, "I want a baby." Although she claims to aspire to a career as a painter, after five minutes in front of the easel she is sidetracked by her more important marital mission. She hums the wedding march as she chases her prospective husband, a prolific and successful novelist. . . .

The professional women on screen who resist these nesting "trends," who refuse to lower their expectations and their voices, pay a bitter price for their recalcitrance. In *Broadcast News*, Holly Hunter's Jane, a single network producer, fails to heed the cocooning call. She's not out there beating the bushes for a husband and she's passionate about her work. Her male co-worker, a single reporter, has the same traits; on him they are admirable, but on her they constitute neurosis. She is "a basket case" and "an obsessive," who dissolves into inexplicable racking sobs in the middle of the day and compulsively chatters directions. "Except for socially," a female colleague tells her, "you're my role model." While the two lead male characters wind up with brilliant careers and full private lives, Jane winds up alone. Her aggressiveness at work cancels out her chances for love. Her attempts to pull off a romantic encounter fail miserably every time. "I've passed some line someplace," she says. "I'm beginning to repel people I'm trying to seduce."

A Baby-Doll Exterior

In these backlash films, only the woman who buries her intelligence under a baby-doll exterior is granted a measure of professional success without having to forsake companionship. In *Working Girl*, Melanie Griffith's Tess, an aspiring secretary with a child's voice, rises up the business ladder *and* gets the man—but she achieves both goals by playing the daffy and dependent girl. She succeeds in business only by combing the tabloid gossip columns for investment tips—and relying on far more powerful businessmen to make the key moves in her "career." She succeeds in love Sleeping Beauty-style, by passing out in a man's arms.

Tess is allowed to move up in the ranks of American business only by tearing another woman down; in the '80s cinema, as in America's real boardrooms, there's only room for one woman at a time. Female solidarity in this film is just a straw man to knock down. "She takes me seriously," the naive Tess confides to her boyfriend about her new boss, Katharine. "It's because she's a woman. She wants to be my mentor." The rest of the narrative is devoted to disabusing Tess of that notion. Katharine, a cutthroat Harvard MBA with a Filofax where her heart should be (the film's ads called her "the boss from hell"), betrays Tess at the first opportunity. The film ends with a verbal cat fight between the Dark and Light Woman, a sort of comic version of *Fatal Attraction*'s final scene, in which Tess orders Katharine to get her "bony ass" out of the office. Not only does Katharine *not* get the man; she doesn't even get to keep her job. . . .

Making Motherhood Alluring

The backlash films struggle to make motherhood as alluring as possible. Cuddly babies in designer clothes displace older children on the '80s screen; the well-decorated infants function in these films more as collector's items than people. The children of a decade earlier were talkative, unpredictable kids with minds of their own—like the precocious, cussing eleven-year-old boy who gives his mother both delight and lip in *Alice Doesn't Live Here Anymore*, or the seventeen-year-old girl who offers her mother both comfort and criticism in *An Unmarried Woman*. In the late 1980s, by contrast, the babies hardly cry.

Women get sorted into two camps: the humble women who procreate and their monied or careerist sisters who don't. *Overboard*'s haughty heiress refuses to reproduce. But by the end of the film—after she is humiliated, forced to scrub floors and cook meals, and at last finds happiness as a housewife—she tells her tyrannical new husband of her greatest goal in life: having "his" baby. Women who resist baby fever, by controlling their fertility or postponing motherhood, are shamed and penalized. In *Immediate Family*, Glenn Close's career woman—an Ivy League-educated realtor—delays and her biological clock expires. After a grueling round of visits to the infertility doctors, she has to hire a teenage surrogate to have a baby for her. . . .

Lost Ground

In 1988, all but one of the women nominated for the Academy Award's Best Actress played a victim. (The exception, fittingly, was Melanie Griffith's working "girl.") The award's winner that year, Jodie Foster, portrayed a rape victim in *The Accused*. The producer of that film was Sherry Lansing.

Lansing released *The Accused* a year after *Fatal Attraction*, and hoped that it would polish up her feminist credentials. The film told the story of a young working-class woman gang-raped at a local bar while a crowd of men stood by and let it happen—a tale based on a grisly real gang rape at Big Dan's tavern in New Bedford, Massachusetts. "If anyone thinks this movie is antifeminist, I give up," Lansing told the press. "Once you see this movie, I doubt that you will ever, ever think of rape the same way again. Those images will stick in your mind, and you will be more sympathetic the next time you hear of somebody being raped."

Did people really need to be reminded that rape victims deserve sympathy? Apparently Lansing did: "Until I saw this film, I didn't even know how horrible [rape] is," she announced. Apparently many young men watching this film needed the reminder, too: they hooted and cheered the film's rape scene. And clearly a society in which rape rates were skyrocketing could stand some reeducation on the subject.

Lansing said *The Accused* should be hailed as a breakthrough movie because it tells America a woman has the "right" not to be raped. But it seems more reasonable that it should be mourned as a depressing artifact of the times—because it tells us only how much ground women have already lost. By the end of the '80s, a film that simply opposed the mauling of a young woman could be passed off as a daring feminist statement.

"Depiction of women has changed in a pro-feminist direction."

American Films Support Feminism

Stanley Rothman, Stephen Powers, and David Rothman

Stanley Rothman is a professor of government at Smith College in Northampton, Massachusetts, and a coauthor of *Watching America: What Television Tells Us About Our Lives*. Stephen Powers and David Rothman have each coauthored several essays on motion pictures. In the following viewpoint, the three authors argue that the film industry supports women by increasingly portraying them in nontraditional careers. Furthermore, they contend that women are presented in a more favorable light than men in similar positions, and that women are depicted as sympathetic characters even when their goals and methods are unfavorable. They conclude that there is no antifeminist backlash represented in the movies.

As you read, consider the following questions:

1. The percentage of women in nontraditional careers is greater in films than in society, according to the authors. Why do they believe this discrepancy is significant?
2. According to the authors, how did the films of the 1940s and 1950s reflect the societal consensus?
3. How have film depictions of romance changed, according to the authors?

From "Feminism in Films" by Stanley Rothman, Stephen Powers, and David Rothman, *Society*, March/April 1993, © 1993 by Transaction Publishers. Reprinted with permission.

Several national magazines and reports on television have proclaimed a backlash against the women's movement. Citing polls to demonstrate that over 60 percent of American women do not regard themselves as feminists, analysts have announced the advent of a new negativity in the treatment of women. A number of books have been published that make the same argument in greater detail.

Susan Faludi's extensively documented and well received book *Backlash: The Undeclared War Against American Women* argues that the backlash against the accomplishments of the woman's movement in the 1960s and 1970s began with the Reagan administration. Among other subjects, Faludi analyzes the treatment of women in motion pictures to prove her case. A prime example of female bashing, she says, is the Glenn Close character in *Fatal Attraction*, the crazed career woman undone by her biological clock. While acknowledging that movies sometimes portray strong competent women, she maintains that many women presented as strong are often simply protecting their young or are dealt with negatively. For example, in *Broadcast News* the feminine lead is obsessed with her job. In *Baby Boom*, on the other hand, a professional woman opts out of the rat race for the sake of a child. . . .

Feminist Critics Are Wrong

Are those feminist critics (including Faludi) who charge a motion picture backlash correct? Our systematic analysis of a random sample of the 100 top grossing films since 1946 shows this to be not so. Broken down by decade, we have created a consistent coding scheme for each film with data on race, gender, class and a whole host of other characteristics. We have classified the goals of characters in each of the films (greed, revenge, romance, and so on) and summarized overall treatment of each character in the film (positive, negative, mixed). Trained coders scored the films using a detailed codebook and instructions. Reliability was tested to assure that it remained at or above 70 to 80 percent. Our coders were primarily female college students. Films will be listed with year of release and ranking for the year by total receipts according to *Variety* magazine.

Our findings differ considerably from Faludi's and critics who share her views. The late 1970s and especially the 1980s witnessed a continuation of a significant pro-feminist shift in women's roles that began in the 1960s. Increasing numbers of women appear in non-traditional occupations, asserting their independence from men in ways that dovetail with revised notions of romance. Non-traditional occupations for women increase from 38 percent in the first two decades after the Second World War to 49 percent in the late 1960s and 1970s; from 1976

98

to 1989 the figure rises again, to 61 percent. Among women in starring and supporting roles we find an even greater increase in the number portrayed in non-traditional occupations, which rises in the 1980s to 72 percent.

This last statistic should give pause to those who see Hollywood either as a mirror of existing social conditions, or as a bastion of reactionary mythmaking. Despite the influx of women into the workforce, this composite image does not represent women's employment in a realistic way. But it is a sure sign that depiction of women has changed in a pro-feminist direction.

Representations of Women from the 1920s to the 1960s

The representation of women in Hollywood films is not an issue of inclusion or exclusion (as in the case with racial minorities). Women appear in nearly all of the 146 top grossing films we analyzed. Leading female characters represent only about 25 percent of all characters for the entire period. This seems to be a consistent and rigid proportioning for men and women in the movies. While women have always appeared alongside men in star and supporting roles in Hollywood movies, their interests and activities were quite distinct from those of men for many years. In movies of the 1920s and 1930s, women first began to appear in strong roles—as played by Marlene Dietrich, Greta Garbo, Mae West, and others. . . .

By the 1940s, the period when our content analysis begins, things had changed. The Production Code [regulations imposed in 1934 to ban movie depictions of premarital sex] had a real impact on the contents of movies by the late 1930s and the war had taken away many boyfriends and husbands. Many more American women had begun to work outside the home as well. In response to this turmoil in American life, Hollywood's female leads became much more interested in romance and family life. These were more ordinary interests that the moguls perhaps had decided were threatened by the war, or compromised by the demands of work. Movies then may have mirrored the societal consensus of the day more closely.

Although many female leads were extraordinary individuals—the roles of Katharine Hepburn and Rosalind Russell were quite powerful—female characters of the 1940s and 1950s would seek to divert men away from pursuing careers, adventure, wealth, or even war or a life of crime, and getting them to channel more of their energy into domesticity. Most leading female characters were young, attractive, and motivated by romance. [For] the heroines in a large number of the films in our sample—*The Egg and I* (1947/8), *Father's Little Dividend* (1951/10), *Seven Brides for Seven Brothers* (1954/9), *High Society* (1956/4), *Love Me Tender* (1957/10), *The Music Man* (1962/7), and many others—life revolves around finding a husband or resolving romantic problems in favor of conjugal happiness. The women characters' goals usually involve getting the men they care about to behave the way a "good" father or husband should. . . .

Although in the earlier movies women often work, the kind of work they do correlates with their roles vis-à-vis romance. Women who hold traditional kinds of jobs usually do so only to survive. They are either housewives, elementary or secondary school teachers, nurses, secretaries, waitresses, or have other occupations conventionally associated with women. When these characters become romantically involved and marry (the two usually go together), work rarely remains important or desirable. . . .

Rating Movie Images

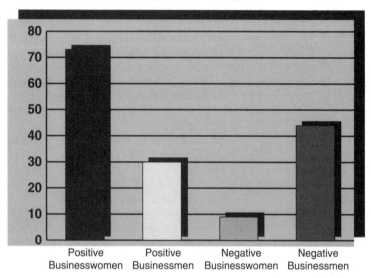

Increasingly since the 1970s, movie women are found in previously elite male jobs, but they are much less likely to be portrayed as villains than men in similar positions.

A significant number of [movie] women hold non-traditional jobs in this period, that is, jobs that were much more likely held by men in the society at the time. These non-traditional roles include college teachers, doctors, lawyers, CEOs, sales managers, military personnel, and other high-paying or otherwise elite jobs. There is, however, an extraordinary catch—the women who hold elite jobs are much more unlikely to be married at a film's opening, and much more interested in romance. Further, until the 1960s, women in lead roles and non-traditional occupations are twice as likely to be motivated by romance as other women. Sixty-four percent of the women, and 68 percent of the elite women, are motivated by romance, as opposed to 30 percent and 28 percent of women in traditional roles. In short, movies of the 1940s and 1950s either present women as already linked to men through marriage, or as pursuing men while working in careers. Even single working women are overwhelmingly portrayed in the earlier period as romantic hopefuls, even though they may not have married. In the later period this correlation between elite occupations and romantic motivation lessens substantially. . . .

Corresponding to emphasis on marriage over work for women in the earlier movies, female characters usually want children and the responsibilities of running a household. Rarely do they express any doubt regarding their suitability for these roles. In spite of the strength of female characters, the social consensus that runs through the films is that men and women serve very different purposes in life. . . .

The Depiction of Sex

It is difficult to overstate the changes in representations of gender roles, and especially of women, since the mid-1960s. Many, if not all, of earlier female characterizations have been modified, or even reversed outright, albeit in complex, interdependent ways. Of course, the relaxation of movie industry self-censorship allowed the introduction of sexually explicit material and by the early 1970s many movies emphasized sexuality in romantic relationships. Yet, the changes were also deeper and more subtle than a quantitative increase in explicit depictions of sex would suggest at first. Although many film theorists and critics have argued that the 1980s witnessed a reactionary trend in representations of women, this is hardly the case. If anything, a liberal attitude on sexuality and social and political issues involving gender has once again transformed Hollywood representation of women since the late 1960s.

The depiction of sex has been the most sensational change since 1965. Hollywood movies before 1965 usually condemn sexual activity outside of marriage. . . . Under the rating system that went into effect in 1968, sexually explicit material became more and more acceptable in films for adults. Sex outside of marriage quickly became an acceptable activity, and as representations of sexual conduct became more daring, women's roles gradually expanded from the predominantly romantic to more complex characterizations. Some movies made not only previous judgments about non-marital sex more problematic, but also the romantic idealism that generally surrounded marriage and family life—sex hardly had to lead to marriage or scandal now, but could function as one aspect of an open-ended entanglement—and a way to sell tickets. . . .

From Romance to "Self Interest"

In movies from the mid-1960s on, the scenarios change rapidly. While romance remains high as a goal for all female characters, "self interest" now is a close second. In the previous decades "self interest," the second most frequent motivation for women, was found in only 28 percent of the sample group. Romance quickly loses its preeminence in women's motivation at the same time as explicit depictions of sex multiply. Many films now represent romance as a secondary concern for women, or at any rate as less consuming than it once was for the myriads of women now in elite professional positions. In the film *The Electric Horseman* (1980/9) Halle (Jane Fonda) is an aggressive investigative reporter who gets her story, despite the interference of romance. Unlike earlier movies, where romance and career often merge into a romantic narrative, in this case they conflict.

In *Mr. Mom* (1983/9) Caroline (Terri Garr), a frustrated housewife with a college degree, becomes a high-powered business executive while her husband stays home and takes care of the kids, again leading to conflict. . . . In *Private Benjamin* (1980/7), female army recruits are put through the same grueling basic training as men. Judy Benjamin (Goldie Hawn) starts out as a blond bimbo but winds up a successful military officer who, in the final scene, punches out her chauvinist fiancé.

While the goal of romance declines substantially for these leading women in non-traditional occupations, for women in traditional occupations romance actually increases in importance as a motivation. This, however, occurs at the same time as the percentage of women in traditional occupations is falling off dramatically and non-traditional occupations are rising.

Even in films where romance figures prominently, it often causes conflicts not present in most earlier films. . . . Sally (Meg Ryan), in *When Harry Met Sally* (1989), is an independent, modern woman, a successful author, determined not to become sexually involved with her best friend Harry (Billy Crystal). The two sleep together eventually but this compromises the friendship and, until the end of the story, fails to bring about a more serious commitment. Both are holding back their feelings for each other. This film provides an interesting view of the contemporary barriers to intimate communication, now just as likely to be a problem for women as for men. Although a more realistic view of modern life, it is quite different from earlier portrayals of women as more willing participants in romance. These characters must find their ways in a bewildering variety of landscapes which simply did not exist in earlier mainstream American films.

Women Presented More Favorably than Men

Along with changes in the representation of sex, romance, and women's occupations come new goals and methods for female characters, particularly in the late 1970s and 1980s. Women's goals, and their methods for achieving them, are now more closely aligned with those of their male counterparts. One important difference: despite greater reliance on antagonism, including greed or malevolence, violence, and the exercise of authority, women in previously elite, male jobs are less likely to be villains than men in similar positions.

Women are presented in a more favorable light than men. Since the mid-1970s sympathetic roles for women have included even tough, sensational vocations as well as elite ones, and finally, highly violent behavior. *The Witches of Eastwick* (1989) is a notable example of the new image of women. The three protagonists, Alexandra (Cher), Jane (Susan Sarandon), and Sukie (Michelle Pfeiffer) are working women who become romantically involved with the devilish Darryl Van Horn (Jack Nicholson). Sukie, mother of six, has been deserted by her husband but still manages to work as a newspaper writer. Jane is recently divorced and works as a schoolteacher. Alexandra is a widow raising one child and working as a sculptor. To rid themselves of their demonic lover, the three must resort to violence and deceit. In spite of being victimized by Darryl and other men along the way, the women manage to win out in the end—beating the devil at his own game. The only negative woman in the movie is Felicia (Veronica Cartwright), the newspaper editor's more traditional wife. She is portrayed as a bible-thumping prude and Darryl sends evil spirits to possess and destroy her. Whether women play business moguls, military heroines, super-cops, or con-artists, they tend to improve the overall image of these professions because as a rule women are more likely to be sympathetic protagonists than men. This is especially true for elite business occupations.

In recent years big business has become a new category of employment for women. They fill positions from which they were essentially excluded in earlier periods, such as CEOs, sales managers and representatives, proprietors, and supervisors. Female characters who have moved into these ranks are rated much more positively than their male colleagues. Susan (Elizabeth Perkins) is such a character in the movie *Big* (1988). Molly (Kirstie Alley) in *Look Who's Talking* (1989) is a CPA [certified public accountant] pursuing her career while raising an infant. The father is an irresponsible, philandering wealthy businessman. In *Moonstruck*, Loretta Castorini (Cher), another CPA, breaks out of her more traditional family role and previous engagement, to pursue her fiancé's brother.

In fact, for the last decade or so, positive businesswomen outnumber businessmen by a ratio of more than two to one: 73 percent of women are rated positively in business, while only 30 percent of the businessmen are positive characters. Businesswomen are also far less likely to be negative figures than men. Only 9 percent received negative ratings in contrast to the majority of businessmen—44 percent. The remaining 26 percent [of businessmen and 18 percent of businesswomen] received mixed ratings. While female characters have always appeared in a larger percentage of sympathetic roles than men, women now represent a formidable and much more legitimate cohort within the business ranks, at the same time that business as a whole appears seamier and more corrupt than it did before.

Motives and Methods

All of the more violent movie heroines of recent years—*Terminator 2*, *Thelma and Louise*, and *V.I. Warshawski*—are highly sympathetic. Thelma and Louise wind up on the run from the law because they have shot and killed a would-be rapist. The actions of the two women, which include various acts of violence, crime, and other wrongdoing, are shown as fully justified. The men in this movie are overwhelmingly portrayed as fools and villains, always trying to take advantage of them. In the end, the two escape only in death, by driving their car over a cliff. American society is essentially portrayed as an immoral and unjust patriarchal culture that subjugates women in almost every aspect of private and public life.

Sharper critiques of specific American institutions in movies of the past twenty-five years correlate with the rising status of female characters. For example, in recent decades the majority of rich men have been portrayed negatively, while few rich women have been so portrayed. In other words, the female characters associated with this elite group are much more rarely associated with its shortcomings, which tend to be embodied in male characters. Another way of viewing the change is to examine the methods female characters use to achieve their goals and how these methods are depicted. For example, corresponding to the substantial increase of women filling non-traditional jobs is a rise in the use of authority or discipline. Women in traditional roles seldom resort to this method.

After 1976, it more than doubles as a method for women in non-traditional occupations. Notably, the rise in the use of authority or discipline correlates with positive character ratings. Examples of this are plentiful. In *Stripes* (1981/5) the two female

MPs [military police] are positive authority figures while Sergeant Hulka (Warren Oates) and Captain Stillman (John Larroquette) are portrayed as idiots. Even the apparently reactionary *Rambo: First Blood, Part I* (1985/2) features Co (Julia Nickson) as a political dissident and guerrilla fighter who aids Rambo (Sylvester Stallone). In *The Enforcer* (1977/8), Kate Moore (Tyne Daly) is Harry Callahan's (Clint Eastwood) unlucky partner. She is killed in the line of duty, but not before she saves Harry's life in a shoot-out with convicts at San Quentin.

In both *Police Academy I* (1984/8) and *Police Academy II* (1985/8) women appear as strong, capable law enforcement officials, even though many male officers are portrayed as silly, incompetent, or both. Many of the female characters in elite professional roles, such as Princess Leiah in the *Star Wars* trilogy, also fit this description. In the past twenty-five years, female characters have more likely been motivated by contemptible impulses, such as greed and malevolence, than they were before. And they are now more likely to be violent, especially those in non-traditional occupations. Violence has become an important new method for all women and, since the mid-1970s, non-traditionally employed women are almost as likely to resort to violence as men.

Moviemakers Are Sympathetic to Women

Based on the shifts in female characters' goals motivated by greed and malevolence, and in their increasing reliance on violent and authoritative methods, we would expect to see a decline in the numbers of positive portrayals overall and a corresponding rise in the negative treatment of women in non-traditional jobs or roles. This is in fact not the case. When male and female characters in elite jobs are rated, women come out far ahead of men.

In recent movies women maintain their advantage over men despite their reliance on negative goals and methods. Women's increased importance in the workforce is a reality of American society, but Hollywood is not a reportorial community.

The Hollywood elite has not discarded old myths for truth, but it has created new myths to replace outmoded ones. Hollywood moviemakers have been relatively sympathetic to the change in women's roles in the past and continue to be so. The backlash described [earlier] exists only in the minds of those who assert it is so, either because they have not fully achieved what they wish to achieve or because they are attempting to rally their troops (or troupes) for further efforts.

"Seldom does TV portray the indignities that blacks routinely encounter, regardless of social or economic status."

Many Television Images of Blacks Remain Negative

J. Fred MacDonald

In the following viewpoint, J. Fred MacDonald argues that while the situation of blacks in television—both behind the camera and on the screen—has somewhat improved since the early 1980s, images of blacks remain unsatisfactory. According to MacDonald, blacks are unrealistically presented either as middle-class citizens, which minimizes the racial inequities present in American society, or as caricatures of demeaning racial stereotypes. MacDonald is a professor of history at Northeastern Illinois University in Chicago and the author of *Blacks and White TV: African Americans in Television Since 1948*, from which the following viewpoint is excerpted.

As you read, consider the following questions:

1. According to the author, what has motivated the television industry to improve its treatment of blacks?
2. MacDonald notes that while television has changed for the better, there has been no "moral reevaluation of racism within U.S. society." What does this prove, according to MacDonald?
3. What are three of the black stereotypes found on television, according to the author?

After decades of racial misrepresentation and damaging bias in U.S. television, the situation for blacks in white TV has been changing significantly since the early 1980s. With networks in decline and national television evolving toward a new relationship with its public, the medium is slowly evidencing a new racial attitude. This is because the infrastructure of the industry is changing. Ultimately, TV is a medium of advertising, and money is its mother's milk. Since American television has always been fueled by sponsors' dollars, it has been dedicated to attracting large audiences for the commercials of its advertisers. If material forces alter this fundamental arrangement, then those in the business must adapt or perish.

New business conditions by the 1990s have made African Americans a prized target audience, one to be respected by programmers and appreciated by advertisers. Although secondary characterizations and stereotyping . . . may endure, before the camera blacks are gradually emerging from predictable, subordinate roles. Behind the camera minority presence remains small, but here, too, there have been modest developments in which blacks have begun to exert influence over program production and content. Together, these changes constitute a breach in the racial logjam that chronically has blocked African Americans from fair and open access to the video industry. These changes also represent a move toward fulfilling the original promise of prejudice-free TV, a condition that seems more realizable in the final decade of the 20th century than at any time in the history of the medium.

Fragile Improvements

But there remains serious weakness in the new attitude of television toward black America. As director Melvin Van Peebles noted on the CNN *Showbiz Today* telecast of April 28, 1989, "Now, television has offered a substantial opportunity—not as substantial as we would like, not as equitable. But on the whole it's moving a little bit." Although created by substantial changes in the structure of television, this movement toward an honest treatment of minorities is still recent and fragile. The improvements of the last several years do not constitute an immutable transformation. The improvements remain defenseless against pressures created by economic calamities, deteriorating international relations, and social and political tensions within the United States.

It is significant that these material changes have not been complemented by any moral reevaluation of racism within U.S. society. When a former Grand Dragon of the Ku Klux Klan and American Nazi Party leader [David Duke] garners almost two-thirds of the white vote in the Louisiana senatorial election in

1990—then nearly wins the governorship of that state in 1991—it is obvious that racial bigotry remains virulent and obvious and rewarding. When civil rights protections find stiff opposition from the President of the United States, Congress, and the Supreme Court, black Americans cannot be reassured that equality and justice are on the horizon. When it is more dangerous for a young black man to walk the streets of urban America than to fight his nation's battle in the Persian Gulf, social fact must sound a sobering counterpoint to any advancement for African Americans in television. And when 43 percent of black children are born officially poor—when black unemployment is more than double that of whites—when a black boy is seven times more likely to be murdered than a white boy—when nearly half the African-American teenagers in Chicago are high school dropouts and there are more black men in Washington, D.C. jails than are graduated from the city's high schools in a year, the United States has clearly failed a sizable portion of its citizens. As a 1991 British assessment of ghetto conditions [by the *Economist*] has declared, "The slums in America's great cities are shameful. They are a damning indictment of the richest country in the world. The problems that fester in them are not peripheral: they constitute America's main domestic challenge today."

In understanding the place of blacks in contemporary TV, there is also a lesson from recent history to consider. Just as social, economic, and political developments in the early 1970s eroded the Golden Age for blacks in the industry [the last half of the 1960s, when the greatest achievements were realized], so too might future realities adversely affect the positive trends of the past several years. Unless their presence takes root in the infrastructure of the business, blacks will always be vulnerable.

What Image?

Adding to the ambiguity of this improving situation is an apparent confusion among blacks about their own image in popular culture. With a greater potential for honest African-American representation, questions are being debated within the black community. Should blacks be shown only as middle class and assimilated, as are most whites, or is this a denial of racial authenticity? Should blacks be portrayed in terms of the urban underclass, especially when such imagery might appear as crude or unaccomplished? Should the folk images of rural blacks—often with characteristics that have fed the distorted, racist stereotypes so familiar in American pop culture—be propagated now as authentic, or should they be buried as anachronistic and self-defeating? Can African Americans dare to accept a full range of racial characters—from the dynamic chairman of the corporate board to the dimwitted buffoon—when the predominantly white audience has a persistent history of prejudice, when black socioeconomic mobility remains constricted, and when television still has not opened its doors to full and unfettered participation by minorities?

In the new television arrangement most people of color have been assimilated into the middle class where they now display the behavioral norms of bourgeois white America. Yet, this "Bill Cosby" image has received its share of criticism, attacked for being unrealistic, unrepresentative, and misleading. Certainly, there is a substantial black middle class whose housing, dress, language, education, income level, value system, and life-style are little different from its Caucasian equivalent. In fact, the black bourgeoisie rose from about 10 percent of the African-American population in 1960 to more than one-third of it by 1991. Moreover, many scholars have long asserted that social class is more crucial than race or ethnicity in determining social behavior. Still, as it did at the time when *Julia* [a 1960s situation comedy about a middle-class black woman] was a popular series, such representation invites criticism for proposing an unauthentic model for blacks.

African American Experience Is Not Revealed

Many people fail to realize that the African American experience in society differs from the average American's experience because prejudice and discrimination have profoundly affected almost all Americans of African ancestry. Therefore it is reasonable to expect that televised persons from this group will reflect aspects of that unique experience, including the needs, interests, concerns, or perspectives written by, for, or about the group. In fact, however, the mainstream values and beliefs of African Americans seen on primetime commercial television have not revealed unique African American experience but rather the perceptions of white producers, sponsors, writers, and owners.

Jannette L. Dates, *Split Image: African Americans in the Mass Media*, 1990.

Importantly, there is a substantial portion of the African-American population that does not meet middle-class criteria. Blacks still earn fifty-six cents for every dollar earned by whites. Many live in substandard housing located in "black sections" of the nation's large cities. Here these disadvantaged people constitute a lower class, even an underclass. They attend devitalized schools, and are victimized by an oppressive political and economic system still unwilling to address adequately their needs.

Too often, they are further hampered by broken homes, drug abuse, poverty, and insufficient job skills.

The frustrating reality of this social element is infrequently depicted in the new video order [the condition of TV since 1983, resulting from the decline of the major networks, technological advances, the arrival of cable, and the globalization of the entertainment business]. Seldom does TV portray the indignities that blacks routinely encounter, regardless of social or economic status. Seldom, too, does the medium present life in the inner city with compassion or understanding. In a report issued in 1989, the National Commission for Working Women of Wider Opportunities for Women concluded that blacks on television were being unrealistically represented. "Real-world racism, which is pervasive, subtle, and blatant, is commonplace in America but virtually invisible on entertainment television," according to the report. It pointed out, too, that 90 percent of the minority characters on TV—and most of these were African Americans—were middle-class and rich, while the working class and the poor made up less than 10 percent of those images. Yet, according to the report, more than 40 percent of minority men and 60 percent of minority women subsist on less than $10,000 annually. The report also criticized TV entertainment for misleading viewers by suggesting that racial harmony and an egalitarian work place were everyday realities, and by offering racial injustice as a matter of individual immorality instead of the result of oppressive social structures.

A Matter of Economics

Nevertheless, there is little doubt that U.S. television has begun to change. After a half-century of moral protestation, some in the industry may have been persuaded that African Americans must be treated fairly because it was the "democratic" or "right" thing to do. But the driving force behind this new video reality is more substantial than any spiritual conversion. When he appeared on a segment of the CBS program *West 57th Street* on May 27, 1989, director Spike Lee well illustrated that the basis for the new openness in Hollywood rested in economics, not ethics. Although he spoke of the motion picture industry, his comments were applicable to TV production as well. "Hollywood only understands economics. I mean, they could hate you, I mean they could call me 'nigger this' and 'nigger that' behind my back, they probably do—you know, 'young nigger upstart,' whatever. But they look at it, when they get their reports from the office, and they see my films are making money." Lee continued, "No matter what they think of me, they're still going to continue to fund them because the films are making money. But if the time ever arises where you stop making money, 'You're outta here!'"

In essence, improved African-American representation in modern television is the result of a simple equation: first, there are many more stations and consequently greater competition for viewers and profits; second, there are sizable minority audiences, the most prominent of which is the black viewership, whose loyalty is now highly desirable; and third, each minority audience appreciates positive depiction of itself on TV. When added together, the resulting programs will attract viewers, make money, and inspire others to create respectful images of minorities. . . .

Premeditated Stereotypes

[However], although cable success and network attrition delivered the message that African Americans constituted a desirable target audience, this was still no insurance against inflammatory racial representation. . . . Derisive racial depiction appeared in two basic forms: occasionally, in episodes of network shows that were otherwise benign, and fundamentally, when built into a recurring series character. . . . While egregious displays of racism might be dismissed as occasional tastelessness or the personal ignorance of individuals, there was something deeply sinister when familiar racial stereotypes appeared premeditatedly as series regulars. During the first two seasons of *Miami Vice*, Charlie Barnett played a silly street informant, Noogie Lamont, whose facial grimaces and addled banter were more appropriate for a minstrel-show endman than an occasional character in this polished Florida police drama. Moreover, his juxtaposition to the other sophisticated black and white personalities in the series only accentuated the distortion inherent in "the Noog man."

Another flagrant case of insensitivity in minority characterization occurred in the fall of 1983 on the short-lived situation comedy *Just Our Luck*. Here, T. K. Carter played Shabu, a black genie liberated from a green bottle, who now proclaimed his willingness to serve his white master "for 2000 years or until your death." Media authority Don Bogle accurately termed Shabu "a 1980s-style slave" and "an embarrassing throwback to past eras of movie coons."

In the hit series *Webster*, the endearing black child, the pickaninny, was reprised by precocious Emmanuel Lewis. Like Gary Coleman and Todd Bridges in *Diff'rent Strokes*, Webster offered a picture of the deracinated youngster living the good life because whites adopted him. Although for one season Webster had a black relative, Uncle Phillip (played by Ben Vereen), during its four-year run (1983-87) this uprooted child's world was defined by the white couple that "rescued" him after his parents

111

had perished in an automobile accident. The racial condescension in this scenario was obvious. The implications for black parenting were damning. At a time when network TV had no series featuring black families, this cute African-American boy was being raised by Caucasians. Predictably, U.S. television has never scheduled a series where a loving black couple "rescued" a white child by adopting him.

As much as the minstrel-show coon or the endearing pickaninny, the sexually neutralized black man possesses a rich history in American popular culture. In this classic characterization, African-American males were rendered romantically unappealing to white women, thereby constituting no rivalry to white male prowess. This was done via exaggerated physical unattractiveness, or diminished intellectual capacity, or a general disinterest in white femininity. Often this image was enhanced with dominating black women who bullied and belittled their weak men, an activity sure to reassure whites that the black male libido was being controlled by this substitute overseer.

Like the other minstrel-show caricatures, this emasculated social type appeared often in U.S. television—from the sexually harmless males depicted on *Amos 'n' Andy*, to their brethren in contemporary video. Nowhere in modern TV was such neutralizing of black manhood more obvious than in *Designing Women*. In a series filled with flirtatious Southern white women, the accomplished Chicago actor Meshach Taylor played the loyal friend and helper, Anthony, to four sexy and available Dixie belles. Always there with assistance or sympathy, Anthony operated around them like an ebony eunuch in a harem of white flesh, never able to touch the tempting merchandise, never even fantasizing about romantic liaison.

Linking Blacks with Crime

But recent series television has not just resurrected vintage stereotypes, it has popularized a new negative type. Although the crime rate in African-American society remains a deplorable reality, there has been little attempt by entertainment TV to explain this social crisis in terms of its roots in poverty, ignorance, discrimination, unemployment, frustration, alienation, and anger. Instead, in television fiction black crime has taken on an exciting mystique. Outlaw behavior has become an asset, in fact, as many black characters have been created as reformed criminals now working for "the system." Even harmless Anthony on *Designing Women* is an ex-convict. From a streetwise con man turned investigative reporter on *The Insiders*, to a comical escapee from a Texas chain gang on *Stir Crazy*, to a paroled murderer now investigating cases for a white female lawyer on *Gabriel's Fire*, entertainment TV has propagated the message that no one knows crime like blacks know crime. Such imagery also has suggested that lawlessness is generic to African-American manhood, and that criminality has its rewards since it provides a useful street education to these crooks-turned-good-guys.

Compounding the linkage of racial minorities to crime, network and local newscasts constantly focus on lawlessness among African Americans. While black-on-black crime statistics are staggering, the constant stream of distressing TV pictures—a bloody corpse on the ground and a drive-by shooting investigated, robbery or rape suspects jailed, drug pushers and addicts, vandalism in the projects—present black urban communities as virtual war zones. Add to this the rash of police actuality shows such as *Cops* and *America's Most Wanted* that entered television in the 1990s, and the impression received is one of rampant inner city outlawry created by uncontrollable black marauders.

The writer Ishmael Reed has lashed out at such imagery, reminding Americans that reality communicated through network television news is a distortion. According to Reed, while TV news associates blacks with drugs 50 percent of the time, in actuality 15 percent of the drug users in the U.S. are black and 70 percent are white. Although the majority of Americans affected by homelessness, welfare, unwed parenthood, child abuse and rape are whites, again TV journalism disproportionately associates these conditions with minorities. In damning "the chief source of information that Americans receive about the world," Reed was blunt. "The networks' reasoning seems to be that if blacks weren't here, the United States would be a paradise where people would work 24 hours a day, drink milk, go to church, and be virgins until marriage."

"A more positive portrayal of Black families [on television] is emerging."

Television Images of Blacks Are Improving

Bishetta Merritt and Carolyn A. Stroman

In the following viewpoint, Bishetta Merritt and Carolyn A. Stroman describe a study of three situation comedies that feature intact black families. They conclude that black family members are depicted as competent individuals, and that familial interactions are less conflictual than previous studies indicated. The authors conclude that these positive representations of black families may encourage positive attitudes and behavior among black children. Merritt is an associate professor in the Radio, Television, and Film Department at Howard University in Washington, D.C. Stroman is an associate professor in the School of Communications, also at Howard University.

As you read, consider the following questions:

1. According to the authors, what is the role of the family in society?
2. What five criteria did the authors use to evaluate the television images of black families? How did they analyze the interactions between characters?
3. According to Merritt and Stroman, why are positive television images of black family life important?

From "Black Family Imagery and Interactions on Television" by Bishetta Merritt and Carolyn A. Stroman, *Journal of Black Studies* 23 (June 1993) 492-99. Copyright © 1993 by Sage Publications, Inc. Reprinted by permission of Sage Publication, Inc.

Most people would probably agree with the assertion that "the family is at once the most sensitive, important, and enduring element in the culture of any people" (A. Billingsley). For it is within the family—the principal socializer—that an individual's personality and identity are formed and norms and values of particular cultures and subcultures are transmitted. Perhaps because of this central role that the family plays in the socialization of individuals, the family has been of great interest to scholars and laymen alike.

Television families have also been of great interest. As L.N. Glennon and R. Butsch pointed out, many of the more than 200 fictional families that have appeared in "family series" since 1946 are known and loved by millions of Americans. The Nelsons (*The Adventures of Ozzie and Harriet*), the Cleavers (*Leave it to Beaver*), the Bunkers (*All in the Family*), the Waltons, the Jeffersons, and so forth, have all become a part of our collective history and culture.

Black families have been represented in television programming scheduling since the 1950s. This viewpoint examines the portrayal of Black family life on commercial television during the 1985-1986 season. Its purpose is twofold: (a) to provide data that, when analyzed in the context of previous studies, will allow for the establishment of a trend of how the Black family has been portrayed on television; and (b) to examine Black family portrayals as a possible model for social learning by children.

Research on Black Family Portrayal

Past research concerning the imagery of Black television families is scarce and generally concentrates on the Black family in situation comedies. One qualitative researcher, Gordon Berry, identified frequent representations of Black, minority, and lower-class life-styles appearing on television and concluded that family presentations are disrupted by parent and sibling aggressive behavior; families show a continuous picture of female-dominated households whether or not a male is present; family life portrays frequent friction between males and females; and family portrayals show children with little supervision and love.

Research by B.S. Greenberg and C.K. Atkin supports some of the above notions. They observed several situation comedies with Black families (*What's Happening, Sanford and Son, Good Times,* etc.) and concluded that Black families are isolated from Whites, are more likely to be without a father, and Black mothers are more dominant when critical family decisions are made.

Greenberg and K. Neuendorf observed the interactions of Black and White families. Their findings indicate that within Black families on television the Black males were more active in family interactions than White males; the Black sons played a more active role than Black daughters or White children; and conflict as the content of family interactions was more prevalent in Black family units when compared to White family units. Are these still the messages emanating from television about Black families? The research described below addresses this question.

The Cosby Show Instills Positive Racial Attitudes

According to the Black publication *about . . . time*: "Bill Cosby may be credited with rediscovering the black family. The key to that discovery is self pride." The show's psychological consultant Alvin F. Poussaint thinks that the singular universality of the Huxtable family may have a potent subliminal impact on society: "This show is changing the white community's perspective of Black Americans. It's doing far more to instill positive racial attitudes than if Bill came at the viewer with a sledgehammer or a sermon." In a later article published in *Ebony*, Poussaint suggests that the Huxtables are dispelling negative stereotypes of Blacks. . . .

There are numerous examples of Black culture on *The Cosby Show*, including the well-known "Abolish Apartheid" sign in Theo's bedroom, the March-on-Washington show, regular mention of Black people and places, the suggestion of Ralph Ellison's *Invisible Man* for a book report, Denise's choice of an all-Black college, music by Ray Charles and the Rayettes, the picture of Martin Luther King, Jr., in Denise's room, the paintings by Black artists in the living room, Afro hairstyles and clothing, Black History Week, a special dinner at a West Indian restaurant, and reminiscences of the old Negro baseball league. In addition, a number of Black performers and personalities have been incorporated into various episodes; . . . particular attention has been devoted to Black musicians, especially jazz artists like Dizzy Gillespie, B. B. King, and Max Roach.

Linda K. Fuller, *The Cosby Show: Audiences, Impact, and Implications*, 1992.

The sample of programs examined for this analysis was limited to half-hour, prime-time, situation comedies that featured recurring, intact Black nuclear families. During the 1985-1986 seasons, three shows met these requirements: (a) the *Cosby Show*, which featured a mother, a father, four daughters, and a son; (b) *227*, which was composed of a mother, father, and one daughter; and (c) *Charlie & Company*, which featured a mother, father, two sons, and a daughter.

One third of each of the shows aired during the season were randomly selected, coded, and analyzed. Coding was done by two persons; coder reliability tests, which were done periodically on all content variables, were always above 90.

Modifications of the definitions used by J. Seggar; J. Hinton, Seggar, H.C. Northcott, and B. Fontes; and M. DeFleur to determine imagery were adopted for use in the present study. These definitions were as follows: (a) role significance—the classification of family member portrayals as major, supporting, minor, and bit parts; (b) dress—the classification of clothing apparel as showy, well dressed, ordinary, or poor; (c) occupational status—the classification of clearly observable tasks being performed that can be classified using the broad occupational categories used by the U.S. Bureau of the Census; (d) competence—the classification of intelligence displayed, the ideas proposed, or the actual successful and affective completion or carrying out of a task as very competent, generally competent, sometimes incompetent, and very incompetent; and (e) wealth—determined by context, possessions, and special access to facilities and things, classified as wealthy, comfortable, ordinary, and poor.

Interactive behavior was coded according to direction—that is, whether the interaction was conflictual or affiliative in nature—and mode—the giving, seeking, or receiving of advice, information, or orders. An interaction began when something was said between one or more of the characters and ended when one of the characters left the scene or a new character entered.

A More Positive View of Black Family Life

The first question to be addressed is what image of Black family life emerges from the three shows included in this study. In contrast to previous shows, where the majority of Black families were lower-class and rather poorly dressed, the families in *227* and *Charlie & Company* are working/middle-class, and the family in the *Cosby Show* is definitely upper-middle-class, with dress ranging from ordinary to well dressed on all three shows. As to overall wealth, the Huxtables (*Cosby Show*) are home owners, relatively wealthy, and live in a New York brownstone that is nicely furnished; the Jenkins (*227*) and the Richmonds (*Charlie & Company*) rent their apartments and enjoy rather ordinary-to-comfortable life-styles.

Occupation-wise, the mother and father on the *Cosby Show* are an attorney and obstetrician, respectively. The mother on *Charlie & Company* is a schoolteacher and the father works for the Department of Transportation. The mother on *227* does not work; initially, the father was a blue-collar worker, but later he was promoted to a professional/managerial position.

Regarding role significance, all of the family members assumed major or supporting roles, and all were portrayed as being competent or very competent. Clearly, these shows offer a different, more positive view of Black family life.

We now examine and compare family role interactions among characters on the three shows. In terms of mode of interaction—that is, giving, seeking, or receiving advice, information, or orders—the data reveal that most of the interactions appearing on all three shows were equal give and take. Specifically, 81% of the interactions on *227*, 83% of those on the *Cosby Show*, and 84% of those on *Charlie & Company* were coded as equal giving and receiving of advice, information, or orders.

Who Is Interacting?

Who is doing the interacting? On *227*, 58% of the interactions were between the husband and wife and 27% between mother and daughter. What is noteworthy is the low, compared to the other two statistics, amount of interaction between the father and daughter. On the *Cosby Show*, the father's interactions with all four of his daughters are approximately the same as with his son, 15% and 16%, respectively. Again, wife-husband interactions account for the largest amount, 31%. Surprisingly, the mother's interaction with her daughter makes up only 7% and with her son, 3%. Sibling interactions account for a substantial portion of the interactions; sister-sister interactions constitute 14% of the total interactions, and brother-sister interactions, 15%. On *Charlie & Company*, as in the other two shows, wife-husband interactions constituted the largest category (37%), followed by father-son (18%) interactions.

The data were then examined in terms of male-female role interactions. Clearly, on the *Cosby Show*, the females are the initiators, initiating over 60% of the interactions. Mrs. Huxtable, as wife and mother, initiates over 30% of the interactions. Interestingly, the father is the one more likely to be the receiver of an interaction, leading the list with 23%. Similarly, over 60% of the interactions on *227* were also female-initiated. Contrast this with *Charlie & Company* where the majority of the interactions are male initiated, with the father and sons each initiating approximately 20% of the interactions. On this same program, males are also most likely to be the receiver of an interaction; the father, husband, and the sons each received more than 15% of the total interactions.

How do these findings compare with those of previous research, particularly those of Greenberg and Neuendorf? The present research found, as did Greenberg and Neuendorf, that the most active pair in Black television families is the wife-husband pair. Although there was a tendency for fathers to interact more with their sons than with their daughters, this was only slightly so and not markedly so as in the pre-1980 shows analyzed by Greenberg and Neuendorf.

Perhaps the most important findings pertain to the low

amount of conflict evident in the interactions. In *Charlie & Company*, 9% of the interactions were characterized by conflict (i.e., one character opposed or attacked the other) as were 10% of those occurring on the *Cosby Show*. *227* had the lowest amount, 4%. This is in contrast to Greenberg and Neuendorf's research, which found Black family interactions characterized by conflictual behavior in 17% of the interactions. Interestingly, the majority of the conflicts involved daughters and sisters. (It should be noted, however, that there was little evidence of siblings being active in conflictual family role interactions as was found and reported in Greenberg and Neuendorf.)

Promoting Positive Attitudes

When compared with previous research, this analysis suggests that a more positive portrayal of Black families is emerging. That is, in this sample of television programs, Black families have both husband and wife present; these spouses interact frequently, equally, and lovingly with each other; and children are treated with respect and taught achievement-oriented values. All of this takes place in an atmosphere that harbors little conflictual behavior.

These findings are important for several reasons. A great deal of the concern expressed about the portrayals of Blacks and their families is related to the perceived impact that television has on children, particularly Black children. Seemingly, positive portrayals will have positive outcomes. Consequently, by portraying Black families in a positive light, these television programs may be providing role models that promote positive attitudes and behavior.

Additionally, it should be noted that some individuals believe that the media, particularly television, shape our ideas and attitudes about what kinds of family structures and interaction are acceptable and appropriate, and what kinds are serious or funny. The media also define for us how spouses and parents and children are "supposed" to relate to each other. The implication here is that because children learn other attitudes and behaviors from the media, it is expected that they would also learn family roles, attitudes, and behaviors from the models presented on television.

As a result, the above-documented step in the direction of improved images of Black family life is to be applauded. There is a need, however, for more shows like the exemplary *Cosby Show* if a balance is to be reached in televised portrayals of Black families.

Periodical Bibliography

The following articles have been selected to supplement the diverse views presented in this chapter.

Wayne M. Barrett — "Hollywood Sex and Violence: We've Seen It All Before," *USA Today*, September 1993.

William Norman Gregg — "The Gay Cultural Explosion," *The New American*, May 31, 1993. Available from 770 Westhill Blvd., Appleton, WI 54915.

The Humanist — "Hollywood Versus America?" January/February 1993. Two articles respond to Michael Medved's book *Hollywood vs. America*.

Raymond Keating — "Hollywood's Views of Capitalism," *The Freeman*, March 1993. Available from the Foundation for Economic Education, Irvington-on-Hudson, NY 10533.

Michael Medved — "Hollywood's Poison Factory: Making It the Dream Factory Again," *Imprimis*, November 1992. Available from Hillsdale College, Hillsdale, MI 49242.

Charles Oliver — "Box of Babel? Why TV's Diversity Is Not a Threat to the Common Culture," *Reason*, July 1993.

Sherri Paris — "Mike Tyson and Clarence Thomas: America as Seen On Television," *New Politics*, Summer 1992.

Fred Pelka — "Dreamworlds: How the Media Abuses Women," *On the Issues*, Winter 1991.

Elayne Rapping — "Gender Politics on the Big Screen," *The Progressive*, October 1992.

Paul Rudnick — "Out in Hollywood," *The Nation*, July 5, 1993.

Society — "Polarizing American Culture," July/August 1993. Several articles on media and mass culture.

Thomas H. Stahel — "America in Black and White," *America*, June 13, 1992. Available from 106 W. 56th St., New York, NY 10019.

How Do the Media Influence Society?

Chapter Preface

In October 1993, a five-year-old Ohio boy set fire to the trailer in which he lived, killing his baby sister. His mother immediately blamed the animated MTV show *Beavis and Butt-head*—which features two pyromaniacal teenaged boys—for giving her son the idea to set his home ablaze. The mother's accusation reflects an ongoing debate about the power of the media to directly influence social behavior—especially violent behavior.

Many people believe a cause-and-effect relationship exists between violence in the media and social violence. Numerous laboratory studies have suggested that viewing media violence during childhood leads to aggressive behavior in adolescence and adulthood. According to freelance writer David S. Barry, "The American Medical Association, the National Institute of Mental Health, the U.S. Surgeon General's Office, the U.S. Centers for Disease Control and the American Psychological Association have concluded that study after study shows a direct causal link between screen violence and violent criminal behavior."

However, such a causal connection between media violence and real-life violence is doubted by many commentators. These critics argue that laboratory studies on media violence lack credibility because they are subject to too many variables, including intentional and/or inadvertent manipulation by the researchers themselves. Freelance writer Mike Males argues that there is a "tendency by even the most conscientious researchers to influence subjects to produce the desired results." Moreover, Males contends that "the coexistence of media and real-life violence suffers from a confusion of cause and effect": He argues that media violence does not cause aggression, but reflects the violence already present in American society.

While some people think the media have the power to control human behavior, others believe their impact is exaggerated. The effect on society of violence in the media is one aspect of the media's influence that is discussed in the following chapter.

"Study after study shows a direct causal link between screen violence and violent criminal behavior."

Media Violence Contributes to Society's Violence

David S. Barry

The average American child will witness 100,000 acts of media violence by the end of elementary school, according to David S. Barry. In the following viewpoint, Barry argues that this increasing barrage of violent images viewed by young people since the 1950s has contributed to a dramatic rise in U.S. violent crime rates. To support his contention, Barry cites numerous studies conducted by the medical community that have proven a direct causal link between media violence and aggressive behavior. Barry is a journalist and a screenwriter.

As you read, consider the following questions:

1. According to Barry, what is the difference between media violence of the 1950s and that of the 1990s?
2. What type of television programming contains the most violence, according to the author?
3. Barry writes that many depictions of violence on television take place out of context and result in no consequences or judgments. Why do you think he makes this point?

"Growing Up Violent: Decades of Research Link Screen Mayhem with Increase in Aggressive Behavior" by David S. Barry. Reprinted with permission from the Summer 1993 issue of *Media & Values*, published by the Center for Media and Values, Los Angeles, California.

123

If you were a teenager in the 1950s, you remember the shock effect of news headlines about the new specter of juvenile delinquency. The book *The Amboy Dukes* and the movies *Blackboard Jungle* and *Rebel Without a Cause* were deeply alarming in their portrayal of teenagers willing to defy their school teachers and beat up other students. The violence portrayed in those stories, terrifying as it was, consisted almost entirely of assaults with fists and weapons which left victims injured, but alive. It was nonlethal violence. The notion of American teenagers as killers was beyond the threshold of credibility.

Since the 1950s, America has [become] almost unrecognizable in terms of the level of criminal violence reported in everyday news stories. In looking for a root cause, one of the most obvious differences in the social and cultural fabric between postwar and prewar America is the massive and pervasive exposure of American youth to television. Behavioral scientists and medical researchers have been examining screen violence as a causative element in America's crime rate since the 1950s. Study after study has been published showing clear evidence of a link. And researchers say that the evidence continues to be ignored as the violence steadily worsens.

Grim Statistics

The statistics about children and screen violence—particularly that shown on television—are grim. You've probably seen figures that show an average of 28 hours of weekly TV watching by children from ages two to 11. For prime-time programming, which contains an average of five violent acts per hour, that works out to 100 acts of violence seen each week, 5,000 a year. But children also watch cartoons, which contain far more violence than adult programming. For Saturday morning cartoon shows, the violence rate spikes up to 25 acts per hour, the highest rate on TV. With children's programming added to the mix, the average child is likely to have watched 8,000 screen murders and more than 100,000 acts of violence by the end of elementary school. By the end of the teenage years, that figure will double.

Those numbers are not mere statistics. They do not occur in a social vacuum, but in a culture and society with a murder rate increasing six times faster than the population. Whether we like to acknowledge it or not, America is in the grip of an epidemic of violence so severe that homicide has become the second leading cause of death of all persons 15 to 24 years old (auto crashes are the first)—and the leading cause among African-American youth. In 1992, the U.S. Surgeon General cited violence as the leading cause of injury to women ages 15 to 44, and the U.S. Centers for Disease Control considers violence a leading public health issue, to be treated as an epidemic.

From the 1950s to the 1990s, America has gone from being one of the safest to one of the most violent countries on earth. Here are some numbers: In 1951, with a population of 150 million, federal crime reports showed a national total of 6,820 homicides, 16,800 rapes and 52,090 robberies. For 1980, with a population of 220 million, (a 47 percent increase) the numbers were 23,000 murders, 78,920 rapes and 548,220 robberies.

The Menace of TV Violence

Turn on your TV virtually any time of any day and you can bring a carnival of murder, mayhem and bloodshed right into your living room. Maybe, like many Americans, you've grown accustomed to it and even expect it. But step back and look at this kaleidoscope of killing through the eyes of a child—and consider what role it's played for America's new generation of ultra-violent killers—and you see what a menace TV violence really is.

Susan R. Lamson, *American Rifleman*, July 1993.

In big cities, changes were more drastic. In Detroit, for instance, the 1953 murder total was 130, with 321 in New York and 82 in Los Angeles. Thirty years later, the Detroit murder tally was up to 726, the New York toll 1,665—and the Los Angeles murder total was 1,126. The fastest climbing sector of the rising crime rate is youth, with the past 10 years showing a 55 percent increase in the number of children under 18 arrested for murder. America now loses more adolescents to death by violence—especially gun violence—than to illness.

A Direct Causal Link

The reason these numbers belong in this discussion is that the medical community sees a direct link between screen violence and criminal behavior by viewers. In panel discussions on this subject, we usually hear claims from TV and movie industry spokespersons that opinion is divided in the medical community. Different conclusions can be drawn from different studies, so the arguments go, and no clear consensus exists. Yet, the American medical establishment is clear—in print—on the subject of just such a consensus. The American Medical Association, the National Institute of Mental Health, the U.S. Surgeon General's Office, the U.S. Centers for Disease Control and the American Psychological Association have concluded that study after study shows a direct causal link between screen violence and violent criminal behavior.

The research goes back decades. The 1968 National Commission on the Causes and Prevention of Violence cited screen violence as a major component of the problem. The 1972 *Surgeon General's Report on TV and Behavior* cited clear evidence of a causal link between televised violence and aggressive behavior by viewers. A 10-year followup to the Surgeon General's Report by the National Institute of Mental Health added far more data in support of the causal link. The NIMH report, a massive study covering an additional 10 years of research, was clear and unequivocal in stating: "The consensus among most of the research community is that violence on television does lead to aggressive behavior by children and teenagers who watch the programs."

A 1985 task force for the American Psychological Association Commission on Youth and Violence came to the same conclusion. A 1992 study for the APA Commission on Youth and Violence took the issue further, examining research evidence in light of its effects or implementation. The finding was that the research evidence is widely ignored. The APA report was authored by Edward Donnerstein, Ph.D., chair of the Department of Communications, University of California Santa Barbara, by Leonard Eron, Ph.D., University of Chicago, and Ron Slaby of the Education Development Center, Harvard University. Their 39-page report . . . states definitively that, contrary to arguments of people in the TV and motion picture industry, there is consistency and agreement in the conclusions drawn by the major medical organizations' studies of media violence.

After discussing a massive number of studies and an extensive body of research material, Donnerstein's study quotes from the 1982 NIMH report: "In magnitude, television violence is as strongly correlated with aggressive behavior as any other behavioral variable that has been measured."

Specifically, the report noted the agreement by the NIMH, the APA and the Centers for Disease Control that research data confirms that childhood watching of TV violence is directly related to criminally violent behavior later on.

Daily Assault

Adding scope to the APA report is a study conducted for the nonprofit Center for Media and Public Affairs in Washington, D.C. The CMPA tabulated all the violence encountered during an 18-hour broadcasting day (a Thursday) in Washington, including cable TV. The tally showed an overall average of 100 acts of violence per hour for a total of nearly 2,000 acts of violence in the 18-hour period. Most of the violence involved a gun, with murder making up one-tenth of the violent acts recorded. A breakdown by channel, or network, showed cable to be far more violent then network broadcasting. WTBS was clocked at 19 violent acts per hour, HBO at 15 per hour, USA at

14 and MTV, the youth-oriented music video channel, at 13 violent acts per hour.

The networks (except for CBS, whose violence content was skewed by the reality show *Top Cops*) were as low in violence content as PBS, which showed two violent acts per hour. ABC showed three violent acts per hour and NBC two. CBS, because of *Top Cops*, was tallied at 11 violent acts per hour. But only one-eighth of the violence occurred in adult-oriented TV entertainment. The bulk of the violence occurred in children's TV programming, with cartoons registering 25 violent incidents per hour—six times the rate of episodic TV drama. Toy commercials ranked with cartoons in violent content. Next were promos for TV shows and movies, which were four times as violent as episodic drama.

The most violent period of daily TV programming was mornings from 6 to 9 a.m. where 497 scenes of violence were recorded for an hourly rate of 165.7. Next was the 2 p.m. to 5 p.m. afternoon slot with 609 violent scenes, or 203 per hour. The morning and afternoon slots compared to 320 violent scenes in prime time, from 8 p.m. to 11 p.m., or 106 per hour, and a late-night rate (from 11 p.m. to 12 a.m.) of 114.

No Consequences

In addition to recording totals, the CMPA examined the context in which the screen violence occurred. The finding was that most TV violence was shown with no visible consequences, nor any critical judgment. A significant amount of the violence occurred in movie promos, where it was shown out of context. Music videos generally present violence without comment or judgment. Similarly, violence in cartoons and toy commercials usually occurs without consequences or comment. More than 75 percent of the violence tallied in the study (1,640 of the nearly 2,000 violent acts) was presented with no judgment as to its acceptability as behavior. Violence was judged criminal in fewer than one-tenth of the incidents. And, ironically, while violence in episodic TV drama and TV movies for adult viewers is subject to close scrutiny for context and suitability, the bulk of the screen violence viewed by children is not.

The studies mentioned above make a compelling argument, particularly when looked at as a group. But a study by Dr. Brandon Centerwall of the University of Washington Department of Epidemiology and Psychiatry takes the discussion much farther. In a study published in the June 1992 *Journal of the American Medical Association*, Centerwall looked for statistical connections between the change in violent crime rates following the introduction of TV in the United States.

Centerwall found this: murder rates in Canada and the U.S.

increased almost 100 percent (92 percent in Canada, 93 percent in the U.S., corrected for population increase) between 1945 and 1970. In both countries, the ownership of TV sets increased in almost the same proportion as the homicide rate.

Centerwall's stark and unmistakable conclusion is this: white homicide rates in Canada, the U.S. and South Africa were stable or declining until the advent of television. Then, in the course of a generation, the murder rates doubled.

The APA study by Donnerstein, Slaby and Eron also makes the point that research evidence of TV violence effects has "for decades been actively ignored, denied, attacked and even misrepresented in presentations to the American public, and popular myths regarding the effects have been perpetuated." Consequently, Donnerstein says, a major education gap exists regarding television's contribution to the problem of violence in America.

Screen Violence Rises

The discouraging point made in both studies is that, despite the massive research evidence of screen violence as a direct contributing factor to America's homicide rate, the screen violence level continues to rise.

As a writer deeply committed to the constitutional guarantees against censorship, I don't like to hear the suggestion of government regulation of movies or TV. But it's time we at least face the evidence of what screen violence is doing to our children, and come to some sober conclusions about our responsibilities to the common good.

"The best evidence . . . shows that [media violence] is a small, derivative influence compared to the real-life violence . . . that our children face."

Media Violence Does Not Cause Societal Violence

Mike Males

According to Mike Males, complaints about media violence are misdirected. In the following viewpoint, Males argues that research into the effects of media violence is unreliable and proves only a minimal relationship between media violence and real-life aggression. Males contends that the true causes of America's violence are its social problems, such as youth poverty, child abuse and neglect, and excessively harsh juvenile justice policies. Males believes that critics attack media violence because it allows them to ignore society's real problems. Males is a freelance writer.

As you read, consider the following questions:

1. Why do critics emphasize the effects of media violence on children and adolescents, according to Males? Does he believe that children are more strongly affected by media violence?
2. According to the author, what age group is responsible for the majority of crimes committed against young people?
3. Males enumerates three "embarrassing problems" with media violence research. What are they?

From "Public Enemy Number One?" by Mike Males, *In These Times*, September 20, 1993. Reprinted by permission of the author.

Forget about poverty, racism, child abuse, domestic violence, rape. America, from Michael Medved to *Mother Jones*, has discovered the real cause of our country's rising violence: television mayhem, Guns N' Roses, Ice-T and Freddy Krueger.

No need for family support policies, justice system reforms or grappling with such distressing issues as poverty and sexual violence against the young. Today's top social policy priorities, it seems, are TV lockout gizmos, voluntary restraint, program labeling and (since everyone agrees these strategies won't work) congressionally supervised censorship. Just when earnest national soul-searching over the epidemic violence of contemporary America seemed unavoidable, that traditional scapegoat—media depravity—is topping the ratings again. . . .

The campaign is particularly craven in its efforts to confine the debate to TV's effects on children and adolescents even though the research claims that adults are similarly affected. But no politician wants to tell voters they can't see *Terminator II* because it might incite grownups to mayhem. . . .

But the biggest question media-violence critics can't answer is the most fundamental one: is it the *cause*, or simply one of the many *symptoms*, of this unquestionably brutal age? The best evidence does not exonerate celluloid savagery (who could?) but shows that it is a small, derivative influence compared to the real-life violence, both domestic and official, that our children face growing up in '80s and '90s America. . . .

The Genuine Causes of Violence

When it comes to the genuine causes of youth violence, it's hard to dismiss the 51 percent increase in youth poverty since 1973, 1 million rapes and a like number of violently injurious offenses inflicted upon the young every year, a juvenile justice system bent on retribution against poor and minority youth, and the abysmal neglect of the needs of young families. The Carter-Reagan-Bush eras added 4 million youths to the poverty rolls. The last 20 years have brought a record decline in youth well-being.

Despite claims that media violence is the best-researched social phenomenon in history, social science indexes show many times more studies of the effects of rape, violence and poverty on the young. Unlike the indirect methods of most media studies (questionnaires, interviews, peer ratings and laboratory vignettes), child abuse research includes the records of real-life criminals and their backgrounds. Unlike the media studies, the findings of this avalanche of research are consistent: child poverty, abuse and neglect underlie every major social problem the nation faces.

And, unlike the small correlations or temporary laboratory effects found in media research, abuse-violence studies produce powerful results: "Eighty-four percent of prison inmates were abused as children," the research agency Childhelp USA reports in a 1993 summary of major findings. Separate studies by the Minnesota State Prison, the Massachusetts Correctional Institute and the Massachusetts Treatment Center for Sexually Dangerous Persons (to cite a few) find histories of childhood abuse and neglect in 60 to 90 percent of the violent inmates studied—including virtually all death row prisoners. The most conservative study, that by the National Institute of Justice, indicates that some half-million criminally violent offenses each year are the result of offenders being abused as children.

Clay Bennett/*St. Petersburg Times*. Reprinted by permission.

Two million American children are violently injured, sexually abused or neglected every year by adults whose age averages 32 years, according to the Denver-based American Humane Association. One million children and teenagers are raped every year, according to the 1992 federally funded *Rape in America* study of 4,000 women, which has been roundly ignored by the same media outlets that never seem short of space to berate violent rap lyrics.

Sensational articles in *Mother Jones* ("Proof That TV Makes Kids Violent"), *Newsweek* ("The Importance of Being Nasty") and *U.S. News & World Report* ("Fighting TV Violence") devoted pages to blaming music and media for violence—yet all three ignored this study of the rape of millions of America's children. CNN devoted less than a minute to the study; *Time* magazine gave it only three paragraphs.

In yet another relevant report, the California Department of Justice tabulated 1,600 murders in 1992 for which offenders' and victims' ages are known. It showed that half of all teenage murder victims, six out of seven children killed, and 80 percent of all adult murder victims were slain by adults over age 20, not by "kids." But don't expect any cover stories on "Poverty and Adult Violence: The Real Causes of Violent Youth," or "Grownups: Wild in the Homes." Politicians and pundits know who not to pick on.

An Excuse for Failed Policies

Ron Harris' powerful August 1993 series in the *Los Angeles Times*—one of the few exceptions to the media myopia on youth violence—details the history of a decade of legal barbarism against youth in the Reagan and Bush years—which juvenile justice experts now link to the late '80s juvenile crime explosion. The inflammatory, punishment-oriented attitudes of these years led to a 50 percent increase in the number of youths behind bars. Youth typically serve sentences 60 percent longer than adults convicted for the same crimes. Today, two-thirds of all incarcerated youth are black, Latino, or Native American, up from less than half before 1985.

Ten years of a costly "get tough" approach to deter youth violence concluded with the highest rate of crime in the nation's history. Teenage violence, which had been declining from 1970 through 1983, doubled from 1983 through 1991. It is not surprising that the defenders of these policies should be casting around for a handy excuse for this policy disaster. TV violence is perfect for their purposes.

This is the sort of escapism liberals should be exposing. But too many shrink from frankly declaring that today's mushrooming violence is the predictable consequence of two decades of assault, economic and judicial, against the young. Now, increasingly, they point at Jason, 2 Live Crew, and *Henry: Portrait of a Serial Killer*.

Dubious Research

The insistence by such liberal columnists as Ellen Goodman and Coleman McCarthy that the evidence linking media violence to youth violence is on a par with that linking smoking to lung cancer represents a fundamental misunderstanding of the difference between biological and psychological research.

Psychology is not, despite its pretensions, a science. Research designs using human subjects are vulnerable to a bewildering array of confusing factors, many not even clear to researchers. The most serious (but by no means only) weakness is the tendency by even the most conscientious researchers to influence subjects to produce the desired results. Thus the findings of psychological studies must be swallowed with large grains of salt.

Consider a few embarrassing problems with media violence research. First, many studies (particularly those done under more realistic "field conditions") show no increase in violence following exposure to violent media. In fact, a significant number of studies show no effect, or even decreased aggression. Even media-violence critic L.R. Huesmann has written that depriving children of violent shows may actually increase their violence.

Second, the definitions of just what constitutes media "violence," let alone what kind produces aggression in viewers, are frustratingly vague. Respected researchers J. Singer and D. Singer found in a comprehensive 1986 study that "later aggressive behavior was predicted by earlier heavy viewing of public television's fast-paced *Sesame Street*." The Parent's Music Resource Center heartily endorsed the band U2 as "healthy and inspiring" for youth to listen to—yet U2's song "Pistol Weighing Heavy" was cited in psychiatric testimony as a key inspiration for the 1989 killing of actress Rebecca Schaeffer.

Third, if, as media critics claim, media violence is the, or even just a, prime cause of youth violence, we might expect to see similar rates of violence among all those exposed to similar amounts of violence in the media, regardless of race, gender, region, economic status, or other demographic differences. Yet this is far from the case.

Inconsistencies and Contradictions

Consider the issue of race. Surveys show that while black and white families have access to similar commercial television coverage, white families are much more likely to subscribe to violent cable channels. Yet murder arrests among black youth are 12 times higher than among white, non-Hispanic youth, and increasing rapidly. Are blacks genetically more susceptible to television violence than whites? Or could there be other reasons for this pattern—perhaps the 45 percent poverty rates and 60 percent unemployment rates among black teenagers?

And consider also the issue of gender. Girls watch as much violent TV as boys. Yet female adolescents show remarkably low and stable rates of violence. Over the last decade or so, murders by female teens (180 in 1983, 171 in 1991) stayed roughly the same, while murders by boys skyrocketed (1,476 in 1983, 3,435 in 1991). How do the media-blamers explain that?

Finally, consider the issue of locale. Kids see the same amount of violent TV all over, but many rural states show no increases in violence, while in Los Angeles, to take one example, homicide rates have skyrocketed.

The more media research claims are subjected to close scrutiny, the more their contradictions emerge. It can be shown that violent people do indeed patronize more violent media, just as it can be shown that urban gang members wear baggy clothes. But no one argues that baggy clothes cause violence. The coexistence of media and real-life violence suffers from a confusion of cause and effect: is an affinity for violent media the result of abuse, poverty and anger, or is it a prime cause of the more violent behaviors that just happen to accompany those social conditions? In a 1991 study of teenage boys who listen to violent music, the University of Chicago's Jeffrey Arnett argues that "[r]ather than being the cause of recklessness and despair among adolescents, heavy metal music is a reflection of these [behaviors]."

The clamor over TV violence might be harmless were it not for the fact that media and legislative attention are rare, irreplaceable resources. Every minute devoted to thrashing over issues like violence in the media is one lost to addressing the accumulating, critical social problems that are much more crucial contributors to violence in the real world. In this regard, the media-violence crusade offers distressing evidence of the profound decline of liberalism as America's social conscience, and the rising appeal (even among progressives) of simplistic Reaganesque answers to problems that Reaganism multiplied many times over.

Virtually alone among progressives, columnist Carl T. Rowan has expressed outrage over the misplaced energies of those who have embraced the media crusade and its "escapism from the truth about what makes children (and their parents and grandparents) so violent." Writes Rowan: "I'm appalled that liberal Democrats . . . are spreading the nonsensical notion that Americans will, to some meaningful degree, stop beating, raping and murdering each other if we just censor what is on the tube or big screen. . . . The politicians won't, or can't, deal with the real-life social problems that promote violence in America . . . so they try to make TV programs and movies the scapegoats! How pathetic!"

Without question, media-violence critics are genuinely concerned about today's pandemic violence. As such, it should alarm them greatly to see policy-makers and the public so preoccupied with an easy-to-castigate media culprit linked by their research to, at most, a small part of the nation's violence—while the urgent social problems devastating a generation continue to lack even a semblance of redress.

"TV teaches people not to read. It renders them incapable of engaging in an activity that now is perceived as strenuous, because it is not a passive hypnotized state."

Television Causes Illiteracy

Larry Woiwode

With its emphasis on visual images, television is undermining language and reading in American society, according to Larry Woiwode, the author of the following viewpoint. Consequently, says Woiwode, 60 percent of Americans read no books after leaving school and 40 percent of the American public is functionally illiterate. Woiwode concludes that television reduces people's ability to think critically and instills in them a superficial and distorted understanding of reality. Woiwode, a novelist, is the author of *Indian Affairs; What I'm Going to Do, I Think;* and *Beyond the Bedroom Wall.*

As you read, consider the following questions:

1. How is television destroying language, according to Woiwode?
2. According to the author, how does television alter the way people perceive human beings?

From "Television" by Larry Woiwode. Reprinted, with permission, from *USA Today* magazine, March 1993, © by the Society for the Advancement of Education.

135

What is destroying America today is not the liberal breed of one-world politicians, International Monetary Fund bankers, misguided educational elite, or World Council of Churches. These largely are symptoms of a greater disorder. If there is any single institution to blame, it is television.

TV is more than a medium; it has become a full-fledged institution, backed by billions of dollars each season. Its producers want us to perch in front of a glazed-over electronic screen, pressing our clutch of discernment through the floorboards, and sitting in a spangled, zoned-out state ("couch potatoes," in current parlance) while we are instructed in the proper liberal tone and attitude by Dan Rather and Tom Brokaw. These television celebrities have more temporal power than the teachings of Aristotle and Plato have built up over the centuries.

Television, in fact, has greater power over the lives of most Americans than any educational system, government, or church. Children particularly are susceptible. They are mesmerized, hypnotized, and tranquilized by TV. It often is the center of their world. Even when the set is turned off, they continue to tell stories about what they've seen on it. No wonder that, as adults, they are not prepared for the front line of life. They simply have no mental defenses to confront the reality of the world.

TV Eats Books

One of the most disturbing truths about TV is that it eats books. Once out of school, nearly 60% of all adult Americans never read a single book, and most of the rest read only one book a year. Alvin Kernan, author of *The Death of Literature*, maintains that reading books "is ceasing to be the primary way of knowing something in our society." He also points out that bachelor's degrees in English literature have declined by 33% since the early 1970s and that, in many universities, the courses largely are reduced to remedial reading. American libraries, he adds, are in crisis, with few patrons to support them.

Thousands of teachers at the elementary, secondary, and college levels can testify that their students' writing exhibits a tendency toward a superficiality that wasn't seen, say, in the late 1970s and early 1980s. It shows up not only in their lack of analytical skills, but in poor command of grammar and rhetoric. I've been asked by a graduate student what a semicolon is. The mechanics of the English language have been tortured to pieces by TV. Visual, moving images—which are the venue of television—can't be held in the net of careful language. They want to break out. They really have nothing to do with language. So language, grammar, and rhetoric have become fractured.

Surveys by dozens of organizations also suggest that up to 40% of the American public is functionally illiterate. That is, our citizens' reading and writing abilities, if they have any, are impaired so seriously as to render them, in that handy jargon of our times, dysfunctional. The problem isn't just in our schools or the way reading is taught—TV teaches people *not* to read. It renders them incapable of engaging in an activity that now is perceived as strenuous, because it is not a passive hypnotized state.

Gary Brookins/*Richmond Times-Dispatch*. Reprinted by permission.

Passive as it is, television has invaded our culture so completely that the medium's effects are evident in every quarter, even the literary world. It shows up in supermarket paperbacks, from Stephen King (who has a certain clever skill) to pulp fiction. These really are forms of verbal TV—literature that is so superficial that those who read it can revel in the same sensations they experience when watching television.

Even more importantly, the growing influence of television, Kernan says, has changed people's habits and values and affected their assumptions about the world. The sort of reflective, critical, and value-laden thinking encouraged by books has been rendered obsolete. In this context, we would do well to recall the Cyclops—the race of giants that, according to Greek myth, predated man.

TV Beats Our Brains Out

Here is a passage from classicist Edith Hamilton's summary of the encounter between the mythic adventurer Odysseus and the Cyclops Polyphemus. On his way home from the Trojan Wars,

Odysseus and his crew have found Polyphemus' cave:

"At last he came, hideous and huge, tall as a great mountain crag. Driving his flock before him he entered and closed the cave's mouth with a ponderous slab of stone. Then looking around he caught sight of the strangers, and cried out in a dreadful booming voice, 'Who are you who enter unbidden the house of Polyphemus? Traders or thieving pirates?' They were terror-stricken at the sight and sound of him, and Odysseus made shift to answer, and firmly too: 'Shipwrecked warriors from Troy are we, and your supplicants, under the protection of Zeus, the supplicants' god.' But Polyphemus roared out that he cared not for Zeus. He was bigger than any god and feared none of them. With that, he stretched out his mighty arms and in each great hand seized one of the men and dashed his brains out on the ground. Slowly he feasted off them to the last shred, and then, satisfied, stretched himself out across the cavern and slept. He was safe from attack. None but he could roll back the huge stone before the door, and if the horrified men had been able to summon courage and strength enough to kill him they would have been imprisoned there forever."

To discover their fate, read the book, preferably Robert Fitzgerald's masterful translation. What I find particularly appropriate about this myth as it applies today is that, first, the Cyclops imprisons these men in darkness, and second, he beats their brains out before he devours them. It doesn't take much imagination to apply this to the effects of TV on us and our children.

Mental Epilepsy

Quite literally, TV affects the way people think. In *Four Arguments for the Elimination of Television*, Jerry Mander quotes from the Emery Report, prepared by the Center for Continuing Education at the Australian National University, Canberra, that, when we watch television, "our usual processes of thinking and discernment are semi-functional at best." The study also argues that, "while television appears to have the potential to provide useful information to viewers—and is celebrated for its educational function—the technology of television and the inherent nature of the viewing experience actually inhibit learning as we usually think of it." Moreover, "The evidence is that television not only destroys the capacity of the viewer to attend, it also, by taking over a complex of direct and indirect neural pathways, decreases vigilance—the general state of arousal which prepares the organism for action should its attention be drawn to a specific stimulus."

How are our neural pathways taken over? We think we are looking at a picture or an image of something, but what we actually are seeing is thousands of dots of light blinking on and off in a strobe effect that is calculated to happen rapidly enough to keep us from recognizing the phenomenon. More than a decade ago, Mander and others pointed to instances of "TV epilepsy," whereby those watching this strobe effect overextended their capacities. *The New England Journal of Medicine* recently honored this affliction with a medical classification—video game epilepsy.

Images Replace Substance

Television also teaches that people aren't quite real. They are images—gray-and-white shadows or technicolor little beings who move in a medium no thicker than a sliver of glass, created by this bombardment of electrons.

The tendency is to start regarding them in the way children think when they see too many cartoons—that people merely are objects that can be zapped, or that can fall over a cliff and be smashed to smithereens, then pick themselves up again. This contentless violence of cartoons has no basis in reality. Actual people aren't images, but substantial, physical, corporeal beings with souls. . . .

Television eats out our substance. Mander calls this the mediation of experience. "[With TV] what we see, hear, touch, smell, feel and understand about the world has been processed for us." When we "cannot distinguish with certainty the natural from the interpreted, or the artificial from the organic, then all theories of the ideal organization of life become equal."

In other words, TV teaches that all lifestyles and values are equal, and that there is no clearly defined right and wrong. In *Amusing Ourselves to Death*, one of the best books on the tyranny of television, Neil Postman wonders why nobody has pointed out that television possibly oversteps the injunction in the Decalogue against making graven images.

Moral Questions Distorted

In the 1960s and 1970s, many of the traditional standards and mores of society came under heavy assault. Indeed, they were blown apart, largely with the help of television, which just was coming into its own. There was an air of unreality about many details of daily life. Even important moral questions suffered distortion when they were reduced to TV images. During the Vietnam conflict, there was much graphic violence—soldiers and civilians actually dying—on screen. One scene that shocked the nation was an execution in which the victim was shot in the head with a pistol on prime-time TV. People "tuned in" to the war every night, and their opinions largely were formed by what they viewed, as if the highly complex and controversial issues about the causes, conduct, and resolution of the conflict could be summed up in these superficial broadcasts.

The same phenomenon was seen again in the Gulf War. With stirring background music and sophisticated computer graphics, each network's banner script read across the screen, "War in the Gulf," as if it were just another TV program. War isn't a program—it is a dirty, bloody mess. People are killed daily. Yet, television all but teaches that this carnage merely is another diversion, a form of blockbuster entertainment—the big show with all the international stars present.

A Fantasy World

In the last years of his life, Malcolm Muggeridge, a pragmatic and caustic TV personality and print journalist, warned: "From the first moment I was in the studio, I felt that it was far from being a good thing. I felt that television [would] ultimately be inimical to what I most appreciate, which is the expression of truth, expressing your reactions to life in words. I think you'll live to see the time when literature will be quite a rarity because, more and more, the presentation of images is preoccupying."

He concluded: "I don't think people are going to be preoccupied with ideas. I think they are going to live in a fantasy world where you don't need any ideas. The one thing that television can't do is express ideas. . . . There is a danger in translating life into an image, and that is what television is doing . . . [thus] falsifying life. Far from the camera's being an accurate recorder of what is going on, it is the exact opposite. It cannot convey reality nor does it even want to."

"It's absurd to say that, when it comes to education and literacy, TV has no strengths, and no place, at all."

Television Can Enhance Literacy

David Bianculli

David Bianculli is a television critic at the *New York Daily News*, a television columnist for the *Philadelphia Inquirer*, and the author of *Teleliteracy: Taking Television Seriously*, from which the following viewpoint is excerpted. Bianculli believes that critics have exaggerated the harmful effects of television. He contends that many television programs have educational potential, and that television renditions of classic literature often inspire viewers to read books. He argues that television and literature are not antithetical, but complementary; if used in conjunction, they supplement each other and enhance overall understanding. Bianculli concludes that television should be accepted as a form of literature.

As you read, consider the following questions:

1. How does Bianculli refute the argument that Americans are "slaves of the 'boob tube' "?
2. What are the different functions of books and television, according to David Attenborough as quoted by Bianculli?

Cleveland State University professor Jane Healy, author of *Endangered Minds: Why Our Children Don't Think*, attacks the long-running PBS [Public Broadcasting System] children's series *Sesame Street* by saying, "It's truly amazing that everyone seems to have bought the notion that the program will teach kids to read, despite the fact that the habits of mind necessary to be a good reader are exactly what *Sesame Street* doesn't teach." Jerome L. and Dorothy G. Singer, a husband-and-wife team of psychologists at Yale, agree. They accuse *Sesame Street* of creating "a psychological disorientation in children that leads to a shortened attention span, a lack of reflectiveness and an expectation of rapid change in the broader environment." Neil Postman, author of *Amusing Ourselves to Death* (and another Big Bird basher) warns, "*Sesame Street* makes kids like school only if school is like *Sesame Street*." The inference is clear: if one of the TV shows most generally accepted as beneficial to children is actually *bad* for kids, then why should parents let kids watch TV at all?

The inference, like the argument, is dead wrong. Empirically, early studies showed that, after six weeks of watching *Sesame Street*, those students were significantly more proficient than nonviewers at the tasks of recognizing letters, associating sound with letters, and identifying different geometric forms. Artistically, *Sesame Street* has developed into a wonderful show; as both a TV critic and a parent, I applaud it, and encouraged my children to watch it. Pragmatically, it's neither the responsibility nor the function of *Sesame Street* to—as Postman puts it—*make* kids like school. That's the teacher's job, and the parent's. *Sesame Street* is there to encourage children while entertaining them—to introduce them to concepts so they'll be more prepared for the scholastic experience when their education truly begins. Anyone who sees *Sesame Street* as an enemy of education, rather than an ally, is misunderstanding the impact and potential of television. Educators who fear TV and run from it are heading in the wrong direction; they ought to use it and run with it. . . .

A Waste of Time?

One commonly voiced complaint about TV is that it robs the viewer of time to do other things—that when children are watching television, for example, they aren't reading, doing homework, or playing outdoors. "They're not playing in the street, either," Peggy Charren [founder of Action for Children's Television (ACT)] says, her flippancy revealing her impatience with that particular attack on TV. Again, this argument against the use of television dispenses with any evaluation of individual worth, and pits medium against medium rather than content against content. It may sound like a sin for a child to watch four hours of television on a Saturday afternoon—but if that child is watching the miniseries version of *Anne of Green Gables*, or a handful of episodes from David Attenborough's nature series *The Trials of Life* (two examples from my own home and neighborhood), I argue that's a fine use of their time *and* their television sets. "Watching *some* TV," says Charren, "especially some terrific television, is as good as going to a terrific movie and reading a terrific book."

The same thing holds for adults, and for entire families. Before reacting with alarm to the latest statistic showing that the average TV household watches seven or eight hours of TV a day, or that the average child will have seen five-thousand hours of TV before entering first grade, ask *how* those viewers are watching—whether it is intently, with the TV set being the focus of their attentions, or as radio with pictures, a background complement to whatever else they happen to be doing. More important, ask *what* they're watching.

Let's take the "eight hours a day" family viewing estimate. For me, an average Monday viewing day might begin with a fifteen-minute look at the Weather Channel, to see how our kids should be outfitted for school. Then, not counting any viewing I'd do as part of my job, the rest of my viewing day probably would include an evening newscast, an hour or two of prime time (on Mondays, *Evening Shade* and *Northern Exposure*), and, if the subject is interesting, *Nightline*. That's close to three hours of "pleasure" viewing just for me, and that's hardly atypical. Give my wife the same viewing allotment, though not necessarily with the same programs, and you're up to six hours a day already. If my two children each watch an hour of TV a day—which, on weekdays, is basically their limit—that's eight hours of family viewing right there. Are we slaves of the "boob tube"? No. Are we sitting there, zombielike, forfeiting all opportunities to interact, exercise or read? No. We're using the television when we want, to watch what we want. People who complain about TV's constant availability, like those who complain about its profane and violent content, seem to forget that every set comes equipped with both a channel changer and an on-off switch. . . .

Shakespeare and *Laverne & Shirley*

Bill Moyers has done more to prove television's worth as an educational force than almost anyone else you could name—yet even he is defensive when it comes to TV's ubiquitousness. Nor does he see it as stealing time only from children. "I guess, overall, television is probably a negative force in our society," Moyers says, "because . . . when you are watching television, you are not doing anything else. You are not talking to your wife, playing with your kids, attending a town meeting, writing a letter to your congressman."

Robert Thompson [an associate professor at Syracuse University's Newhouse School and an advocate of television as a serious subject] has heard that argument many times before—so many times that his response to it is immediate and passionate. "The assumption there," he says, "is that by doing one thing, you're not doing the other. By watching television, you're not learning to read. You never hear a music professor say, 'You attend so many ballets; you should be attending operas.' No one says that when someone is listening to good music, or taking a trip to the science museum, those activities are all taking away from time they could be spending reading."

Modern Literacy

By defining [television and literacy] in conventional terms—TV as the one-eyed, one-way monolith, literacy as traditional reading and writing—many of our social prophets have induced us to ignore the unparalleled activism of our nascent viewers and readers. That words are no longer words alone but ingredients in the moving landscapes wrought by video, computers, and optical discs, provoking alternative skills, is ignored. When a child learns to type, draw, and store words on his personal computer at the age of seven or eight, he taps powers of invention and recall beyond anything available to the average student, chalk and table in hand one hundred years ago.

Douglas Davis, *The Five Myths of Television Power*, 1993.

In Thompson's own academic circles, he says, his support of television as a subject worthy of scholarly scrutiny often is misconstrued as an assault on reading and literacy. "Because you're arguing in defense of television," he says, "they think you're therefore arguing for abolition of study of the classics. To them, it's like matter and antimatter. I don't think intellectuals can understand that a person could in the morning read Shakespeare, and in the afternoon laugh at *Laverne & Shirley*."

And since the same time-wasting arguments were leveled at radio before TV, and at movies before radio, and at theater before the movies, and at certain kinds of books and newspapers before that, it's a position that grows less convincing with each repetition. Blame television for a drop in the literacy rate, and in national Scholastic Aptitude Test scores, if you want to. But even if you could prove a direct link, which is doubtful, that would merely identify the problem, not solve it. Television isn't going away—not until another, more popular mass medium usurps it. And even if television *is* part of the problem, it's also part of the solution. . . .

Even older viewers can become more literate—and experience more literature—by watching the right kinds of television. In *Fields of Vision*, British writer D. J. Enright—no great fan of television—admits that "television adaptations of Charles Dickens, Anthony Trollope, Jane Austen, among others, have the effect of sending some viewers back to the novels, to renew acquaintance, to spot what has been left out, to clear up obscurities caused by truncation. The effect on other viewers may be to send them to the novels for the first time; pious hope would have it so." That hope may be pious, but it's not mistaken. TV producer William Perry generated many TV adaptations of stories and novels by Mark Twain, including the excellent PBS dramatization of *Life on the Mississippi*, starring David Knell as young Sam Clemens. "When we released *Life on the Mississippi*," Perry said in 1989, "we ran a survey of libraries around the country. And for the month that followed that show, the circulation of Twain's book had gone up 50 percent—and that was true of other Twain books as well." To those who say TV fosters illiteracy, Perry says to tell them "to ride the subway after *Shogun* has been on."

Valuable Adaptations

Robert Geller, another longtime advocate of TV as a "literate" medium, created *American Short Story*, that fine American-literature precursor to *American Playhouse*. The twin joys of *American Short Story*, launched in 1977, were its tasteful adaptations of wonderful stories and its reliance upon gifted young talent. Shelley Duvall in F. Scott Fitzgerald's *Bernice Bobs Her Hair*. LeVar Burton in Richard Wright's *Almos' a Man*. Outside of the *American Short Story* umbrella, Geller has continued to work with literary adaptations—from 1979's *Too Far to Go*, an NBC telemovie amalgam of John Updike stories that was later released theatrically, to *Seize the Day*, a 1989 *Great Performances* dramatization of the Saul Bellow story, starring Robin Williams. During his *American Short Story* years, Geller recalls, "I would get fascinating letters from kids I least expected to hear from. I don't want to turn this into Spencer Tracy and *Boys Town*, but I'd hear from boys who had never read Fitzgerald, girls who had never read *Bernice*, and what resonated through them." As for the idea that TV can inspire reading, Geller says, "Go to bookstores after *Lonesome Dove* is shown. That's proof. It's not sophisticated proof—but that's proof."

Some would call it heresy to discover that Geller's adaptations of Fitzgerald and Updike share library space with the printed originals—but it's been that way since 1988, when the John T. and Catherine R. MacArthur Foundation arranged for the duplication and dissemination of selected PBS programs at special rates to public libraries. Episodes of *American Short Story* and *American Playhouse* are included, along with Perry's version of *Life on the Mississippi* and a half-dozen dramatizations from *The Shakespeare Plays* series. The same package included such landmark nonfiction works as *Alistair Cooke's America*, Jacob Bronowski's *The Ascent of Man*, Kenneth Clark's *Civilisation*, *A Walk through the 20th Century with Bill Moyers*, Fred Friendly's *The Constitution: That Delicate Balance*, and two superb nature series from David Attenborough, *Life on Earth* and *The Living Planet*. It should be pointed out that these quality packages were by no means the first videotapes to cross the threshold of public libraries. In fact, more than four-thousand libraries nationwide had already established video-lending facilities when the PBS package was organized.

Intellectual Neighbors

The thought of books and videos as intellectual neighbors, if not equals, is relished by David Attenborough himself. In his nature documentaries, he uses television astoundingly well, both as a personal communicator and an effective educator. His ambitious and lengthy series *The Trials of Life* is, quite simply, a television masterpiece; its companion book, written by Attenborough, is more complementary than duplicative. Taking advantage of the TV medium to create interest in a book with the same title, then taking advantage of the strengths of the printed page to add and reorganize other information in that book, is a trick used by Moyers (in *The Power of Myth*, among others), Attenborough, and others equally comfortable in print and on TV. It's accurate to say TV does some things better than others, and that TV should never supplant reading. But it's absurd to say that, when it comes to education and literacy, TV has no strengths, and no place, at all.

"One has to analyze what it is that television does best," Attenborough says, entertaining the concept of teleliteracy [fluency in the television medium] quite seriously. "What television does best is to light flames of enthusiasm, and to give smells and whiffs and sparks of excitement. And what it doesn't do, not nearly as well, is carry on abstract lines of thought, which is what books are good at. . . .

"TV can be used in a multitude of ways, just as printing can. There are some differences, of course. You can't go back as easily as you can in a book. But it's like generalizing about printing: It's what it *means*, it's what people put *into* it. Television is good at igniting. It is not so good at carrying ideas, even simple ideas. . . . You won't be able to go into enormous detail. In the ideal circumstance, you produce a double package.". . .

There's a well-known quote by Ed Murrow describing the then-fledgling medium of television in enthusiastic yet reserved tones. "This instrument can teach, it can illuminate; yes, and it can even inspire," Murrow said. "But it can do so only to the extent that humans are determined to use it to those ends. Otherwise, it is merely wires and lights in a box." That's the famous portion of Murrow's quote, and it has lasted more than a generation as the TV equivalent of the "garbage-in, garbage-out" (or GIGO) warning label leveled at the computer industry. However, Murrow's remarks didn't quite end with that memorable "wires and lights in a box" phrase. Next came a plea to include television in the arsenal of national education and enlightenment: "There is a great, perhaps decisive battle to be fought, against ignorance, intolerance and indifference. This weapon of television can be useful."

In 1955, some twenty years before the introduction of the home videocassette recorder, Murrow and producer Fred W. Friendly collaborated on a book version of *See It Now*—one of TV's earliest hardbound spinoffs. The book reprinted some of the best transcripts from the show's first four seasons, including interviews with physicist J. Robert Oppenheimer and poet Carl Sandburg, and Murrow's controversial report, defending an Air Force officer accused of Communist ties, called "The Case of Lieutenant Milo Radulovich." Back in those pre-VCR days, publishing the transcripts in book form was the best means of saving the content of those shows for posterity, and for serious study and prolonged enjoyment. In the foreword to the hardcover version of *See It Now*, Murrow and Friendly collaborated on a passage that explained their comfort with TV words on a printed page. They weren't just making a case for TV and literacy; they were arguing for the concept of TV as literature.

"We expect," Murrow and Friendly wrote, "that all good literature has not been written on a typewriter or with a pen or dictating machine. We believe that Sandburg talks as well as he writes, that Sir Winston Churchill converses as well as he orates, that President Eisenhower ad-libbed the best copy he ever wrote." Listing some of the other individuals interviewed for the *See It Now* reports, Murrow and Friendly remarked that some of them "may never write a book, but under the pressure of the moment and armed with the conviction born of conflict, they composed compelling literature."

Periodical Bibliography

The following articles have been selected to supplement the diverse views presented in this chapter.

Carl M. Cannon — "Honey, I Warped the Kids," *Mother Jones*, July/August 1993.

Brandon S. Centerwall — "Television and Violence: The Scale of the Problem and Where to Go from Here," *The Journal of the American Medical Association*, June 10, 1992. Available from 515 N. State St., Chicago, IL 60610.

Stephen Chapman — "TV Violence: False Crisis with False Solutions," *Conservative Chronicle*, October 13, 1993. Available from PO Box 11297, Des Moines, IA 50340-1297.

John Condry — "Thief of Time, Unfaithful Servant: Television and the American Child," *Daedalus*, Winter 1993.

Amitai Etzioni — "Lock Up Your TV Set," *National Review*, October 18, 1993.

Joan Zoglman Fischer — "The False Idol in the Living Room," *The Family*, February 1993. Available from 50 St. Paul's Ave., Boston, MA 02130-3491.

Norman Goldberg — "Corporate Corruption of Culture and Art," *Political Affairs*, August 1992.

Media & Values — "Children and Television: Growing Up in a Media World," Fall 1990/Winter 1991.

Media & Values — "Media and Violence: Part One: Making the Connections," Summer 1993.

Jon Remmerde — "TV Guide," *The Sun*, November 1991. Available from 107 N. Roberson St., Chapel Hill, NC 27516.

Carl Rowan — "What Makes Little Johnny So Violent? TV?" *Liberal Opinion Week*, July 19, 1993. Available from 108 E. Fifth St., Vinton, IA 52349.

Utne Reader — "The Future of Reading," July/August 1993.

The World & I — "TV or Not TV?" June 1992. Available from 2800 New York Ave. NE, Washington, DC 20002.

Should the Media
Be Regulated?

Chapter Preface

In May 1990, San Francisco public television station KQED filed a lawsuit in the U.S. District Court asserting its right to videotape the execution of condemned murderer Robert Alton Harris. Although KQED lost the lawsuit and was denied permission to film the execution, its efforts raised questions about the degree of regulation the media should be subjected to in covering one of America's most divisive moral issues—capital punishment.

The proposal to televise executions has supporters among both proponents and opponents of capital punishment. Some death penalty backers contend that televising the event would deter crime by making clear the unpleasant consequences of criminal acts. Many capital punishment opponents favor televising the procedure for different reasons; they believe that exposing the public to the barbaric reality of the punishment would incite a backlash against it. According to *Time* magazine's Jill Smolowe, these critics argue that "if Americans want the death penalty, they should face the consequences of their action squarely. If they cannot bear the thought of watching public executions, then they may realize that it does not make moral sense to permit executions in private either."

Those who oppose televising executions also come from both sides of the death penalty debate. Some proponents of the death penalty fear that opening the process up to public scrutiny would evoke too much public sympathy for the condemned. "Our compassion for the murderer whose life is cut short before our eyes may overcome our sense of justice," says law professor Ernest van den Haag. Some opponents of capital punishment maintain that televised executions would resemble the countless acts of violence on television every day; thus televising executions would desensitize people to publicly sanctioned killing by reducing it from a morally significant event to a television entertainment spectacle. According to *Time*'s Lance Morrow, "People pay millions to watch terminators and terminations. They have a taste for it. The distinction between actual death and special effects gets blurry in this culture. It thins to vanishing. Reality and unreality become ugly, interchangeable kicks."

Television's entrance into the debate over capital punishment reveals how central the media have become to U.S. society. Furthermore, it illustrates the complex interplay of factors that influence decisions about when and how to control the media. The debate over televising executions is one issue considered in the following chapter on the regulation of the media.

> "The 1st Amendment cannot be ignored in our discussions of electronic media regulation."

Regulating Television Violence Would Threaten Free Speech

Patrick D. Maines and Danny Goldberg

Patrick D. Maines is president of the Media Institute—a Washington, D.C., research organization that specializes in communications policy and First Amendment issues. In Part I of the following viewpoint, he argues that government threats to regulate television's violent content jeopardize free speech. In Part II of the viewpoint, Danny Goldberg contends that regulating television violence would harm American culture by eliminating one aspect—however unpleasant—of reality. Goldberg is senior vice president of Atlantic Records and chair of the American Civil Liberties Union Foundation of Southern California.

As you read, consider the following questions:

1. According to Maines, how might parental advisories hinder depictions of the "social impact of violence"?
2. According to Goldberg, whose job is it to teach children about violence?

"Beware the Real Evil of Violence Warnings" by Patrick D. Maines, *Los Angeles Times*, August 2, 1993. Reprinted by permission. "Parents, Not Government, Should Tune Out TV Gore" by Danny Goldberg, *Los Angeles Times*, August 15, 1993. Reprinted by permission.

I

The threat of government regulation has prompted the networks—ABC, CBS, NBC and Fox—to impose coercive regulations on themselves. They have sought to buy time by agreeing "voluntarily" to run parental advisories before and during "excessively violent" programming.

The networks are reacting to those who are concerned—and rightly so—about violence in society. But to view this strictly as a violence issue is to risk overlooking the critical point: If government is thinking of imposing restrictions on program content, the issue becomes a constitutional one involving the 1st Amendment.

What Limits?

There is no guarantee that, under mounting pressure from government and interest groups, the networks would limit advisories only to those programs offering "gratuitous" violence. Nor is there a guarantee that critics of TV violence will be content with advisories only.

Rep. Edward Markey, chairman of the House subcommittee on telecommunications, wants to mandate that television sets carry "V chips," which, when activated by parents, would block out all programming carrying a "violence" rating, regardless of the violence's context.

In the meantime, parental advisories are red flags for interest groups like the Rev. Donald Wildmon's American Family Assn. Such groups target the sponsors of "objectionable" programming without regard to the context of the objectionable material.

Fox's "America's Most Wanted" and "Cops," both widely respected by law enforcement, have come under fire for their depictions of actual violent behavior.

Fictional portrayals of the social impact of violence could also be jeopardized. ABC's miniseries "War and Remembrance" contained realistic and necessarily graphic depictions of Nazi atrocities. To gloss over such brutalities would have been a public disservice. Yet parental advisories could make such programming easy prey for activist critics.

The high-profile warnings adopted by the networks will be featured in all program advertising and TV listings, and will only make boycotts of sponsors easier. Advertisers are justly skittish.

Legitimizing Censorship

Infinitely more dangerous than the parental advisories themselves, however, is the precedent the advisories set. By bowing to congressional pressure, the networks have tacitly admitted that government can, if it so chooses, regulate television content.

If the content of entertainment programming can be dictated by government, what about the content of so-called reality programming? Programs like "Hard Copy" and "Inside Edition" not only blur the line between entertainment and news, but also have received some of the harshest criticisms for their depictions of violence.

It may be premature to worry about warning labels being applied to actual newscasts, but even hard-news shows are being attacked for violent content.

Feiffer © 1993 Jules Feiffer. Reprinted with permission of Universal Press Syndicate. All rights reserved.

One might wonder where the 1st Amendment enters the discussion. It doesn't. TV watchdogs and their congressional allies skirt free-speech issues by defining TV violence as a "public health" issue. Rep. Charles Schumer has stated that we "must approach television violence as a public-health crisis as we have with the danger of smoking."

Once government asserts a public-health interest in TV violence, however, controlling that violence through various forms of content censorship could quite easily be seen as a reasonable means of advancing the government's interest.

The 1st Amendment cannot be ignored in our discussions of electronic media regulation—whether the regulation is in the form of legislation or threats of legislation. With ever-increasing amounts of information reaching consumers through electronic means, defending free speech in the electronic media is very much in the real public interest.

II

Sen. Paul Simon and several of his purportedly liberal cohorts in Congress think they can help me and my wife raise our daughter Katie. He was in Hollywood in August 1993 to lecture television producers about violence on TV. Meanwhile, Rep. Edward J. Markey of Massachusetts has proposed a bill that would require all newly manufactured TV sets to include a chip that would allow parents to block out "violent" programming.

Among the issues left unclear amid all the sound bites is how violence is to be defined. Will the vaunted chip be programmed to shut out the evening news, with its real-life murders or body-contact sports? Will the definition include slapstick comedy like that of the Three Stooges, or the Westerns from the '50s, like "Have Gun Will Travel"? Will it preclude families from seeing a PBS showing of Kenneth Branagh's version of Shakespeare's "Henry V," with dead bodies strewn everywhere? Is there truly a single "family" standard of violence incorporating the attitudes and values of Jews, Catholics, atheists, Muslims, Baptists and Quakers, rural and urban, rich and poor, college-educated and illiterate? Who will set the standards?

Now, I admit my wife and I are not very happy when Katie, who just turned 3, runs around the house pretending to shoot us or our cat. But I can't see how Congress can help us. Katie doesn't even watch regular TV—just videos we control. Her exposure to guns comes from friends at preschool.

Guns are part of American culture and have been since long before TV and movies were invented. When I grew up in the '50s, network TV aired many Westerns in which people got shot and died. My parents taught me to hate violence; the job of teaching Katie that violence is evil is ours.

A Destructive Cure

Washington's latest assault on the entertainment business is reminiscent of the "healers" in the Middle Ages who prescribed leeches for serious illnesses. Not only did the removal of "sick blood" fail to cure the disease; the treatment, however well-intentioned, seriously weakened the patient. Similarly, politicians who beat up on entertainment, whatever their motives, are making easy headlines but weakening the culture—and doing nothing to help parents or children.

To be sure, every adult will, at one time or another, detest a portion of the popular entertainment to which their children are exposed. Undoubtedly, some parents support the attacks on Hollywood. But are the members of the public who watch supposedly offensive entertainment all morally inferior to those who don't? Is there really no room for a clash of cultural images in a moral society? Are politicians and pundits and social scientists really better equipped to guide entertainment than the free marketplace?

A belief in a free marketplace of entertainment does not preclude criticism. We have decided that Katie is too young to see "Jurassic Park," and we now feel we made a mistake by allowing her to see the video of "Wizard of Oz." The witch was too scary.

It's helpful to read reviews, to ask friends for advice and to impose a moral context for evaluating entertainment. Criticism is not only constitutionally protected, it is righteous. But there is all the difference between criticism that advocates one idea or aesthetic over another and blacklisting that seeks to prohibit controversial ideas and images from being exposed at all. Contrary to the platitudes of modern-day blacklisters, moral decisions are made in a more complex and mysterious way than decisions about what kind of toothpaste to buy.

A Blander America?

Unfortunately, many kids grow up with little parental supervision, and, perhaps, politicians have some wistful hope that curtailing violence on TV will make these "latchkey children" better citizens when they grow up. The reality is unsupervised kids are unlikely to stay home and watch bland TV if they can visit their friends and see the gory stuff. Even if they stayed home, everything we know about leaving kids to grow up by themselves tells us that absence of guidance is infinitely more damaging than anything on TV.

Ironically, Simon can be seen, playing himself, in the movie "Dave," in which he advocates a full-employment bill that, in real life, he no longer actively supports. Rather than pass gun-control legislation and help American families, Congress seems to be saying "let them eat sit-coms."

Entertainment is not supposed to "solve" problems; it is supposed to allow people to alternatively escape from them or think about them. There is no evidence that repressing art or entertainment improves the moral character of people.

So, no thanks, senators and congressmen, I do not want my daughter growing up in a blander America in which artists are punished for exploring the dark side of life. Picasso, Alfred Hitchcock, Bruce Springsteen, William Faulkner, Martin Scorsese and the Greek tragedians are among the artists who could not have searched for truth under the bureaucratic eye of Congress. Unfortunately, there is pain and ugliness in the world. We will not raise moral children by pressuring for a culture that ignores real life.

*"If television is a business like any other,
Congress should legislate an end to the industry's
abuse of our children."*

Regulating Television Violence Would Not Threaten Free Speech

Newton N. Minow, Craig L. LaMay, and Megan Rosenfeld

In 1961, Newton N. Minow called television a "vast waste-land"—a statement that has since become famous. Minow is director, and Craig L. LaMay is assistant director, of the public-service television project of the American Academy of Arts and Sciences. In Part I of the following viewpoint, which defends efforts to reduce television violence, they argue that since the airwaves are public property, television content should reflect the public interest. Furthermore, to the extent that the television industry is a business, it is subject to government regulation. In Part II of the viewpoint, Megan Rosenfeld, a staff writer for the *Washington Post*, argues that the television industry uses the First Amendment to protect its freedom to make profits, not its freedom of speech.

As you read, consider the following questions:

1. According to Minow and LaMay, how does self-interest affect the marketplace? On what "premise" is society's dedication to free speech based?
2. Why is the television industry addicted to violence, according to Rosenfeld?

Under the threat of congressional action, ABC, CBS, NBC and Fox television networks have agreed to begin labeling the violent programming they purvey in the nation's living room.

This initiative comes at a time when the American people are more concerned than ever before about television's troublesome effect on our youngest citizens. They have been joined by the American Psychological Assn. and the American Academy of Pediatrics, both of which have labeled the glut of TV violence a national health issue, as important and neglected as cigarette smoking was in the 1960s.

"Our Air"

To be sure, television is about ideas, and even bad ideas are protected by the First Amendment. But television is also about the private use of a valuable public property, the broadcast spectrum. Like anyone else who uses public property, broadcasters are not free to do with it whatever they please. Their 1st Amendment rights are not absolute, but depend on the access to the broadcast spectrum granted to them by the public.

Despite their agreement on violence ratings and despite congressional concern—the 1993 inquiries in the Senate and the House are only the latest of many, extending over 40 years—broadcasters are likely to go on treating the public airwaves as their personal property. To many of them, any concession amounts to self-imposed censorship. "If we censor television," asks a recent *Broadcasting* magazine editorial, "who will decide how much violence on TV is too much, and what kind, and in what situations?"

The violence ratings, whatever their shortcomings, provide a good answer to this rhetorical question: If we, the people, want to, we can provide for better television and give our children healthier viewing experiences. And we can do it because, as the broadcasters like to say, "It's our air." All that's required is for us to change the way we think about this important medium, free enterprise and free speech.

We have been living for too long according to the seductive social theory that the individual pursuit of self-interest will automatically promote the general welfare. At the same time, many economists have ridiculed the idea of public interest, citing Adam Smith's famous dictum that he "never knew much good done by those who claim to trade in the public welfare."

Applying the same notion to speech, one recent FCC [Federal Communications Commission] chairman declared television a business no more significant than any other and characterized a television set as a mere "toaster with pictures."

Not surprisingly, the result has been a television system for children that has by turns trivialized and ignored the idea of social and personal responsibility. Dick Wolf, the producer of "Miami Vice" and the NBC show "South Beach," said in the fall of 1992, "I have an 8-year-old and a 5-year-old. They've never seen any of the shows I've ever produced. They shouldn't be watching them." Should yours?

Free Speech and Moral Responsibility

Anyone who has actually read Adam Smith knows that our "marketplace of ideas" is at best a caricature of his economic marketplace: Unbridled self-interest, Smith wrote in "The Wealth of Nations," corrodes the moral context the market requires in order to function. Without moral responsibility, and if necessary government intervention, the market soon falls apart.

The market for free speech—a metaphor popular with free-speech absolutists—is sustained the same way. Indeed, our dedication to free speech and our abhorrence of censorship are based on the premise that ours is a society committed to individual moral responsibility.

Signe Wilkinson/Cartoonists & Writers Syndicate. Reprinted with permission.

With respect to television violence, then, our dilemma is simple. If television is a business like any other, Congress should legislate an end to the industry's abuse of our children. If instead television is protected from government intervention as a vital part of our national communications, we must demand greater moral responsibility from those who use the public airwaves, or risk letting the whole system of free expression fall apart.

Make no mistake—it is those broadcasters and Hollywood producers who speak ominously of censorship who through their moral negligence are the greatest of the dangers to our 1st Amendment freedoms.

And to our children.

II

I was sent to the Capitol Hill press conference at which the major networks announced their plan to label violent television shows. . . .

There has been a lot of moaning in reaction to these labels. One side, the anti-violence lobby, says they're a palliative, a crumb tossed at the mob to stall legislators from actually regulating the airwaves, a license to produce even more violence as long as it's labeled. The other side, the so-called "creative community" and the civil liberties dogmatists, is crying about artistic freedom and the First Amendment. Labeling, they say, is the first step down the slippery slope of censorship. "I think we are being enormously scapegoated," producer Dick Wolf ("Law & Order") told the *Washington Post*. "If you listen to Congress, it's [as if] television is the root of all social ills in this country."

Oh, please. I find myself curiously unmoved by television producers covering themselves with a First Amendment flag. As far as I'm concerned, they have abrogated their rights to freedom of speech by being so resolutely unconcerned about the impact of what they produce. That includes the 100,000 acts of violence, ranging from a "menacing threat with a weapon" (226 examples in one day's monitoring by the Center for Media and Public Affairs) to "serious assaults excluding use of guns" (389 incidents), that the average child will have watched by the end of elementary school. Too often, television is not about protecting speech, but protecting a business, and pretending otherwise is foolish. . . .

We have an unfortunate tradition in this country of putting the "rights" of adults before the needs of children. You can see that demonstrated every day in courthouses, classrooms and social-work bureaucracies everywhere. Television is no exception: Every socially useful change that has been made in recent years—eliminating cigarette and liquor advertising; setting aside early evening hours for "family" viewing—has been forced down the networks' throats. Somehow, I am not convinced that they want to use the First Amendment in my family's interest. . . .

Do people watch violent shows because they want violence or because that is what's there? If television producers really confronted the issue, they would have to admit that throwing another fistfight or choke hold into the script is an easy way to create tension and drama, while doing it with words and nonviolent plot twists is much harder. I suspect it is the "creative community" that is addicted to violence, not the viewers.

One way to find out how big the audience for violence really is would be to segregate all the violent shows onto one channel—the V Network, we'll call it—which would be available to cable subscribers, for a fee. If that works we can move on to the Stupid Sitcom Network, the Humiliating Game Show Channel and the Grotesque Talk Show Broadcasting System, and make things a lot easier for the consumer. . . .

I am not a person who wants to eradicate all trash on television. Nor do I think Looney Tunes should be listed among the most violent shows, as the National Coalition on Television Violence does. I have friends, and even relatives, who write for and act on television, and other friends who would love to do so. I am happy to assert my responsibility as a parent and issue dictums that make my children think I am Cruella de Vil. I know that little boys will draw pictures of guns, and always have drawn pictures of guns, regardless of how much violence they see on television. And I do not think a television show causes someone to go out and commit murder; it just gives them an excuse after the fact.

But I admit it: If there were such a thing as Taste Police, I would want to be the chief. We all think we know what's best, especially when it comes to our children. And tell me, have the presidents of NBC, CBS, ABC and the schlock-specialists at Fox Broadcasting done such a great job looking out for our interests?

I have always believed that television is a tool you should teach your children to master, not avoid, because it is unavoidable. Throwing it out is a solution, but that doesn't teach children to make choices. In my household, we don't allow television on school nights, for example, and we try to limit it at other times. But the pull of the black box in the corner is always there, and rare is the day that my kids don't ask, "Can I watch TV?" And then, "Why not?"

Some Help

I could use some help. I feel as if I spend too much time as a parent censoring and saying no, and fighting off the unceasing lures thrown out by the Howard Stringers of the world [Stringer is president of the CBS Broadcast Group]. . . .

So, for now, I'll take the labels. I would prefer that the creators of television would produce less violence (and less garbage in general), but perhaps this initiative will help make that happen. It is, at least, an acknowledgment that what they put on the air really does affect human life, and for that I am grateful.

Previously, network executives sold advertising on the premise that commercials would prod us lowly viewers to buy products, but refused to admit that the programs surrounding the commercials could possibly influence anyone to do anything.

I hope the industry, including the cable operators and independent producers who refused to sign on to the two-year labeling experiment, will take seriously the companion plan to sensitize producers, writers and program developers to violence. The objective is to do for violence what they did for seat belts, drug use, and cigarette and alcohol consumption—glamorize the good stuff and downplay the bad. There is a real possibility that nothing will change. In that case I will have no choice: I will have to take the television out and throw a bomb at it. I sure hope nobody else will be hit by the flying debris.

*"There is a constitutional right to televise
executions."*

The Press Has the Right
to Televise Executions

Jeff Angeja

In the following viewpoint, Jeff Angeja argues that the constitutional right of the press to televise executions is guaranteed by
the First, Fourteenth, and Eighth Amendments. According to
Angeja, the two criteria required to guarantee the right of access
to an event under the First Amendment are met in the case of
executions. First, executions have traditionally been open to the
public. Second, televising executions would serve as a positive
governmental role by allowing the public to monitor the criminal justice system and by enabling the community to experience
the catharsis the event provides. Angeja is a contributor to the
Hastings Law Journal, a journal of the University of California,
Hastings College of the Law in San Francisco, California.

As you read, consider the following questions:

1. What two arguments does Angeja use to support his view
   that an execution is an open process?
2. According to Angeja, in what two ways are the electronic
   media superior to the print media at reporting executions?
3. How does the Fourteenth Amendment support the press's
   right to televise executions, according to the author?

Imagine twenty-six people standing in silence, unable to remove their eyes from a person strapped into a chair inside an airtight chamber. Cyanide splashes into acid and shatters the silence of the death chamber as gas fills the air like thick fog. The condemned writhes in pain in her death throes. While twenty-six witnesses watch in silence, millions of television viewers watch with them in the privacy of their own homes. Does the broadcast media have the right to televise an execution? This [viewpoint] argues that it does.

Whether the death penalty should be used as a means of punishing criminals presents one of the most hotly debated topics in our society. This [viewpoint] does not attempt to resolve that controversial issue. However, television has thrust a new controversy into this arena of debate: Is there a constitutional right to televise executions? In the summer of 1991, San Francisco's public television station, KQED, sought to televise the execution of Robert Alton Harris. The warden at San Quentin Prison, Daniel Vasquez, allowed neither electronic equipment nor writing implements into the execution chamber. KQED sued unsuccessfully in federal district court asserting a constitutional right to televise executions. . . .

Focusing on California's execution procedure, this [viewpoint] argues that there is a constitutional right to televise executions based on the First, Fourteenth, and Eighth Amendments. . . .

[*Richmond Newspapers v. Virginia* and other Supreme Court] cases establish a First Amendment right of access to a particular process when: 1) that process has been traditionally open and 2) press access serves a positive structural role in the functioning of that process. When these criteria are satisfied, the right may be overcome only by an exclusion scheme narrowly tailored to serve a compelling state interest. If the execution process has traditionally been open, and if camera access plays a positive structural role in the execution process, then the broadcast media's First Amendment right of access should extend as far as the execution chamber.

The History of Public Access to Executions

Executions were traditionally open in this country. At the "time of our earliest decisions upholding capital punishment, a substantial portion of California's residents had witnessed executions," [*People v. Anderson,* 1972]. Currently, however, California conducts executions within the walls of San Quentin Prison.

Although California's executions occur in San Quentin, which is generally closed to the public, the executions are still sufficiently open to the public to satisfy the first prong of the Court's test for establishing a First Amendment right of access. G. Mark Mamantov has noted that "historical momentum would appear to favor closing executions, rather than opening them to the press and public." Unlike courtrooms, which are open to the public, the execution chamber is closed to the public. Nevertheless, two arguments support the view that executions are sufficiently "open" to warrant a right of press access.

First, the warden is required to select twelve official witnesses and fourteen media witnesses to attend all executions. A process that includes members of the general public, even if limited in number, cannot be said to be completely closed. The only standard a witness must meet is that she be reputable. Presuming that the witness is reputable, the execution process is open to her and therefore not completely closed.

Second, consider the nature of a prison and the necessity of maintaining security within it. Consider the physical space limitations within an execution chamber. The "closed nature" of the execution process can be seen as a function of the physical limitations of both the execution chamber and the prison environment, which are designed to prohibit freedom of movement, rather than a policy judgment to close executions to the public.

Surrogates for the Public

These two arguments strongly support the notion that the fourteen media witnesses serve as surrogates for the public at large; the press provides the public with an eyewitness account of the execution. In fact, the current policy requires the media witnesses to "give their pool commentary and recounting [sic] to the other assembled media." Thus, the media witnesses act as surrogates for the non-witness media. The media witnesses simultaneously act as surrogates for the public in that part of the standard by which they are selected includes "the broadest cross-section of media format and greatest circulation/viewers." This selection criterion acknowledges the structural importance of the press as the eyes and ears of the public. As Chief Justice Burger stated in *Richmond Newspapers v. Virginia*: "[P]eople now acquire [information about trials] chiefly through the print and electronic media. . . . This 'contribute[s] to public understanding of the rule of law and to comprehension of the functioning of the entire criminal justice system. . . .' "

Although the execution chamber may not be located in the center of the town square, this [viewpoint] asserts that the chamber is as open as space and security limitations allow, and is open to the surrogates of the public. Thus, the execution process was traditionally open and remains sufficiently open to satisfy the first criterion of the *Richmond Newspapers* test.

Chief Justice Burger and Justice Brennan spelled out the positive structural roles that the press may play in securing and fostering a republican form of self-government. First, as Justice

Brennan stated in his concurrence in the judgment of *Richmond Newspapers*, "Implicit in this structural role is not only 'the principle that debate on public issues should be uninhibited, robust, and wide open,' but also the antecedent proposition that valuable public debate . . . must be informed." Second, "public access to court proceedings is one of the numerous 'checks and balances' of our system, because 'contemporaneous review in the forum of public opinion is an effective restraint on possible abuse of judicial power.'" Third, the open process accords with the notion that "justice must satisfy the appearance of justice." Finally, an open process serves a therapeutic or cathartic purpose within the community:

> Civilized societies withdraw from both the victim and the vigilante the enforcement of criminal laws, but they cannot erase from people's consciousness the . . . urge for retribution. The crucial prophylactic aspects of the administration of justice cannot function in the dark; no community catharsis can occur if justice is "done in a corner [or] in any covert manner."

The camera is ideally suited to perform all four of these functions in the execution process. First, the death penalty is a hotly debated subject: both the public and the Court are divided regarding its constitutionality. According to the Court's theory of the structural role of the press in a republican system of government, such debate must be informed to be effective. Televising executions would not only provide a greater amount of accurate information, it would also spark renewed debate.

The Eyes and Ears of America

In this age of talk-show politics and televised town hall meetings, the lens and the microphone have become the eyes and ears of America. The public is thus denied effective access to an event when television cameras are excluded therefrom. . . . An execution might not be pretty, and it might not be entertaining, but it is our undertaking, and our responsibility. The First Amendment should serve to ensure that all of our undertakings are carried out with our knowledge, and with our blessing.

Neil E. Nussbaum, *North Carolina Central Law Journal*, vol. 20, no. 2, 1992.

Second, television access would enable the entire nation to act as a check on the government. As it stands, it is difficult for anyone but the selected fourteen witnesses to serve as "watchdog" over the state during its final act in the gravest of criminal proceedings. Indeed, the state must be watched most carefully in this lethal context. Television would serve this role better than the print media and thus should be granted access to the execution chamber.

Third, television creates an open process and a respect for the judicial system in the spirit of the Court's declaration that "justice must satisfy the appearance of justice." Satisfying the appearance of justice is especially important in the context of an execution, where error cannot be reversed. The criminal justice system faces more difficulty in maintaining the public's respect for the legitimacy of the death penalty when executions remain hidden from public scrutiny than it would if the public were permitted to examine the process directly. As the Court observed, "People in an open society do not demand infallibility from their institutions, but it is difficult for them to accept what they are prohibited from observing."

Finally, television access to the execution chamber would foster the community catharsis of which Chief Justice Burger wrote. Burger asserted that the open process serves a prophylactic purpose by quelling society's retributive urge. Insofar as the death penalty assuages the urge for both vigilante justice and retribution, this purpose would be further served by televising executions. The fourteen media witnesses in the execution chamber perform, to the degree that they are able, the structural roles necessary to a republican form of government. But because the television camera performs these roles better than any other medium, the electronic media should have a right of access to the execution chamber.

Electronic vs. Print Media

The electronic media is superior to the print media both qualitatively and quantitatively. Qualitatively, the camera has several advantages over the newspaper. For example, the print media must filter the sights, sounds, and smells of the entire prison experience and execution process through the memory and notes of a writer. As such, the experience is subject to the writer's potential biases and faults. In contrast, the cliché "a picture is worth a thousand words" rings true in this setting. A television image can convey exactly what a spectator would see if she were present within the execution chamber. Justice Stewart acknowledged this crucial difference in his concurrence in the judgment of *Houchins v. KQED:* "A person touring Santa Rita jail can grasp its reality with his own eyes and ears. But if a television reporter is to convey the jail's sights and sounds to those who cannot personally visit the place, he must use cameras and sound equipment." Other courts have acknowledged the camera's superiority as well: "[V]isual impressions . . . add a material dimension to one's impression of particular news events. Television film coverage of the news provides a comprehensive visual element and an immediacy, or simultaneous aspect, not found in print media."

The electronic media can also claim a quantitative superiority over the print media. Sixty-five percent of all adults acquire most of their news from television. Newspapers finish second at forty-two percent, radio third at fourteen percent, and magazines fourth at four percent. Television has led all other media as the primary source of news since the early 1960s and has enjoyed at least a twenty point lead over newspapers since 1980. "Whereas nearly all American homes have at least one television set which is on an average of seven hours each day, only about half of all Americans buy daily newspapers" [according to David N. Kuriyama]. Most striking of all is that only two percent of Americans derive their news from sources *exclusive of television*. By televising executions, the media would substantially increase the accuracy and availability of information and thereby foster public debate, thus contributing to the formation of a societal consensus regarding the standard for cruel and unusual punishment. For evidence of television's pervasive role in our society, one need only recall recent events such as the Gulf War, the confirmation hearings of Justice Clarence Thomas, and the Los Angeles riots, during which time most people were glued to their television sets. Given the vast superiority in terms of viewers of the electronic media, to deny electronic media coverage of executions is to unduly restrict the structural role that the public, through the surrogacy of the camera, must play in the legal process. The camera is best able to fulfill the role of the press contemplated in the First Amendment. . . .

Equal Protection Support for the Right of Access

Under the Equal Protection Clause of the Fourteenth Amendment, a state may not treat similarly situated individuals differently. By allowing members of the print media to have access to the execution chamber with the tools of their trade, but denying members of the electronic media access to the execution chamber with the tools of their trade, the state arguably violates the Equal Protection Clause. . . .

San Quentin's execution procedures actually deny *all* reporters the use of the tools of their trades, and therefore do not violate the Equal Protection Clause on their face. However, the court in *KQED v. Vasquez* held that the warden could not prohibit the tools of the print media. By denying similar access to the electronic media, San Quentin's practice would deny equal protection.

In addition to protection under the First and Fourteenth Amendments, the television media's right of access to the execution chamber derives additional support from a nexus with the Eighth Amendment. This [argument] assumes that death as a punishment for certain crimes comports with the Eighth Amendment's prohibition of cruel and unusual punishment, and focuses instead on the constitutionality of the mode of execution. The Court has ruled that the meaning of cruel and unusual punishment must be determined by reference to contemporary community standards. An examination of the multitude of factors that enter into a societal determination of the criteria for cruel and unusual punishment is beyond the scope of this [viewpoint]. But regardless of the substance of the debate, it is clear that without complete and accurate information informing the discussion, a contemporary societal standard of cruel and unusual punishment with regard to the mode of execution will neither fully evolve nor accurately reflect the judgment society might render if it were allowed to witness live executions through the medium of television. Complete and accurate information facilitates the evolution and formation of any consensus. Televised executions would provide complete and accurate information in a medium superior to any other in terms of its ability to convey an image of the execution to the public. Thus, the availability of the most complete and accurate information through televised broadcasts of executions would promote the development of a contemporary community standard of cruel and unusual punishment against which particular modes of execution might be judged. This nexus between the First Amendment's guarantee of freedom of the press and the Eighth Amendment's prohibition of cruel and unusual punishment validates the structural role of the press in the execution process and bolsters the constitutional protection of the broadcast media's right of access to the execution chamber. . . .

The best decision is an informed decision. Through television, the electronic media can provide the most accurate information to the American citizenry, save for those few citizens who witness the execution in person. As a result, televised access to the execution chamber would both allow the public to arrive at an informed determination of the social acceptability of the death penalty, and facilitate the evolution of a fully informed contemporary societal standard of decency with regard to the mode of execution.

In conclusion, the television media may assert a First Amendment right of access to the execution chamber based on the historical and structural criteria established in *Richmond Newspapers* and reaffirmed in other cases. This right of access is further supported by the Fourteenth Amendment's Equal Protection Clause. Finally, the television media may invoke additional protection by positing a nexus between its First Amendment freedoms and the Eighth Amendment's prohibition of cruel and unusual punishment. The inescapable conclusion is that *KQED v. Vasquez* was wrongly decided; the media should have a constitutional right to televise executions.

"The press does not have a First Amendment right to attend or televise an execution."

The Press Does Not Have the Right to Televise Executions

Dane A. Drobny

In the following viewpoint, Dane A. Drobny concedes that executions were open to the public in the past, but he contends that social and political changes have transformed them into closed events. Therefore, the right of the press or the public to attend executions is not guaranteed under the First Amendment. Furthermore, even if individual states grant the press permission to attend executions, they are not required to allow them to film the procedures. Drobny concludes that the print media are adequate for reporting executions. Drobny is a graduate of Washington University School of Law in St. Louis, Missouri.

As you read, consider the following questions:

1. According to Drobny, on what basis did KQED assert that it had the right to televise an execution?
2. What two functions did public executions serve, according to Drobny? Why did executions become privatized?
3. According to Drobny, barring the press from televising an execution does not deny them effective access to it. Why not?

From Dane A. Drobny, Note, "Death TV: Media Access to Executions Under the First Amendment," 70 *Washington University Law Quarterly* 1179 (1992). Reprinted with permission.

The debate over the media's right to televise executions has intensified. . . . State legislators on both coasts of the United States have considered legislation which would enable television stations to broadcast executions. Not only have articles on the issue appeared in newspapers and magazines all over the country, but even a talk show host has discussed the subject with a panel of experts over the nation's airwaves.

The nation's courts have also contributed to the debate. A federal district court in California prevented a television station from videotaping and broadcasting the execution of a convicted murderer in the gas chamber in 1991. In *KQED v. Vasquez*, the court held that the prohibition of cameras at executions was a reasonable and lawful regulation. This holding is consistent with the Fifth Circuit's decision in *Garrett v. Estelle*. In *Garrett*, the court denied a television reporter's request to televise Texas's first execution since 1964, and held that the media has no First Amendment right to televise an execution.

The issue of media access to executions has complex and important political and legal dimensions. Politically, the issue implicates the debate over capital punishment. Legally, the issue raises questions concerning the media's First Amendment right to gather information.

This [viewpoint] attempts to preempt any political resolution of the issue by resolving it in a strictly legal arena. . . . [It] analyzes the issue within the proper legal framework and concludes that the press does not have a First Amendment right to attend or televise an execution.

The Media's First Amendment Right to Gather Information

The First Amendment to the United States Constitution provides that "Congress shall make no law . . . abridging the freedom . . . of the press." Generally, the Supreme Court has interpreted this constitutional clause to provide the press with the right against prior restraints and against *post hoc* burdens on publication. However, denying press access to a prison for the purposes of filming and broadcasting an execution relates most directly to the press's right to gather information. Although the Press Clause of the First Amendment includes the right to gather information, it may not extend far enough to provide television stations the right to witness and film executions. . . .

In *Pell v. Procunier*, the Court restricted the right to gather information. The Court held that prison regulations that prohibited reporters from interviewing prisoners did not violate the reporters' rights to gather news under the First Amendment. The Court stated that although the government cannot interfere with the freedom of the press, it need not provide the press with information not available to the public generally. Because the public did not possess the right to interview specific prisoners upon request, the Court concluded that denying this access to the media did not violate its right to gather news. The Court ruled that the media has no constitutional right of access to prisons or prisoners greater than that accorded the general public.

In *Richmond Newspapers v. Virginia*, the Court adopted a framework for determining whether the media has specific rights of access. The Court concluded that "[a]bsent an overriding interest," the press and the public must have access to criminal trials. Writing for a plurality of the Court, Chief Justice Burger examined the history of criminal trials in England and the United States; he found that throughout American history, criminal proceedings had been open to the public and the press. The Chief Justice attributed this to the value the public places on the trial process as one of the most significant features of democratic government. Although the First Amendment does not explicitly guarantee the right to attend criminal trials, the plurality concluded that the First Amendment implies this right of access. Thus, by tracing the historical development of the right of access to criminal trials, the Court established that the press and the general public have a constitutional right of access to criminal trials.

Refining the Right of Access

The Court refined its method for addressing right of access questions in *Globe Newspaper v. Superior Court*. The Court invalidated a Massachusetts statute that required the exclusion of the press and public from criminal trials during the testimony of a sex offense victim who was a minor. The Court applied the *Richmond Newspapers* test for determining whether the First Amendment affords a particular right of access. First, the Court must determine whether the particular proceeding "has been open to the press and the general public." Then the Court must consider whether "the right of access [to the specific proceeding] plays a particularly significant role in the functioning of the judicial process and the government as a whole." Applying this test to the facts of *Globe Newspaper*, the Court reaffirmed that the First Amendment affords the press and public a right of access to criminal trials. Although this right of access is not absolute, the "state's justification in denying access must be a weighty one." The Court found that the state failed to demonstrate a compelling interest to justify the automatic ban.

A divided Court attempted to define the extent of constitutional protection of press access to government institutions in *Houchins v. KQED*. Chief Justice Burger stated that the First Amendment did not require prison officials to grant the media access to a prison or to allow reporters to use a camera or tape recorder when reporting on prison conditions. The Court expressly limited its decision to whether the First Amendment afforded the press a "special" right of access. Relying on *Pell*, the Court reasoned that the First Amendment does not guarantee media access to government property or "sources of information within the government's control." The Court concluded that absent a legislative decree to the contrary, the press does not have a more powerful right of access to a prison than the Constitution affords the public.

Violence Without Horror

Today's children, reared on television, have seen, by age 18, 40,000 people die right in their living rooms. In the event of televised executions, will there really be a distinction for them that the person on the tube this time is *real*? And do we want the type of nation, a generation from now, whose citizens have been brought up on both fictional and actual violence, and for whom neither elicits much horror?

Charles Colson, *Christianity Today*, July 22, 1991.

In his concurrence, Justice Stewart agreed with the Chief Justice that the Constitution does not provide the media with a special right of access. However, Justice Stewart contended that when the government grants access, it must provide the press with effective access. Effectively conveying the conditions of a prison to the public may involve some use of a reporter's video camera and tape recorder. Justice Stewart concluded that the limitations on public access, when applied to the press, may serve to restrict the press from effectively conveying prison conditions to the public. The Court did not reach consensus as to the extent of access the Constitution affords the press. . . .

KQED v. Vasquez

A federal district court in California considered whether the media has the right to televise executions in *KQED v. Vasquez*. In *KQED*, a public television station brought suit challenging the constitutionality of a California state prison policy which prohibited stations from videotaping executions. The station claimed that the policy violated the First Amendment because it unjustifiably prohibited the media from effectively reporting the events at an execution. Citing Justice Stewart's concurrence in *Houchins v. KQED*, the station contended that when the government provides access to public institutions, the government must provide "effective" access.

The station argued that the very reason the state provided press access to executions was so that the press could relate the details of an execution to the public. After contending that the media needs to utilize the tools of their trade to accomplish this purpose, KQED claimed that the Supreme Court's rulings in the right to access cases supported its arguments. Applying the test articulated in *Globe Newspaper*, the station asserted that the history of public executions, combined with the importance of "[a]ccurate citizen awareness" in a democratic society, creates a "presumption of openness" guaranteed by the Constitution. KQED contended that because the state lacked a compelling interest to defeat this presumption, the First Amendment prohibited the state from precluding the media from televising an execution.

In contrast, the prison warden argued that the regulation prohibiting the media from filming executions did not violate the Constitution. Relying on *Pell v. Procunier*, the defendant contended that the media has no right of access to an execution because the state does not afford the *public* the right to witness an execution. In addition, the warden strongly suggested that the two factors articulated by the Court in *Globe Newspaper* for determining questions of media access do not create a "presumption of openness" with respect to executions. The defendant concluded that if the public does not have the right to film an execution, then neither does the media. The state need demonstrate only that the regulation is "reasonable," because the restriction on filming executions "is only a 'time, place and manner' restriction." Thus, the defendant contended that the First Amendment does not provide the media with the right to film executions.

In a convoluted oral opinion, the court stated that the First Amendment does not provide the press with an absolute right to gather news. Concluding that the press has no special right of access beyond that afforded to the public generally, the court emphasized that the state does not hold its executions open to the public. Nevertheless, the court refused to permit the prison to completely bar the press from attending executions. Although the court refused to arbitrarily exclude the press from attending executions, it held that prison officials can limit the degree of access afforded to the media. The court ruled that the policy was "valid and necessary" to guarantee the safety of prison personnel involved in the execution.

A More Appropriate Legal Framework

None of the courts that have addressed the issue of whether the First Amendment grants the media the right to videotape and broadcast an execution analyzed the question within the correct legal framework. Focusing only on whether state law provided the general public with the right to attend executions, these courts failed to decide if the Constitution guarantees the public such a right. The Supreme Court provided the proper framework for addressing the media's constitutional right to access in *Globe Newspaper*. Analysis of the issue within this framework reveals that the First Amendment does not provide the press with the right to attend or televise executions.

Courts considering the issue first should have resolved whether executions "historically ha[ve] been open to the press and general public." An examination of the history of public executions in both England and America illustrates that the public and the press initially had the right to attend executions. However, due to changes in sociopolitical attitudes, they lost this right. For all practical purposes, public executions ceased in America in the latter part of the nineteenth century. Therefore, in contrast to the public's right of access to criminal trials, history does not demonstrate an unbroken tradition of press and public access to executions. In *Globe Newspaper*, the Court stressed that the right of access to a criminal trial "remained secure" throughout American history. Conversely, legislators over a century ago abolished the public's right to attend executions. The conclusion that the right has not "remained secure" precludes a finding that executions "historically ha[ve] been open to the press and general public."

Executions Are No Longer Public

The courts that addressed the issue of televising executions also should have analyzed whether "the right of access to [public executions] plays a particularly significant role in the functioning of the judicial process and the government as a whole." An examination of American history illustrates that *public* executions served a very specific function in the United States. Generally, public executions reinforced the power of a new republic and provided a means for the condemned person to repent for his crime and seek salvation. Public executions served significant judicial and governmental functions for two reasons. First, they demonstrated that the new republic would not tolerate unlawful action by its citizens. Second, through the ritual of the prisoner seeking repentance, public executions demonstrated that the republic also possessed the capacity to forgive those who broke its laws and threatened its power. Therefore, the sociopolitical climate in the nation allowed public access to executions to serve important purposes during an early period in American history.

However, as the republic strengthened and society started to embrace privacy and disfavor public disorder, state legislatures throughout the country privatized executions. Consequently, the role that executions played in "the judicial process and the government as a whole" changed. Society executed its prisoners to achieve goals of deterrence and retribution, rather than to convey outdated civic and religious messages. Therefore, the presence of the public was no longer necessary to facilitate the role that executions played earlier "in the functioning of the judicial process and the government as a whole."

Accordingly, because executions historically have not been open, and because *public* executions ceased contributing significantly to democratic society, the Constitution does not contain a "presumption of openness" with respect to executions. Since the First Amendment only affords the press the same rights of access as those afforded to the public, the media has no constitutional right to attend executions.

No Right to Film

Yet the question remains whether the press has the right to film executions if the state provides the public, and consequently, the press, with access to executions. In *Houchins v. KQED*, the Court emphasized that the Constitution only requires the state to provide the same *type* of access to the media that it affords the public. Thus, if the state forbids the public from filming executions, then the Constitution does not require the state to allow the media access to film executions.

Justice Stewart's concurrence in *Houchins v. KQED* stressed that the state must provide the press with effective access. Even under this formulation, however, the state still need not allow the press to film executions. Denying the media the right to film an execution does not deny the press effective access to the execution. The press can continue to effectively transmit the happenings of an execution through written text. The press can effectively report the details of any deviation from proper execution procedure in a newspaper or magazine article. Allowing the media to televise executions will not further the purpose of increasing the effectiveness of the media's reporting to an appreciable extent. Rather, a videotaped execution will most likely only sensationalize the death of a criminal.

More importantly, televising executions will transform private executions back into public executions. The decisional law relating to press access and the right to gather information illustrates that courts cannot make this transformation under the guise of providing for effective reporting without stretching the First Amendment beyond its appropriate scope. Only state legislatures, motivated by public opinion, have the power to catapult executions back into the public arena. Because an execution is not dignified or aesthetically pleasing, legislators ultimately will have to decide whether they want this type of "program" to appear on American television. . . .

Although each court which addressed the issue of media access to executions incorrectly analyzed the subject, all of the tribunals arrived at the correct conclusion. Although the press has a constitutional right to gather information, this right does not extend into the execution chamber. Neither opponents nor proponents of capital punishment should exploit the deaths of condemned criminals in order to wage their battles concerning the death penalty. The press adequately informs the public about the details of executions through the nation's newspapers and magazines.

"Operational security and the need for surprise are essential elements of warfare, and require a controlled press."

Restrictions on War Coverage Are Necessary

Karl Tage Olson

During the 1991 war in the Persian Gulf, the movements and communications of U.S. news reporters were controlled. Many critics complained that these restrictions were unconstitutional. However, in the following viewpoint, Karl Tage Olson argues that such restrictions are constitutional because the conditions that guarantee a First Amendment right of access are not met in the case of warfare. Although Olson concedes that a free press is essential for a democratic society, he believes that some restrictions on the press are necessary in order to protect the security of troops and to maintain the secrecy of strategic information. Olson is former editor in chief of *Drake Law Review*, a journal published by the students of Drake Law School in Des Moines, Iowa.

As you read, consider the following questions:

1. According to the author, why does press coverage of warfare fail to meet the two conditions for First Amendment protection?
2. Why are media pools necessary, according to Olson?
3. According to the author, why does the existence of satellite communications bolster the need for security reviews of news stories?

From Karl Tage Olson, Note, "The Constitutionality of Department of Defense Press Restrictions on Wartime Correspondence Covering the Persian Gulf War," 41 *Drake Law Review* 511 (1992). Reprinted with permission.

News executives severely criticized the government's decision to deny media representatives access during the initial deployment of United States forces to the Persian Gulf. Proponents of a "right to access" argued the First Amendment guarantees the press a right to speak, publish, *and gather information.* . . .

The Supreme Court has suggested that any claim to a right of access must be premised on two conditions: (1) showing the place sought to be accessed has historically been open to both the media and the public, and (2) showing the right of access "plays a particularly significant role in the functioning of . . . the government as a whole."

The press claims a well-established First Amendment right to gather information and report on events happening in an "open" area. Yet, military operations historically have not been held "open" to the public. Access is usually limited to accredited members of the press. Additionally, in commando-type raids like the failed attempt to rescue American hostages held in Iran, neither the press nor the public is given access. Furthermore, media access to military operations arguably fails to play a "significant" role in the functioning of our government and its ability to wage war. The ability of the media to independently report on the conduct of a war does not contribute significantly to the government's ability to wage war. Operational security and the need for surprise are essential elements of warfare, and require a controlled press.

The Importance of the Press

It is difficult, however, to imagine the United States involved in a major war without some form of independent media coverage. Correspondents marched with the Army of the Potomac during the Civil War, huddled in the trenches with our troops during World War I, and stormed the beaches of Normandy in World War II. Any suggestion that the executive branch could "completely" deny media access during a prolonged military operation when American service personnel are fighting and dying is inconsistent with past practice. More importantly, a total ban on access runs contrary to the spirit and intent of the First Amendment. . . . The underlying rationale for a free press is two-fold. First, a free press serves as a check against abuse of government authority. Second, a free press, like free speech, serves a necessary self-governing function.

Our democratic form of government requires the informed participation of its citizenry. The people choose who shall govern. They elect the President and the Congress. The President serves as Commander in Chief of the Armed Forces and conducts the nation's foreign policy. The Congress makes law, collects taxes, and declares war. A free press ensures the citizens of this country are informed about public matters and are prepared to discharge their civic rights in an intelligent manner. James Madison wrote: "A popular government, without popular information, or the means of acquiring it, is but a Prologue to a Farce or a Tragedy; or, perhaps both. Knowledge will forever govern ignorance: And a people who mean to be their own Governors, must arm themselves with the power which knowledge gives."

Journalists Cannot Be Trusted

Freedom of access for journalists requires freedom of movement. And freedom of movement, especially given modern communications technology, means freedom for journalists to determine the content of reporting without supervision by the military. The question is, Can they be trusted to make those determinations responsibly? Sadly, ample evidence exists that they cannot.

Ted Smith, *The World & I*, April 1991.

A complete denial of access would place the American people at the mercy of its government for information. The press, as an agent for the public, would be unable to perform its self-government and checking functions. It would become nothing more than a propaganda machine of the government—merely passing to the American people official government communiqués on the conduct of war. Without access there could be no check on the accuracy of the government's claims; there could be no independent assessment of the government's performance; and there could be no informed basis on which the American people could discharge their civic duties. Government controlled information could conceivably become as biased and inaccurate as Iraqi broadcasts were to the Iraqi people during the Gulf War. Such a scenario would be unthinkable in our democracy.

Access Must Be Limited

Although a policy that categorically denies media access to military operations is unthinkable, so too is a policy that grants unlimited access to the media. Operational security requirements and national security interests demand some degree of governmental secrecy and control. Unlimited media access could seriously jeopardize military operations and lives. The American public should not expect to be informed of every major troop movement, bombing mission, or enemy target. Consequently, access to military units, briefings, and installations must be limited if war is to be waged successfully.

In his concurrence in *Richmond Newspapers, Inc. v. Virginia*,

Justice Brennan recognized the right of access was not absolute. He specifically addressed the need to balance the First Amendment with other compelling interests such as national security. Brennan wrote:

> [T]he First Amendment has not been viewed by the Court in all settings as providing an equally categorical assurance of the correlative freedom of access to information. Yet the Court has not ruled out a public access component to the First Amendment in every circumstance. Read with care and in context, our decisions must therefore be understood as holding only that any privilege of access to governmental information is subject to a degree of restraint dictated by the nature of the information and countervailing interests in security and confidentiality.

Controlling the media's access to information in a theater of operations, therefore, requires a balancing test under the First Amendment.

In *Globe Newspaper Co. v. Superior Court*, the Supreme Court concluded that when government "attempts to deny the right of access in order to inhibit the disclosure of sensitive information, it must be shown that the denial is necessitated by a compelling governmental interest and is narrowly tailored to serve that interest." The exigencies of war necessitate restraint on access. The power to wage war means "'the power to wage war successfully.' It extends to every matter and activity so related to war as substantially to affect its conduct and progress," [the Supreme Court stated in *Hirabayashi v. United States*].

Assuming for the sake of argument that the media has a limited right of access to military operations, the next logical question is whether the military's "media pool" and "security review" requirements are permissible restraints on the media's right to collect information.

Are Media Pools Justifiable?

During the Persian Gulf War, the military provided access to accredited members of the media on the condition that they follow DOD [Department of Defense] guidelines. An essential feature of these guidelines was the use of media pools, in which media personnel agreed to share stories and photographs with their colleagues. Media representatives not participating in these pools were denied access to United States forces.

The pools were organized by the Joint Information Bureau ("JIB"), which provided daily sign-up sheets for press pool activities. Usually, the number of reporters registered for an activity exceeded the quota established by the JIB. Reporters fortunate enough to make the quota would travel under the supervision of military escorts to their predetermined destinations. Once there, they had to deal with time constraints, escort supervision, and military censorship before piecing a story together.

Reporters insisted the pooling requirement was an attempt to thwart serious media coverage of military operations. Specifically, they argued the pooling requirement limited their ability to gather information. Military officials maintained the pooling arrangement was a necessary means for ensuring operational security, protecting United States forces, and ensuring the safety of journalists. Assuming operational security is a compelling government interest and access can be controlled, the pooling arrangement is the military's primary means for limiting media access.

Globe requires, however, that military access restrictions be narrowly tailored to serve the compelling government interest. Thus, the fundamental question is whether pooling arrangements constitute narrowly-tailored restrictions aimed at achieving operational security and the protection of United States forces.

Pools Are Necessary

In peacetime, the media do not enjoy unlimited access to military installations or military training exercises. Given the exigencies of war and the need for increased security, the media should not be given greater freedom in wartime. The military cannot unleash hundreds of correspondents in a developed theater of operations and expect to maintain maximum security. An intelligent reporter with unlimited access conceivably could acquire sufficient information to accurately detail military plans and strategy. A leak of this information could seriously hamper or even defeat entirely such plans and strategies.

Because of operational security concerns, reporters should not be allowed to transmit footage of American marines and soldiers practicing how they intend to breach minefields. It would be unconscionable to allow correspondents to transmit footage of the latest Scud missile attacks, detailing information that could aid the enemy in launching more accurate attacks in the future. The slightest bit of information intercepted by the enemy could tip American battle plans and cost lives. Access to information must be controlled if war is to be waged successfully. Pooling arrangements provide the necessary framework for limiting media access. The media may be indignant, but they must recognize an uncontrolled press corps on the battlefield poses a potential threat to human life and the war effort. Government cannot allow this potential threat to go unchecked.

Security Review Requirements Are Essential

The media opposed the security review requirements established by the Pentagon even more stringently than the pooling requirements. The pooling requirements limited the media's ability to gather information. The security review requirements, on the other hand, interfered with the media's ability to disseminate information once it was acquired. Pentagon officials insist security reviews are necessary to ensure military operational security; critics, however, argue the security review requirements constitute a prior restraint on free speech and are therefore unconstitutional. . . .

Military history and case law support the government's position to censor certain information in time of war. For example, in *Near v. Minnesota*, the Supreme Court stated:

> "When a nation is at war many things that might be said in time of peace are such a hindrance to its effort that their utterance will not be endured so long as men fight and that no Court could regard them as protected by any constitutional right." No one would question but that a government might prevent actual obstruction to its recruiting service or the publication of the sailing dates of transports or the number and location of troops.

In this age of satellite communications, information can be transmitted and received within seconds. Information broadcast to the United States can just as easily be intercepted and received in Baghdad. A security review of all material ensures that the enemy does not receive information it could use against United States forces during war.

There is, of course, potential for government abuse. Military officials could easily suppress any story under the pretext of operational security. Yet, the media guidelines specifically state material will not be censored "for its potential to express criticism or cause embarrassment." The intent behind the security review is to ensure that troop strengths, locations, missions, and tactics are not inadvertently released. If a dispute does arise regarding whether information should be censored, the ground rules provide an appeal process.

Restraint on the Press Is Constitutional

The media serve two important functions—a checking function and a self-government function—that among other things enable the American public to make wise and informed decisions about government. The Founding Fathers deemed a free press so essential to a democracy that they guaranteed its freedom in the First Amendment. Implied in this guarantee is a limited right of access for media personnel to gather information.

The public, however, cannot investigate every public matter. In most matters of public importance, the media operate as agents of the public. Historically, the public has been denied access to the battlefields where American forces are fighting. They have relied instead on information provided by our government and by a free press.

Our system of government demands the press be afforded limited access to military operations. Operational security and the safety of United States forces are compelling interests justifying some restraint on media access and publication. Pool arrangements and reasonably administered security reviews are narrowly-tailored to serve these compelling governmental interests and are, therefore, both constitutional and appropriate mechanisms to reconcile these competing interests.

*"The government's limitations on press coverage
of the Persian Gulf war were unconstitutional."*

Restrictions on War Coverage Are Excessive

The Committee on Civil Rights of the Association of the Bar of
the City of New York

In the following viewpoint, the Committee on Civil Rights of
the Association of the Bar of the City of New York contends that
restrictions imposed on the news media during recent military
operations—especially the war in the Persian Gulf—were unconstitutional. The committee argues that the press has a constitutional right of access to combat zones and troops unless the military demonstrates "compelling" security reasons to bar them,
which it refused to do during the Gulf War. The committee
states that censorship of information distorts the democratic
process of public debate that inevitably surrounds the country's
involvement in war.

As you read, consider the following questions:

1. According to the committee, why was the Sidle panel set up?
   What policy did the panel advocate?
2. Who controls the military, according to the authors?
3. For what purpose should press pools be used, in the authors'
   opinion?

From "Military Restrictions on Press Coverage: The Unacceptability of the Pentagon's
Policies During the Persian Gulf Conflict" by The Committee on Civil Rights, The
Association of the Bar of the City of New York, *The Record* of The Association of the Bar of
the City of New York, vol. 46, no. 8, December 1991. Reprinted with permission.

Like any other arm of the United States government, the armed forces exist to serve the people. The especial importance of democratic control of those forces has been recognized since the birth of our government. This democratic control requires unfettered debate, so that the country may make the openly considered choices that are central to our national strength.

But meaningful debate is not possible without meaningful information. For this reason, the military forces of the United States are obliged both to permit the press physical access to combat operations and to limit any interference with journalists' reports to the absolute minimum necessary to protect operational security. During the 1991 hostilities in the Persian Gulf, the Pentagon's discharge of this obligation was inadequate. The actions of defense authorities in confining journalists to press pools, as well as in delaying or censoring their accounts for reasons other than the physical protection of troops, were inconsistent with our heritage and demeaned our principles.

These failures represent both a breach of the government's duty today, and a danger for the future. We are concerned by the prospect that the success of the military during the last ten years in keeping information about combat operations from the American public may, in the absence of strong public protest, create a precedent that will prove dangerous to civilian control of the military. "If a nation expects to be ignorant and free," Thomas Jefferson wrote, "it expects what never was and never will be." The citizenry cannot—without risking the very values for which the nation fights—surrender into governmental hands the decision concerning which facts it needs to know.

The Press Must Be Free

Throughout American history, including the war in Vietnam, the press corps has had virtually unfettered access to the scenes of military operations, and the only restraints imposed on the transmission of information have been those minimal ones necessary to insure operational security.

When the United States invaded Grenada in October 1983, however, the military physically prevented reporters from travelling to the island, and then severely restricted the movements of those who were eventually allowed to land. This unprecedented policy—which significantly restricted the flow of information to the public—was widely denounced, and repudiated by the panel which the Pentagon itself set up to re-consider the issue (the Sidle panel).

That panel specifically affirmed the correctness of the policy that had been followed in all previous wars, that is, the press must be free to use its own resources to travel to combat scenes; in circumstances where that is impractical (e.g. a quick strike on a distant target), the military must assist the press in obtaining physical access to the location of the fighting. Press pools are to be used only to implement this second responsibility. Press pools are a second-best mechanism to be relied upon only to the extent that independent access is not possible. In that event, they should be used for the minimum time possible as a mechanism to assure timely press presence at the combat scene. Press pools, in short, are devices that should be used exclusively to increase—not decrease—access.

Media Must Have Access

The events in Grenada, Panama and the Persian Gulf demonstrate the need for clear judicial guidelines establishing the permissible scope of media access to the battlefield. . . . While the military may impose reasonable restrictions on the media, such as the institution of a press pool, these restrictions must be administered in a manner which allows all stages of a military operation to be covered by at least some members of the media. Although the First Amendment does not guarantee unlimited access to the battlefield, press restrictions must be narrowly tailored to accomplish a legitimate purpose and to provide as much media access as is reasonably possible.

David A. Frenznick, *Pacific Law Journal*, vol. 23, 1992.

Nonetheless, despite this explicit re-affirmation of its own policies, the military also imposed Draconian restrictions on the coverage of the invasion of Panama in December of 1989. Once more, the Pentagon's own subsequent review (the Hoffman report) strongly criticized the Department of Defense for its "excessive concern for secrecy," which exacerbated the effect of the misleading claims that were later made by government officials.

The efforts of the Pentagon to restrict the physical access of the press to areas of military operations thus have a short and dubious pedigree, one which hardly justifies the restrictions that the Defense Department imposed on coverage of the Persian Gulf hostilities.

The Restrictions on Persian Gulf Coverage

Notwithstanding these self-criticisms and promises of change, as well as vigorous protests from the press to a preliminary proposal, the Pentagon, during January of 1991, issued rules forbidding any coverage of the combat in the Persian Gulf except by reporters in official press pools, who would be accompanied by military escorts, and whose reports would be subject to censorship at the source. Reporters travelling on their own would be subject to detention and revocation of their press credentials.

In actual operation, the rules proved highly restrictive. At best, stories were significantly delayed. At worst, the presence of military "minders" inhibited honest reporting, and the military command used its control over access to cajole or pressure reporters either into favorable coverage or into no coverage at all. Most pervasively, the breadth and competitiveness of the coverage that one would expect from some 1,600 journalists representing a broad range of media were significantly curtailed by a system that, at maximum, could put only 192 journalists with combat units in the field.

Unconstitutional Limits

While the Defense Department is constitutionally entitled to broad discretion in its conduct of military operations abroad, it has been firmly established that the first amendment provides protection for journalists' reports of military activities. These same protections should apply to reporters' access to combat zones and troops.

The first amendment gives the press a right of access to many events that the government carries out in the name of its citizens. Considering the lessons of history, the importance of public access, and the availability of less restrictive alternatives, the courts have often overturned governmental restrictions inhibiting the ability of the press to act as a surrogate for the public. Even where there was no question as to the legitimacy of the reasons for closure, the courts required the government to prove that its means were narrowly tailored to serve those ends.

While no decided case directly addresses governmental restrictions on the reporting of combat operations, an application of the analysis contained in existing case law reveals that the government's limitations on press coverage of the Persian Gulf war were unconstitutional. The historical record demonstrates that this country has had a tradition of openness with respect to combat operations. The public's interest in access, another key element of the test, could hardly be more compelling. The Pentagon itself did not defend its policy as the least restrictive alternative. On the contrary, the Defense Department explicitly took the position that the denial of access was for its own convenience, and would be lifted at its own convenience.

This is not good enough. A key reason that the first amendment establishes a right of access is to overcome the danger inherent in the government's deciding whether there will be independent witnesses to its proceedings. If that right of access is ever to be overcome, it should only be after the same sort of compelling showing as is necessary to censor journalists' reports. But the Pentagon itself appropriately disclaimed any such censorship right in the case of the Persian Gulf conflict; hence, the access limitations were legally unjustified.

Access to the Facts

Since the conclusion of hostilities in the Persian Gulf, the Pentagon has consistently sought to defend its media policies by saying that it provided ample information. This evades the central question, which is not the quantity—or even the accuracy—of the information, but the independence of its source. The Constitution does not require the military to hold press briefings; it does require the military to allow journalists to enter combat zones and to do their jobs.

We are aware of the military's interest in attempting to put facts in the most favorable light. As long as its officials adhere to the truth and an unfettered press can make sure that they are doing so, it is entirely appropriate for the Department of Defense to publicize its views and respond to any challenges to those views. Indeed, political wisdom emerges from such interchanges.

But the process is distorted unless the people have access to the facts. Only when the people have access to the facts can they determine, first, that the government might be adding "spin," and, second, whether they are convinced, or would choose to put some different interpretation on the information. To restrict freedom of inquiry is to inhibit sound policymaking by distorting the normal give-and-take of public debate. Overzealous censorship by the military will only intensify the backlash when the failures and tragedies are revealed. The antidote is to reveal more of the truth sooner. After all, the military forces operate under civilian control precisely because of our profound national commitment to the belief that the best political choices are made by a citizenry who know the truth.

Every one of this country's wars has engendered passionate public disputes. However, turbulence is necessary for a democratic country to wage war and still remain a democratic country.

We conclude that the military must allow the press physical access to combat zones and troops and not interfere with journalists' reports unless it demonstrates that there is a compelling justification of insuring operational security and that the interference is the absolute minimum necessary for that purpose.

The Pentagon violated these standards during the Persian Gulf conflict, thus undermining the vital constitutional role of the press as a check on the actions of government.

We encourage the Pentagon to use press pools, but only to increase access, not reduce it. When employed, press pools should be as large and diverse as possible; the selection of the pool's membership should be left to the press; and the military should allow the timely use of its communications facilities to enable the press to transmit information as promptly and as freely as it could using its own equipment.

We deplore the fact that these principles, which have been repeatedly endorsed, not only by civil liberties organizations, but also by the Pentagon itself, were so brusquely violated during the Persian Gulf war. No short-term gains can justify such a policy. For to the extent that we cease to be a country where each of us may justly bear some responsibility for each war we fight, all of us are the losers.

Periodical Bibliography

The following articles have been selected to supplement the diverse views presented in this chapter.

Martha Bayles	"Fake Blood: Why Nothing Gets Done About Media Violence," *The Brookings Review*, Fall 1993.
Leo Bogart	"Shaping a New Media Policy," *The Nation*, July 12, 1993.
Peggy Charren	"It's 8 P.M. Where Are Your Parents?" *The New York Times*, July 7, 1993.
Charles Colson	"Prime-Time Executions," *Christianity Today*, July 22, 1991.
David A. Frenznick	"The First Amendment on the Battlefield," *Pacific Law Journal*, vol. 23, 1992. Available from 3401 Fifth Ave., Sacramento, CA 95817.
Thomas W. Hazlett	"Child's Play," *Reason*, January 1991.
David A. Kaplan	" 'Live, from San Quentin . . .': Should a TV Station Broadcast an Execution?" *Newsweek*, April 1, 1991.
Richard Miniter	"The Press: Jealous of Its Freedoms, Careless with Ours," *Liberty*, May 1991. Available from PO Box 1167, Port Townsend, WA 98368.
Neil E. Nussbaum	" 'Film at Eleven . . .'—Does the Press Have the Right to Attend and Videotape Executions?" *North Carolina Central Law Journal*, vol. 20, no. 2, 1992. Available from School of Law, North Carolina Central University, Durham, NC 27707.
Robert Scheer	"Violence Is Us," *The Nation*, November 15, 1993.
Ted Smith	"The World's First TV War," *The World & I*, April 1991. Available from 2800 New York Ave. NE, Washington, DC 20002.
Jack Valenti	"Hollywood, the Rating System, and the Movie-Going Public," *USA Today*, September 1993.
Thomas Winship	"Free Societies Require a Free Press," *USA Today*, September 1992.

5 CHAPTER

How Do the Media Affect Politics?

Chapter Preface

On February 20, 1992, Ross Perot entered the presidential race during an appearance on the CNN talk show *Larry King Live*. Perot's use of a talk show to declare his candidacy was unprecedented in American politics. Furthermore, the support Perot engendered among the electorate forced the other candidates to follow his lead in what became known as the "talk show campaign." Along with Perot, candidates Jerry Brown and Bill Clinton repeatedly appeared on talk shows. Even George Bush, who at first resisted the trend, was eventually forced by his lagging popularity to join the talk show campaign trail.

Many commentators believed the talk show campaign improved American democracy by bringing the candidates closer to the people. *Business Week*'s Deidre A. Depke argued that talk shows in which candidates responded to questions posed by live audiences and phoned in by viewers created a "direct link" between politicians and voters. This direct link served the voters well, some argued, because it minimized the ability of traditional journalists, pundits, and image-makers to manipulate political messages and influence public opinion. According to John Leo, a contributing editor for *U.S. News & World Report*, the talk show campaign established a "direct connection between candidates and voters, with no professional journalists around to filter the messages or to impose their own judgments and agendas."

While some applauded the talk show campaign, others saw it as a threat to the democratic process. For example, some commentators argued that in turning to talk shows, politicians were merely fleeing the substantive questions of knowledgeable reporters for the more amiable queries of less-informed television hosts. Others criticized the talk show trend for reducing serious political discourse to trivial banter. Terry Eastland of the Washington, D.C., Ethics and Public Policy Center feared that with a pervasion of talk show politics in America, "thought could be reduced to a banal lowest common denominator, and with it the contribution to deliberative democracy that a well-reasoned argument might make."

Whether the new marriage of politics and talk shows enhances or degrades American democracy, few question the importance of the mass media in the political realm. Politicians tailor their words and images for media audiences, while viewers struggle to discern the truth amid a cacophony of competing and conflicting media signals. The viewpoints in the following chapter debate various issues that arise at the intersection of politics and the media.

"Candidates are learning to act, speak, and think in television's terms. In the process they are transforming speeches, debates, and their appearances in news into ads."

Media Campaigns Hinder U.S. Politics

Kathleen Hall Jamieson

The media's emphasis on sound bites has reduced all forms of political speech to ads, according to Kathleen Hall Jamieson. In the following viewpoint, she argues that in the arena of U.S. political campaigns, pithy assertions have replaced serious argumentation, and knee-jerk attacks have taken the place of meaningful engagement. Jamieson is the dean of the Annenberg School for Communication at the University of Pennsylvania in Philadelphia, and she is the author of *Packaging the Presidency: A History and Criticism of Presidential Campaign Advertising*, and *Dirty Politics: Deception, Distraction, and Democracy*, from which this viewpoint is excerpted.

As you read, consider the following questions:

1. What is included in a "full menu of discourse," according to the author?
2. Why do you think the author equates network news with "peg boards used to assess children's hand-eye coordination"?
3. How does the media's emphasis on sound bites influence speechwriters, according to Jamieson?

The strategy perspective that pervades campaign coverage deprives the public of an ability to judge the legitimacy of candidate discourse. And candidates have no interest in providing a corrective since they have nothing to gain and everything to lose by taking clear stands on controversial policy issues. . . . Increasingly, campaigns have become narcotics that blur our awareness of problems long enough to elect the lawmakers who must deal with them. . . .

Full Menu of Discourse vs. Ad "McNuggets"

A campaign composed of publicized broadcast speeches, advertising, debates, citizen call-in programs, press conferences, press interviews with candidates, and analytic recapitulative news invites an office seeker to engage in extended argument that defines its terms, locates policy positions in an historical context, compares them to the available alternatives, argues the comparative advantage of the proposed policy, and then uses dramatic personal appeals to anchor it in the citizenry.

While not a guarantor that a campaign will be engaged and substantive, when both major candidates participate in a full menu of discourse, the odds of finding specificity and substance go up. When this mix is present, ads enable the candidates to digest claims argued elsewhere while appealing to their chosen audiences unfiltered by reporters or editors. When complemented by expository speeches, debates, and press conferences, the telegraphy of ads is useful. The expository forms give the ads substance to digest. The debates and press conferences can hold candidates accountable for the claims made in other generic forms. All of this changes when campaign discourse is transmogrified into ads.

In the political world of 1988, candidates conceived all forms of public communication as parts of a choreographed whole. In successful campaigns, each amplifies the other to create a single sense of the candidate and his opponent, a single set of simplified messages, driven home through frames of reference forged in the electorate early and reinforced throughout the campaign. In 1988, in other words, the once broad menu of discourse was reduced to ad McNuggets. . . .

Television has accustomed us to brief, intimate, telegraphic, visual, narrative messages. Candidates are learning to act, speak, and think in television's terms. In the process they are transforming speeches, debates, and their appearances in news into ads. At the same time, a focus on explaining polls and divining strategy is producing in news what one would ordinarily call ads. This accumulation of tendencies is changing the way in which candidates attack and defend and minimizing the protections a vigilant press can maintain against distortion, deception, and distraction in political discourse.

In recent campaigns, survival of the briefest has become the political norm. The hour-long political speeches of radio days have given way to thirty-second ads and ten-second soundbites. Where an hour-long speech was accepted as usual on the stump in the nineteenth century, today's presidential candidate will deliver an average stump speech in under seventeen minutes. Increasingly, nationally *broadcast* political discourse and our exposure to it come in bite-size morsels. That is true of answers in debates, which have dropped to one and two minutes; candidate soundbites in CBS, ABC, and NBC evening news, which Dan Hallin argues dropped to 9.8 seconds in 1988; and presidential campaign ads, which have dropped in modal length from thirty minutes in 1952 to thirty seconds in 1988.

Speeches Reduced to Strings of Disjunctive Soundbites

As C-SPAN viewers are aware, politicians often fail to structure ideas into coherent speeches or bridge them with transitions. Rather than building arguments, their campaign speeches have adapted to the demands of the press and the dispositions of the mass public by stringing together one-liners and anecdotes. No camera crew will have to look long for a soundbite; no intricate argumentative structure will drive viewers away.

Texas State Treasurer Ann Richards' speech at the 1988 Democratic Convention is illustrative. It contains her memories of summer nights listening to the grownups talk; one letter from a constituent; references to granddaughter Lily—the visual tie to the Democratic attempts to identify themselves with the future by aligning themselves with children; and thirty-second soundbites. The speech alternates between identification and apposition. I am like you. I care; we Democrats care. George Bush isn't like you; he doesn't care. We've had to work for what we've gotten; he hasn't. "Twelve years ago, Barbara Jordan, another Texas woman, made the keynote address to this convention and two women in 160 years is about par for the course. But if you give us a chance, we can perform. After all, Ginger Rogers did everything that Fred Astaire did. She just did it backwards." CUT. "For eight straight years George Bush hasn't displayed the slightest interest in anything we care about. And now that he's after a job he can't get appointed to." CUT. "He's like Columbus discovering America. He's found child care. He's found education." CUT. "Poor George. He can't help it. He was born with a silver foot in his mouth." CUT.

The best way to teach the structure of most contemporary political persuasion is to invite students to examine Jay Leno's monologues. "Moving right along here" is more of a transition than links the disjunctive soundbites in much public speech.

195

"The young people who do speeches for major politicians," claims Reagan and Bush speechwriter Peggy Noonan, "[don't write] a serious text with serious arguments, they just write soundbite after soundbite." Noonan did little more. Her speeches for Reagan at Point de Hoc and after the *Challenger* explosion are storytelling, not argument; the convention acceptance speech she crafted for Bush, little more than uplifting description and assertion.

'...Political campaigns seem so simplistic and superficial...
In the 20 seconds we have left, could you tell us why?...'

Clay Bennett/*St. Petersburg Times*. Reprinted by permission.

In prime-time television, we grant the hypothetical reality of the characters on the screen. From its first moments, we recognize the characters who populate "Murphy Brown" as surely as we do those on "Designing Women." We accept the compression of days and weeks into half-hour programs. The time usually spent sleeping, eating, and getting from place to place no longer exists in this telegraphed world. We grant that it is representative as well. Even though interrupted by commercials and station breaks, we do not question the reality it posits. We grant it a coherence it intrinsically lacks.

Adopting a telegraphic line from actor as gunslinger Clint Eastwood, nominee George Bush sounded tough and decisive at the Republican Convention on August 18, 1988, when he said, "The Congress will push me to raise taxes, and I'll say no, and they'll push, and I'll say no, and they'll push again, and I'll say to them, 'Read my lips. No new taxes.'"

In this snippet, we see operating the form that has come to characterize American televised discourse. The statement is digestive and short. It telegraphs a familiar persona. It reduces that abbreviated telegraphic message to a narrative captured in the primal archetype of physics: force and resistance to force. The verbal form suggests a defense of principle. As important is the fact that the words were repeated throughout the campaign in news. In the process, they gained the repetitive force of advertising in the credible context of news.

When abbreviated discourse is unanchored in traditional speech, it tends to deal in simplifying identifications and appositions that caricature the complexity of issues. Although it occurs in a speech, "Read my lips" is such a simplifying telegraphic statement. That fact supports my earlier claim that campaign speeches have now become soundbite-filled ads strung together with transitions.

"Read my lips. No new taxes" can warn a celluloid gunslinger that Boot Hill is in his immediate future; it cannot of itself articulate an economic philosophy or an argument for how one can meet government's promises without new revenue.

Such soundbites function as do such abbreviated viscerally visual forms as torn Social Security cards or menacing convicts. Both sacrifice two of the preconditions of ethical judgment: the time to consider options and with it the ability of a conscious agent to grant informed consent.

Debate Answers as Ads

The late 1980s witnessed a trend toward adlike candidate responses in debates. In the debates of the 1988 presidential general election, the candidates' one- and two-minute answers to reporters' questions repeated the claims and evoked the images of their ads. Out of the 1988 debates came two attack ads, one Democratic, one Republican. The Democrats replayed the exchange between vice presidential candidates Bentsen and Quayle that culminated in Bentsen's claim that Quayle was no John Kennedy. Dismissive laughter was added to the ad's audio track. The Republicans paid for time to air and rebut Dukakis's denial that he had raided his state's pension fund to balance the budget.

Where the Kennedy-Nixon debates anchored themselves in references to candidate speeches, the Dukakis-Bush debates tied themselves to evocation of newscast pseudo-events and ads. The presence of a live, candidate-picked audience transformed answer after answer into ad material. Just as laugh tracks once cued audiences to chuckle at the "right" moments of sitcoms, the laughter and boos signaled responses to debate answers.

In political campaigns, the interrelation among news, advertising, and debates is prismic. Each reflects, refracts, or refocuses the other in seemingly endless turns. From Dukakis in his tank to Quayle claiming kinship with JFK, clips from news and debates slip into ads to magnify one's own successes or indict an opponent. In news, reporters recount strategies behind ads, posit their effectiveness, and occasionally note the accuracy and fairness of an ad's claims. To underscore supposedly decisive moments, segments of debates replay in ads and news.

Where's the Beef?

Speaking in soundbites requires a capacity to digest and simplify; those issues or discussions that defy digestion into sound and sightbites are not the stuff of which television or winning campaigns are made. Whatever else one says about Gary Hart in 1984, he offered some thoughtful, substantive alternatives on defense policy. Indeed, he had written a book and delivered a number of major speeches outlining proposed reforms in a level of detail uncharacteristic of most modern political discourse.

When, in a March 1984 primary debate, Walter Mondale turned to him and said, "When I hear your new ideas, I'm reminded of that ad, 'Where's the beef?'," the Minnesotan had used the rapier of the soundbite to skewer Hart. Hart's incapacity in that moment was in part a function of the forms in which contemporary discourse traffics.

In the seconds left in the likely sound clip, Hart couldn't articulate his defense alternatives. "Vice President Mondale cleverly has picked up the slogan from a fast food chain and tried to suggest that there are no ideas or issues when he knows full well that they are in the form of a book, in the form of strategy and position papers—quite detailed, quite elaborate," responded Hart feebly. "The fact of the matter is that other candidates or the press or whomever really isn't interested quite often in what industrial policies are, what these detailed ideas are." In that brief telegraphic moment, substance was dispatched by the slogan of a hamburger chain. Later, we learned that Mondale had not even seen the Wendy's ad that propelled "Where's the beef?" into the national vocabulary. He had been handed the line by an aide. . . .

Interview and News Conference Answers as Ads

The Bush-[Tom] Brokaw interview on NBC on October 31, 1988, provides an illustration of the interview answer as ad.

Brokaw: "Your campaign has had a good deal of success on the whole law and order issue in the course of this campaign. That surprise you? Given the fact that in your administration, Michael Deaver and Lyn Nofziger, who had both served in it, were convicted? We have the National Security Adviser, John Poindexter, who has been indicted. Oliver North has been indicted. You had a top environmental administrator who was convicted. Given all of that, have you been surprised that you've been able to do as well in the law and order thing?"

Bush begins to answer the question and then, catching himself, delivers an adbite instead: "No. Because I think the law and—I'll tell you, one of the most moving moments in this campaign for me personally, not just sound bites or backdrops, was when Matt Byrnes, the Lieutenant, ex-Lieutenant on the New York Police force, handed me the badge of his fallen son. And he was doing it because I think he knows I am committed to backing up the local policeman, the guy with the badge, out on the cutting edge in the neighborhood."

"Candidates give their prepared message of the day, regardless of the question. This detracts from the give-and-take of the information process," lamented network correspondent Harry Smith. "We get accused of reducing the campaign to soundbites, but when we *do* ask a serious question, the candidates are so trained to speak succinctly that soundbites are all we get."

For Brokaw's viewers, Bush recreates a story played out on an earlier newscast, recalled in an earlier debate, and viewed again in the Bush election eve program. The message: Bush is tough but caring. Its effect: to displace Brokaw's question about indictments and convictions in the Reagan-Bush administration. There is no propositional relationship between Brokaw's question and Bush's answer.

When faced with a question about his commitment to the confirmation of his Supreme Court nominee, Bush used the same technique more bluntly. "Any questions that you ask me will be answered with the statement, 'I support Clarence Thomas,'" he said. . . .

Soundbites as Ads

In 1988 the candidates reached the largest number of viewers in environments in which assertion was the norm. From Labor Day until election eve, each presidential candidate had eight opportunities five days a week to gain access to a national audience on morning, evening, and late night network news. With the exception of "MacNeil/Lehrer," what was most likely to be excerpted from the candidate's speech of the day was a dramatic attack on his opponent set in a visually reinforcing environment. The major speeches of the campaign that lacked such moments, including Bush's major speech on agricultural policy and Dukakis's major speech on defense, received no network news treatment.

With the exception of candidate interviews, network news is somewhat like the peg boards used to assess children's hand-eye coordination and spacial processing. These boxlike fixtures contain holes of various sizes and shapes. The child is handed a bag of cut-out blocks. The goal of the exercise is getting each block inside the box through the appropriate hole as quickly as possible. The strategy schema provides holes for blocks that are small and helps construct the narrative that answers the question, Who is winning and why? The hole demands short statements that do not require additional contextual explanation from the reporter, do not require additional editing, and will be compatible with the reporter's story line. Any pithy attack on the opponent will do.

In 1978 I was invited to appear on network television for the first time. Wanting to do a good job, I was particularly careful in the pre-interview to define my terms and lay out the available evidence for my arguments. After talking with me for more than a half hour, the producer of the segment laughed and said, "Look professor, I know you are an expert in this area. That's why we want you on the show. But when we say you are an expert, it means you are an expert. You don't have to tell us how you got to your conclusions, just give us the bottom line." In the fourteen years since that experience I have learned that a soundbite is actually an assertion. Whether it is warranted by evidence or not cannot usually be known by the reader or viewer. By certifying the interviewee as an "expert," reporters ask their audiences to take the existence of evidence on faith.

Assertion vs. Argument

Network news accustoms audiences to assertion not argument. Over time, it reinforces the notion that politics is about visceral identification and apposition, not complex problems and their solutions. It also accustoms politicians and quoted academics to think and speak in assertions.

Speechwriters produce and candidates deliver what is rewarded with newsplay. Over time, assertion—not argument— has become the norm for candidate speeches. Indeed, the goal of the campaign comes to be getting the same soundbite into the soundbite hole of each of the networks. Interestingly, that soundbite is not necessarily the thesis of the speech. More often it is an attack on an opponent.

If the goal of a speech is producing a widgetlike soundbite in a prefabricated environment, then some facets of argument fall to the wayside. One does not dare note the legitimacy of anything the opponent has done or said. Doing so runs the risk that that moment of equanimity will be the one played on news. Banned too is discussion of substantive similarities between candidates. One does not accurately summarize the case for the other side, even if only to rebut it. Nor ought one to tie evidence to one's claims lest in the process the claim expands beyond the size of the soundbite slot and as a result is shunted aside. "Stepping on your own message" is shorthand for letting the reporters or the opposing campaign shape the content of your soundbite. As those who watched C-SPAN and the "MacNeil/Lehrer NewsHour" are aware, both Dukakis and Bush delivered important, cogent, well-argued speeches on the stump in 1988. In some instances their central claims and the rationale behind them did reach the nation's living rooms through network evening news. More often, they did not.

When I argued earlier that all forms of campaign discourse were becoming adlike, I meant in part that they were substituting assertion for argument and attack for engagement.

I don't mean to suggest that short assertive statements are necessarily superficial. When a voter is fully informed about an issue and needs only to know whether the candidate is of like mind, such assertions as "I favor *Roe v. Wade*" or "I favor the death penalty for drug lords" are useful and efficient. But if the voter is seeking an understanding of the rationale that has led the candidate to this conclusion or is trying to determine which position to embrace, soundbites aren't very helpful. They can tell a voter *what* a candidate believes, but not *why*. And many issues are too complex to be freeze dried into a slogan and a smile.

Transforming telegraphic assertion into argument requires data and a link between the data and the claim. Engagement goes a step further by differentiating between the espoused position and that of one's opponent and arguing the comparative advantages of one over the other. . . .

The likelihood that the public will be misled is minimized if the candidates' views are available and tested by each other and by the press, if they are expected to engage in warranted argument, and if they accept responsibility for defending their own claims and the claims others offer on their behalf.

Of course, none of this ensures that most citizens or most voters will pay a whit of attention. But it would increase the probability that those who are interested have "adequate" if not "equal" "opportunities for discovering and validating, in the time permitted by the need for a decision, what his or her preferences are on the matter to be decided" [in the words of Robert Dahl].

"Despite cries that campaigns have become less substantial in the television era, . . . campaign communications increase the accuracy of voters' perceptions."

Media Campaigns Enhance U.S. Politics

Samuel L. Popkin

Samuel L. Popkin is a professor of political science at the University of California, San Diego. He has served as a consultant on polling and strategy to the George McGovern, Jimmy Carter, and Bill Clinton presidential campaigns, and he has assisted with polling and election coverage for CBS news. In the following viewpoint, he argues that media campaigns do not reduce the quality of political discussion. Rather, he believes they enable voters to make informed decisions about candidates and issues. Popkin concludes that bigger and louder campaigns are needed to attract greater participation in the political process.

As you read, consider the following questions:

1. According to Popkin, why has the proliferation of media and communications channels fragmented the electorate?
2. The author writes that "big brother is not gaining on the public." How does he support this assessment?
3. How does the "stop and think" experiment support Popkin's argument that campaigns are not trivial?

From "Campaigns That Matter" by Samuel L. Popkin. In *Under the Watchful Eye*, Mathew D. McCubbins, ed. Washington, DC: CQ Press, 1992. Reprinted with permission.

There is something rather miraculous about the fact that citizens believe that leaders selected by balloting are entitled to govern, even though election campaigns are commonly criticized as tawdry and pointless affairs, full of dirty politics, dirty tricks, and mudslinging. Critics want to turn down the noise level of campaigns and focus them on more important issues. On the other hand, they want more people to vote. However, these goals are contradictory: refined, decorous campaigns will not raise more important issues, mobilize more voters, or overcome off-stage mutterings about race and other social issues. Not surprisingly, most proposals for reforming campaigns fail to indicate how the reforms would affect voters or improve the system.

Most reformers do not look closely at how voters respond to campaigns nor at the people they wish to sanitize. Contrary to the reformers' views, voters are not passive victims of mass media manipulators or campaign consultants. They are able to navigate campaigns and make sense of the bits and pieces of information gleaned from these sources. Voters learn from campaigns because they know how to read the media and the politicians—that is, because they reason about what they see and hear. The better we understand voters and how they reason, the more sense campaigns make and the more we see how campaigns matter in a democracy. Indeed, I argue that because campaigns do actually help voters make their ballot choices, we need bigger, necessarily more expensive campaigns to get voters interested and involved in elections. . . .

Information Shortcuts

It is easy to demonstrate that Americans have limited knowledge of basic textbook facts about their government and the political debates of the day. However, evaluating citizens only in terms of factual knowledge is a misleading way to assess their competence as voters because it fails to acknowledge the importance of using information shortcuts. . . .

Voters use information shortcuts in assessing the personal characteristics of the candidate and his or her issue positions. A candidate's past positions will be used to estimate those in the future. When voters are uncertain about past positions, they will accept as a proxy information about the candidate's personal demographic characteristics and the groups with which he or she has associated. And since voters find it difficult to gather information about the performance of politicians outside their district or state, they will accept campaign competence as a proxy for competence in elected office as an indication of the political skills needed to handle the issues confronting the government. . . .

People use shortcuts when choosing a candidate. Faced with an array of candidates, some much better known than others, and all known in different ways that make comparison difficult, voters will seek a clear and accessible criterion for comparing them. This usually means looking for the sharpest differences between the candidates, which are then incorporated into narratives that make it possible to compare the candidates without spending the time and energy needed to make independent evaluations of them. When people compare candidates on the basis of the most obvious differences rather than the most important, they are conducting the equivalent of a Drunkard's Search, looking for their lost car keys under the streetlight only because it is easier to search there. . . .

The Growing Importance of Campaigns

Changes in government, society, the mass media, and the nomination process have made campaigns more important today than they were fifty years ago when modern studies of them began. The electorate consists of many more diverse and overlapping constituencies; a more educated citizenry cares about more issues; there are many more communications channels through which specific segments of the electorate are organized and mobilized; and the primary nominating process leaves parties more divided at the start of the campaign. Each of these changes means that the process of making one distinction paramount in voters' minds is more difficult. . . .

The proliferation of media and channels has increased segmentation of the electorate. As a result, the general campaign has a bigger job, requiring candidates to transmit more messages through more channels than in the past. When the national political conventions were first telecast in 1952, all three networks showed the exact same picture at the same time because there was only one national microwave relay; today, with the proliferation of cable systems and satellite relays, television can show over 100 channels. A voter can receive feedback about a presidential speech or campaign from a variety of religious, ethnic, liberal, conservative, and lifestyle-oriented channels; by 1992 even a comedy channel was offering commentary on state of the union messages. Fifty years ago the only news services were the Associated Press and United Press International; in the 1960s and 1970s papers like the *New York Times* and the *Washington Post* established news services with their own emphases. As channels and options have proliferated, and as commuting time has increased and two-career families have become more common, the proportion of people watching mainstream networks and their news programs has also dropped. This makes the job of integrating segments of the electorate more difficult and expensive.

There are also a great many more specialized radio and TV

programs and channels, magazines, newsletters, and even computer bulletin boards that enable people to keep in touch with others holding similar views outside their immediate neighborhoods or communities. Such extended groups are not new, and modern communication technology is not necessary to mobilize them, as a look back at the abolitionist and temperance movements reminds us; however, more channels to mobilize such groups are available today, and the groups they have nurtured are more numerous. . . .

Words and Impressions

After seeing the presidential candidates on NBC's "Today Show," the Larry King program, and the Phil Donahue show, it is possible at the very least to get a sense of what kind of person the candidate is and how he responds to various issues. . . . Most of us vote for the person we feel most comfortable with and feel will speak to our needs and concerns. All the words may be quickly forgotten, but the impression of the candidate stays in the mind.

Joe Saltzman, *USA Today*, September 1992.

The expansion of communication media [has] increased voters' exposure to individual candidates, particularly to personal information about them. This increases the importance of campaigns because it gives voters more opportunities to abandon views based on party default values in favor of views based on candidate information. There are also more opportunities to shift from views based on a candidate's past record to views based on his or her campaign image. . . .

More Campaigning

Successful reform is possible only if we begin by examining how voters actually reason and then alter the system to provide more of the information and stimulation they need to reduce the chance of unacceptable outcomes. If voters engage in a Drunkard's Search for the keys to political choice, then campaigns should give them more, not fewer, streetlights to look under. The place where the candidates are shining their lights may not be the best spot to find information about the issue of greater concern to a voter. But at least when people look where the candidates are shining their lights, they are likely to find some electoral key.

I believe that voter turnout declined between 1960 and 1990 because campaign stimulation, from the media and personal interaction, is also low and declining, and there is less interaction

205

between the media and the grass-roots, person-to-person aspects of voter mobilization. The lack of campaign stimulation is also responsible for the large gap in this country between the turnout of educated and uneducated voters. . . .

More campaign competition among the candidates, and more voter exposure to this competition, would allow them more time to move from personal character to general political competence and to introduce questions about the past record of the candidates. In the 1984 Democratic primary, Walter Mondale had to ask, "Where's the Beef?" to force Gary Hart to come to grips with specific policy proposals. The more time and stimulation in such campaigns the better.

If government is going to be able to solve our problems, we need bigger and noisier campaigns to rouse voters. It takes bigger, costlier campaigns to sell health insurance than to sell the death penalty; it takes more time and money to communicate about complicated issues of governance than to communicate about racism. The cheaper the campaign, the cheaper the issue.

Campaigns cannot deal with any substance if they cannot get the electorate's attention and interest people in listening to their music. Campaigns need to make noise. Restricting television news to the MacNeil-Lehrer format and requiring all the candidates to model their speeches on the Lincoln-Douglas debates won't solve America's problems.

Are Campaigns Trivial?

There are two important criticisms of a policy to encourage bigger campaigns. The first is the "spinmaster" objection: contemporary political campaigns are beyond redemption because strategists have become so adept at manipulation that voters can no longer learn what the candidates really stand for or intend to do. Significantly, this conclusion is supported by two opposing arguments about voter behavior. One is that voters are staying home because they have been turned off by fatuous claims and irrelevant advertising. The other is that people are being manipulated with great success by unscrupulous campaign advertising, so that their votes reflect more concern about Willie Horton, school prayer, or flag burning (the so-called issues of the 1988 election) than about widespread poverty, the banking crisis, or global warming.

The second objection is that popular concern about candidates and government in general has been trivialized, so that candidates fiddle while America burns. In the various versions of this critique, voter turnout has descended from its postwar highs because today's political contests are waged over small differences on trivial issues. . . .

Both of these critiques argue that contemporary campaigns

are trivial and irrelevant, that advertising and even the candidates' speeches are nothing but self-serving puffery and distortion. This general argument is especially appealing to better-educated voters and the power elite; campaign commercials remind no one of the Lincoln-Douglas debates, and today's bumper stickers and posters have none of the resonance of the Goddess of Democracy in Tiananmen Square or Boris Yeltsin astride a tank. But elitist concerns are not the test of this argument; the test is what voters learn from campaigns. There is ample evidence that voters *do* learn from campaigns. Of course, each party tries hard to make itself look better than the other side. Nonetheless, voter perceptions about the candidates and their positions are more accurate at the end of campaigns rather than at the beginning, and exposure to campaigns is still the best assurance that their perceptions are accurate.

Campaigns Increase Voters' Understanding

Campaign focus on an issue leads to less voter misperception, not more. When the stakes are raised and more information becomes available, voters acquire more accurate perceptions. The more they care about an issue, the better they are able to understand it; and the more strongly the parties differ on an issue, and the more voters hear about it, the more accurate their perceptions become. There is no denying that misperception is always present in campaigns, but it is also clear that communications do affect choices, making voters more, not less, accurate in their perceptions about candidates and issues.

Despite cries that campaigns have become less substantial in the television era, research has supported the findings given in *Voting* [the classic study of the 1948 election, written in 1954] that campaign communications increase the accuracy of voters' perceptions. Pamela Johnston Conover and Stanley Feldman, examining the 1976 general election, found that projection, or false consensus, declined as learning proceeded during the campaign; misperceptions occurred "primarily when there [was an] absence both of information and *strong* feelings about the candidate." Contradicting the claim that voters' perceptions are "largely distorted by motivational forces," Jon Krosnick found that voters in the 1984 election were "remarkably accurate in their perceptions of where presidential candidates [stood] relative to one another on controversial policy issues." And in 1988 it was not misperception about Michael Dukakis but the popularity of Ronald Reagan that was critical for George Bush; the lesson of 1988, Alan Abramowitz has concluded, is that "what matters most [is] . . . what issues the voters are thinking about."

In addition to reducing misperception, campaign information also helps people connect issues to government and parties. In

1984, according to Abramowitz, David J. Lanoue, and Subha Ramesh, "Voters who followed the presidential campaign closely were more likely to connect their personal financial situation with macroeconomic trends or government policies. . . . Attributions of responsibility for changes in economic well-being are based in part on cues received from the political environment and particularly from the mass media." Thus in a world in which causal reasoning matters but voters have only limited knowledge of government, campaign communications heighten awareness of how government affects their lives while reinforcing policy differences between parties and candidates.

Voters Not Manipulated by Media

The mind of the voters is not a tabula rasa to be easily programmed and manipulated. Voters remember past campaigns and presidents, past performance that failed to match promise. They have a sense of who is with them and who is against them; they make judgments about unfavorable news, editorials, and advertisements from hostile sources, ignoring some of what is favorable to those they oppose and some of what is negative to those they support. In managing their personal affairs and making decisions about their work, they collect information that can be used as a reality test against campaign claims and media stories. They notice the difference between behavior that has real consequences and mere talk.

Big brother is not gaining on the public. This is a finding to keep in mind at all times, for many criticisms of campaigns simplistically assume that voters are misled because politicians and campaign strategists have manipulative intentions. This assumption is not borne out by the evidence; voters know how to read the media and the politicians better than most media critics acknowledge.

Critics of campaign spinmasters (and of television in general) are fond of noting that campaigners and politicians intend to manipulate and deceive, but they wrongly credit them with more success than they deserve. As Michael Schudson has noted, in the television age, whenever a president's popularity has been high, it has been attributed to unusual talents for using television to sell his image. He notes, for example, that in 1977 the television critic of the *New York Times* called President Carter "a master of controlled images," and that during the 1976 primaries David Halberstam wrote that Carter "more than any other candidate this year has sensed and adapted to modern communications and national mood. . . . Watching him again and again on television I was impressed by his sense of pacing, his sense of control, very low key, soft." A few years later this master of images still had the same soft, low-key voice, but now it was interpreted as indicating not quiet strength but weakness and indecision.

As these examples suggest, media critics are generally guilty of using one of the laziest and easiest information shortcuts of all. Assuming that a popular politician is a good manipulator of the media or that a candidate won because of his or her media style is no different from what voters do when they evaluate presidents by reasoning backward from known results. The media need reform, but so do the media critics. One cannot infer, without astonishing hubris, that the American people have been successfully deceived simply because a politician wanted them to believe his or her version of events. But the media critics who analyze political texts without any reference to the actual impact of the messages do just that.

Stop and Think

The second objection is that campaigns are sideshows in which voters amuse themselves by learning about the differences between irrelevant candidates who debate minor issues while the country stagnates and inner cities explode. Many also assume that the negativism and pettiness of candidates' attacks on each other encourage a "pox on all your houses" attitude. These attitudes suggest a plausible hypothesis, which can be tested in a simple experiment, one that can be thought of as a "Stop and Think" experiment because it is a test of what happens if people stop and think about what they know of the candidates and issues and tell someone what they know. First, ask a random sample of people across the country what they consider to be the most important issues facing the country, then ask them where the various candidates stand on these issues. Next, ask them to state their likes and dislikes about the candidates' personal qualities and issue stands and about the state of the country. After the election, find out whether these interviewees were more or less likely to vote than people who were not asked to discuss the campaign. If the people interviewed voted less often than those not interviewed, there is clear support for the charge that trivia, negativism, and irrelevancy are turning off the American people and suppressing turnout.

In fact, the National Election Studies done by the University of Michigan's Survey Research Center, which houses the Center for Political Studies, constitute precisely such an experiment. In every election since 1952, people have been asked what they care about, what the candidates care about, and what they know about the campaign. After the election, people have been interviewed again and asked whether they voted; then the actual voting records have been checked to see whether the respondents did indeed vote. The results convincingly demolish the trivia and negativism hypothesis. In every election, people who have been interviewed were more likely to vote than other Americans. Indeed, the expensive and difficult procedure of verifying turnout against voting records by personal reinterview was initiated because scholars were suspicious of the fact that the turnout reported by respondents was so much higher than the actual turnout of all Americans as well as the turnout reported in surveys conducted after the election. Thus respondents in the National Election Studies, after two hours of thinking about the candidates, the issues, and the campaign, were more likely to vote than other people and also more likely to try to hide that they did not vote! Moreover, if people are reinterviewed in later elections, their turnout continues to rise. And, while an interview reduces nonvoting in a presidential election by up to 20 percent, an interview in a local primary may reduce nonvoting by as much as half.

When people put the pieces together they are turned on, not turned off. Indeed the 1991 Louisiana gubernatorial election between Edwin Edwards and David Duke demonstrates this; people will turn out in record numbers to choose between an unabashed rogue and a former Klansman as well as Nazi sympathizer when the campaign is big enough to keep people mobilized.

As Peggy Noonan has noted of the 1988 campaign, "There should have been more name-calling, mud-slinging and fun. It should have been rock-'em-sock-'em the way great campaigns have been in the past. It was tedious." Campaigns cannot deal with any substance if they cannot get the electorate's attention and interest people in listening to their music. Campaigns need to make noise. The use of sanitary metaphors to condemn politicians and their modes of communication say more about the distaste for American society of the people using these metaphors than about the failings of politicians.

Campaigns are essential in any society, particularly one that is culturally, economically, and socially diverse. If voters look for information about candidates under streetlights, that is where candidates must campaign, and the only way to improve elections is to add streetlights. Reforms only make sense if they are consistent with the gut rationality of voters. Ask not for more sobriety and piety from citizens for they are voters not judges; offer them instead cues and signals that connect their world with the world of politics. . . .

Before we attempt to take the passions and stimulation out of politics, we ought to be sure that we are not removing the lifeblood as well. The challenge to the future of American campaigns, and hence to American democracy, is how to bring back the brass bands and excitement in an age of electronic campaigning.

"Bart Simpson's critique of society is more trenchant than that of most newspaper columnists."

The Popular Media Reflect American Politics

Jon Katz

Jon Katz is the media critic for *Rolling Stone*, an entertainment magazine published in New York City. In the following viewpoint, he argues that the news presented in traditional newspapers and news broadcasts—what he calls the "Old News"—is increasingly irrelevant, especially to young people. Taking its place, according to Katz, is the "New News," which includes all the proliferating forms of the popular entertainment media, such as rap music videos and TV sitcoms. These sources, says Katz, accurately and thoroughly reflect the issues that affect most Americans, such as the economy, racial tensions, gender relations, and politics (the 1992 presidential election was approaching when this viewpoint originally appeared).

As you read, consider the following questions:

1. What political message is contained in *Thelma & Louise*, according to Katz?
2. According to the author, how has the "New News" surpassed the "Old News" in its coverage of racial issues?

"Rock, Rap and Movies Bring You the News" by Jon Katz. This article originally appeared in *Rolling Stone* magazine, March 5, 1992. Copyright © 1992 by Jon Katz. Reprinted by permission of Brandy & Brandt Literary Agents, Inc.

It's a shame Oliver Stone wasn't running one of the networks when the Bush administration decided journalists couldn't cover the gulf war. Nobody denied that conspiracy. Stone would have surely gone berserk, storming past the blue cabanas, over the berms and into the desert with his own camera-armed legions to bring back riveting pictures and shocking notions, like war is hell.

It's a shame, too, that Sinéad O'Connor wasn't providing network commentary in place of one more former general touting new weapons. When she refused to have the national anthem played at her concerts, she went further out on a limb than any of the major news organizations did on behalf of their silenced correspondents.

Too bad, as well, that instead of one of those evening-news suits, Bruce Springsteen isn't reporting on the economy. Springsteen seemed to know years ago that the jobs weren't coming back. The networks are still waiting for confirmation from the White House.

Pooped, Confused, and Broke

Straight news—the Old News—is pooped, confused and broke. Each Nielsen survey, each circulation report, each quarterly statement, reveals the cultural Darwinism ravaging the news industry. The people watching and reading are aging and dying, and the young no longer take their place. Virtually no major city daily has gained in circulation in recent years (the *Washington Post* is one of the few exceptions). In the last decade, network news has lost nearly half its audience. Advertising revenues are drying up.

In place of the Old News, something dramatic is evolving, a new culture of information, a hybrid New News—dazzling, adolescent, irresponsible, fearless, frightening and powerful. The New News is a heady concoction, part Hollywood film and TV movie, part pop music and pop art, mixed with popular culture and celebrity magazines, tabloid telecasts, cable and home video.

Increasingly, the New News is seizing the functions of mainstream journalism, sparking conversations and setting the country's social and political agenda. It is revolutionizing the way information reaches people and moves among them. It is changing the way Americans evaluate politicians, and, shortly, elect them.

Think of Walter Cronkite or Ted Koppel if you want to get an image of the Old News. The voice is grave, resonant with the burden of transmitting serious matters—White House communications strategies, leaks from State Department sources, leading economic indicators. The stories are remote (from Yugoslavia, Nairobi, Beijing) or from institutions that feel as remote

(Congress, Wall Street, the Supreme Court). The reporters of the Old News cluster there, talking to one another, mired in an agenda that seems increasingly obtuse and irrelevant.

In January 1992, the New News is absorbed with a different agenda: On the eve of Martin Luther King's birthday, Public Enemy focuses the country's attention on his broken dream through its furious new video, an imagined enactment of the killing of Arizona state-government officials. In New York City, inner-city parents are taking their children to see *Juice* to educate them about the consequences of street violence. *JFK*—assaulted for weeks by the Old News as reckless and irresponsible—has prompted the chairman of a congressional committee that investigated the assassination to ask for the release of all government documents on the slaying. The kids on *Beverly Hills, 90210*—"The only show on TV that portrays teen life as it really is," says the editorial director of *16* magazine—are struggling with divorce, sex and AIDS.

Meanwhile, the remnants of the Old News slowly begin to gather in the bleak towns of New Hampshire for another presidential campaign. Only a few years ago, the three networks virtually hosted the presidential campaigns. Great media encampments took over entire motels in New Hampshire, with producers and technicians stuffed into trailers like a circus come to town. But ABC, CBS and NBC have already announced there will be no vast encampments on the primary trail or at the conventions this year. Day-to-day coverage will be left to cable. One network that has said it will offer more campaign coverage than it did in 1988 is MTV.

Blurred Borders

Once, the borders were clear and inviolate: Newspapers, newscasts and newsmagazines covered serious events; pop culture entertained us. But in the past generation, the culture sparked by rock & roll, then fused with TV and mutated by Hollywood, ran riot over the traditional boundaries between straight journalism and entertainment.

Now the list of issues addressed by the New News—far from the front pages and evening newscasts—is growing steadily. We're exposed to gender conflict in *Thelma & Louise*; money blues, sexual conflicts and working-class stress on *Roseanne*; motherhood, corporate takeovers and journalistic ethics on *Murphy Brown*.

Bart Simpson's critique of society is more trenchant than that of most newspaper columnists. Movies like *Boyz n the Hood* and *Straight Out of Brooklyn* and rappers like Public Enemy and Ice Cube deal with race more squarely than *Nightline*. No wonder Chuck D calls rap the CNN of black America.

213

In the same way that middle-class blacks rarely appear in the traditional media, disaffected working-class whites don't seem to exist in the world Old News covers. Analysts looking for clues to David Duke's popularity would do better to listen to Guns n' Roses and Skid Row songs than to scan newscasts and newspapers for the source of white resentment.

The country's ascendant magazine is not a newsmagazine but a New News magazine. *Entertainment Weekly* focuses on what editors used to call the back of the book—the arts and culture material once ghettoized behind the important stuff. But today, the back of the book is the book. In its January 17th [1992] cover story, "JFK: The Film and the Furor, What's Behind the Backlash," *EW* dramatically illustrated how popular culture and major stories have steadily converged on one another over the past three decades, redefining what news is and who gets to cover it.

Toward Popular Empowerment

I think it is encouraging that our political discourses and processes have become more entertaining, more energetic, more popular, because it means that public issues are, in some way or other, being talked about and argued about instead of being ignored. And that, for me, is a necessary if not sufficient condition for popular empowerment.

Elayne Rapping, *The Progressive*, April 1993.

It didn't happen overnight—more like thirty years. Bob Dylan's vision of rock & roll helped mainstream music move from entertainment to political expression, an Op-Ed page for millions of kids who would never have dreamed of reading—or agreeing with—a newspaper editorial. Following in the tradition of shows like *All in the Family*, TV producers and writers broke free of the censors and produced broadcasts like *Hill Street Blues*, *St. Elsewhere* and *L.A. Law*, presenting life more and more as viewers experienced it, not as the networks wanted it seen.

So did tabloid telecasts and made-for-TV movies, which dramatized, reenacted and reinterpreted issues like sexism, child abuse, alcoholism and homosexuality. Hollywood helped define Vietnam in *Apocalypse Now*, racial hatred in *Do the Right Thing*, the takeover culture in *Wall Street*. Emerging cable technology gave viewers and programmers vastly more choices, breaking open the New News. Pop culture—America's most remarkable invention since the car—had spawned a new information culture.

The modern news media—the Old News—was formed in the

years after World War II. Major newspapers and instantly powerful network-news divisions chose Washington and New York as their headquarters, and presidential politics, the economy and foreign affairs—the cold war, mostly—as their preeminent beats. In its heyday, the Old News showed us the murder of John Kennedy, took us to the moon, then helped drive a president from office and end a war.

Other stories—the sexual revolution, the role of race, dramatic changes in the relationship between people and their jobs, the evolution of pop culture, a rebirth of spiritualism—were covered sporadically and incompletely by the Old News. They often sprang up away from well-staffed bureaus in a handful of major cities, thus making them harder for Old News to cover. They were a sideline, never the main event.

But for the New News—and for much of America—they were *the* event. Women, blacks, Hispanics, gays and Asians had launched an ongoing political and cultural revolution against middle-class white males, who continue to dominate most institutions, including the news media. In some countries, revolutions are violent, bloody affairs settled in the streets. In America, they are slugged out in music videos, movies and cable shows.

In the resulting turmoil, the Old News and the new have taken off in opposite directions, diverging more and more dramatically in content, packaging and audience. Although Americans can watch, in living color, a war or the description of an alleged rape, almost no major daily deigns to use color photographs, and most anchors are still white and male.

The Decline of the "Old News"

As Old News habits have ossified, its audience has evaporated. Newspaper readership has been declining for thirty years. According to a *Times Mirror* study, seventy-one percent of people between the ages of seventy and seventy-nine read a daily newspaper, but only forty percent of people between the ages of eighteen and twenty-nine do. Of people under thirty who are married with children, only thirty percent read a paper daily.

The median age of the *New York Times* subscriber is forty-two, *Time* magazine's is thirty-eight. In contrast, *Entertainment Weekly*'s is thirty-one, *Rolling Stone*'s is twenty-six. Among shows that teenagers watch most often, *The Simpsons* and *Beverly Hills, 90210* rank at the top; *60 Minutes* ranks 110th.

The Old News seems bewildered and paralyzed by the dazzling new technologies competing for its audience, clucking like a cross old lady chasing noisy kids away from her window. Editors and producers prefer "serious topics" to the New News culture. In the same way they once fussed over rock & roll, most newspapers and news shows were too busy attacking Nintendo addiction to notice that more than 50 million entertainment systems had taken up residence in American homes, literally redefining what a TV set was and what it did. In 1991, the Nintendo hot line got 2 million calls from players needing help in ascending yet another level of Tetris or Super Mario Bros. 3.

All the while, news organizations puzzled about why kids were leaving in droves. Interactive video-jukebox systems and sports channels, round-the-clock local-news channels, video shopping and scores of movie and entertainment channels helped to create a new video culture for the young, a profound change in leisure time that the Old News kissed off as a teen fad.

Resisting Change

Stung by the mounting evidence that Americans' passions and concerns increasingly lie elsewhere, Old News institutions do appear unnerved. They've launched promotional campaigns, experimented disdainfully with color, commissioned marketing studies. ("Perhaps we should start a kids' page?") But it's mostly fussing. Every time real change is broached—two years ago, CBS tried reenactments on *Saturday Night With Connie Chung*—the guardian crows of the old order shriek the innovators into submission.

The networks sneered as CNN haltingly began to construct the most efficient and responsive electronic news-video-gathering machine in history. The newspaper industry's most dramatic response to the New News—*USA Today*—was greeted by the business with the same enthusiasm with which the human body greets a foreign invader. It was dubbed McPaper and dismissed as insubstantial, shallow and, worst of all, TV-like.

Its owner, Gannett, which owns eighty-one newspapers and admits to being alarmed about newspapers' shrinking and aging circulation, recently published a handbook for its editors. It says with shocking bluntness that papers have failed to recognize "key topics that shape readers' lives" and are filled with "dull, formula-based writing" and that newsrooms are "isolationist, elitist and afraid of change."

Spotting Major Stories

All the facts add up to a story that, Gannett's urgings notwithstanding, journalism doesn't want to hear. The Old News has clung desperately to the view that the New News culture, like pornography, is nothing but trash and will eventually just go away. Yet journalistically, the New News is often superior to the old at spotting major stories and putting them into context.

All last summer, men and women were talking about men and women. Movies like *Thelma & Louise* and made-for-TV dramas like CBS's *Rape of Dr. Willis* clearly reflected the outrage that co-

216

alesced around the Anita Hill-Clarence Thomas confrontation. The view of men as insensitive, frequently hateful creatures who don't get it was also advanced in movies like *The Doctor*, in which a surgeon has to get cancer before he learns how to be compassionate, and *Regarding Henry*, whose hero learns the meaning of life only after he gets shot in the head. *Beauty and the Beast* might be the timeliest animated film ever made: The heroine is courageous and brainy; the two major male characters are a prince who's turned into a beast so that he can learn how to love and a macho man who is a beast, period.

If the white men in the U.S. Senate had spent more time at the movies and less watching Old News Sunday-morning talk shows, they might have heard the sound of thousands of women cheering when Thelma and Louise blew up that tanker truck. They might not have been so shocked when women all over the country exploded in fury at the Judiciary Committee's failure to explore Anita Hill's charges.

One of the most interesting scoops in the Thomas affair—an exclusive interview with the justice's wife—was secured by *People*. And just three weeks after the hearings, the characters on *Designing Women* spent an episode watching footage of the hearings and vigorously arguing both sides. For millions of Americans, it was a more relevant hashing of the matter than they would get on any Sunday-morning gasathon.

Foreshadowing Racial Tension

Other news stories have been foreshadowed by the New News. The FBI was so alarmed by the rap group N.W.A's "Fuck Tha Police" that it cautioned local police departments against N.W.A's performing in their cities. Yet just two years later, in a stunning example of the new video culture's news-gathering potential, a bystander videotaped the brutal beating of Rodney King by the Los Angeles Police Department, the very force N.W.A was warning its listeners about.

There is, in fact, almost no story Old News has struggled to come to grips with more dramatically and unsuccessfully than race. America seems continually stunned by episodic explosions of racial hatred—by the murder of Yusuf Hawkins in New York, the violent black-Hasidic confrontations in Brooklyn in the summer of 1991, the chord struck by David Duke.

Still overwhelmingly owned, staffed and run by whites, and white males in particular, the media are stymied and discomfited by racial issues. After decades of ignoring brutal racism, they seem to have lurched from one extreme to the other. Now they're so desperate to avoid the appearance of racism that they seem frozen by the subject.

The members of the media are able to quote demagogues and

activists, but they're unable to advance the country's understanding of ghetto fury, to portray and represent the view of the black middle class or to explore white anger and confusion. Few issues in American life generate so much mythology, yet the intrigues of the White House chief of staff are covered in far greater detail. Spike Lee is far ahead of his mainstream journalistic competitors on racial issues. So is Ice Cube: "They have the authority/To Kill a minority/Fucking with me cause I'm a teenager/With a little bit of gold and a pager."

Police advocates don't make many albums, but there's plenty of white backlash to racial tensions evident in white rock, as well as worry about bleak economic futures. Perhaps the leading white working-class New News columnists at the moment are the members of Guns n' Roses, whose "Right Next Door to Hell," from *Use Your Illusion I*, is a national anthem for working-class anger:

> When your innocence dies
> You'll find the blues
> Seems all our heroes were born to lose
> Just walkin' through time
> You believe this heat
> Another empty house another dead-end street.

Skid Row sounds like John Chancellor in comparison. From the album and song *Slave to the Grind*: "You got me forced to crack my lids in two/I'm still stuck inside the rubber room/I gotta punch the clock that leads the blind/I'm just another gear in the assembly line."

Rap and rock—music listened to by the same kids the Old News is fretting about losing—are describing a different world than the one reflected on evening newscasts and in daily papers. Washington journalists were abuzz for months in anticipation of the *Washington Post*'s seven-part series on Vice-President Dan Quayle, reported and written by Old News royalty David Broder and Bob Woodward. But the tens of thousands of words lavished on Quayle told us more about the remote agenda of the Old News than it did about the vice-president.

A Dark Strain in American Life

The most explosive assault the New News has made on the Old is Oliver Stone's *JFK*. Its release has sparked less a free-for-all discussion of a recent historical event than a modern-day heresy trial. Stone set out to upend conventional wisdom, centering his film on Jim Garrison's largely discredited theories. It is unclear why so many Americans remain skeptical about the Warren Commission's findings—only nineteen percent believe in the lone-gunman theory, according to polls—yet clearly they do. Whatever the accuracy of his theory, Stone—whose *Platoon, Wall*

Street and *Born on the Fourth of July* were dramatically journalistic in their efforts to reflect different cultures at crucial times—has tapped into this dark strain in American life.

The Old News condemns Stone as irresponsible because he is advancing disproved theories and crackpot speculation as truth. The Old News is crying foul, incensed that someone has crossed over into their turf.

Yet it is Stone's movie, not years of columnizing by the Old News, that is likely to force the release of Kennedy-assassination documents the government is keeping under wraps. The license Stone took—and the risk—in reinventing a seminal story in the country's history illustrates why the New News is gaining so dramatically on the Old: It is willing to heed and explore the passionate and sometimes frightening undercurrents in American life.

An Odd Country

The United States is an odd country, a lot stranger than the stilted language or narrow conventions of the Old News can explain. Remember the fascination with *Twin Peaks*? Americans seem to know—though surely not from reading it or seeing it in most journalism—that their country is violent, troubled and brooding, in almost desperate need of mythological symbols like those advanced by the cultural historian Joseph Campbell.

Elvis Presley's death and afterlife so boosted supermarket-tabloid sales that they have become a permanent part of the New News. As Greil Marcus shows in his new book *Dead Elvis*, Americans are as obsessed with Presley's death as they are with Kennedy's assassination.

We don't really know why, and how could we? Both stories fall just this side of prostitution to most of the reporters assigned to cover, say, the White House. Stone's assassination theories may or may not have been correct, but his journalistic instinct was sure. He hit one of the rawest nerves in American history, demonstrating at the very least that to many Americans the Kennedy assassination is far from a settled matter.

In their anger at Stone, the guardians of journalistic and cultural propriety are saying that Americans aren't capable of drawing their own conclusions, that only journalists operating in conventional ways and within conventional boundaries can be entrusted with weighty or controversial issues. The anger of the Old News demonstrates anew one of its most self-destructive streaks—a patronizing contempt for the young. Much of the criticism leveled at Stone suggests that Americans who weren't alive when Kennedy was shot are too ignorant or impressionable to see beyond Kevin Costner's earnest face, as though people under thirty can't grasp that a Hollywood film is one person's vision, not the provable truth.

A youthful audience is no guarantee that a New News product is journalistically superior; what is significant is that younger viewers and readers find conventional journalism of no particular use in their daily lives. In fact, given that the media make so much out of fairness and objectivity, it's a puzzle why so few people of any age trust it or its conclusions.

Mainstream journalism frequently checkmates itself. In worshipping balance over truth, objectivity over point of view, moderation over diversity and credibility over creativity, the Old News gives consumers a clear choice. Consumers can have a balanced discussion, with every side of an issue neutralizing the other, or they can turn to singers, producers and filmmakers offering colorful, distinctive, often flawed but frequently powerful visions of their truth. More and more, Americans are making it clear which they prefer.

Younger audiences raised on New News traditions of outspokenness and hyperbole appear to understand that Public Enemy and Oliver Stone are not always to be taken literally. These New News communicators speak to states of mind, to anger at real issues like poverty and hopelessness, to disenchantment with jingoistic institutions and to a common perception that mainstream news organizations don't tell the whole truth or at least don't much reflect their truth.

Stone's *JFK* will have to stand the ultimate capitalist media test, the same one every newspaper, TV station, magazine and Nintendo dealer faces: People will buy it, watch it, read it, believe it. Or not. At least Stone has made it clear where he stands.

An Uncertain Future

It's simply not possible to know yet whether the rise of the New News is good or bad, healthy or menacing. How about all of the above? The final form the Old News will take is unclear, and New News technology and content is still rapidly evolving.

This year Time Warner will unleash another Godzilla on the Old News—in New York, a twenty-four hour local cable news channel will begin broadcasting. For the first time, *truly* local news—fires, high-school sports, board-of-education hearings on condom distribution—will be on TV. Advertisers like pharmacies, copy shops and bridal salons will have an affordable electronic medium to advertise on.

Another billion-dollar shoe waiting to drop, ferociously opposed by its competitors, will come from the Baby Bells. Now that the federal courts have given the regional phone companies permission to enter the information market, they'll use computers and existing and future transmission technology to offer new kinds of electronic travel, shopping, banking and commercial services, including news.

In the new world of twenty-four-hour electronic news, can print or commercial broadcasting remain in the breaking-news business, as both so stubbornly insist on doing? Will newspapers ever stop running banner headlines over black-and-white photos that appeared live on TV twenty-four hours earlier? It seems they'd rather die.

The best vantage point from which to watch the dramatic collision of the competing news cultures will be living rooms across the country, as the Old News struggles to come to grips with its quadrennial Super Bowl-cum-Olympics—the presidential election. If the Old News is right, and only it can be trusted to capture and shape major events, then the country is heading straight for a civics nightmare in which challengers can't get coverage and issues can't be raised, because Americans, wired into their personal entertainment complexes, are too busy to think about who should occupy the White House.

This time around, CNN and C-SPAN will be on all the time, for politicians desperate to communicate with their peers and for political junkies who want to see crucial votes or speeches. But fewer regular prime-time programs will be preempted. Except for the Democratic convention in New York, a cab ride across town, the anchors will be watching most of the campaign on studio monitors. A few troops—Sawyer, Chung—will be running around with their Star Trek earphones, but it will be a pathetic echo of the glory days for the Old News.

Maybe there's a better way. Maybe the New News should field a team of its own this year. Don Henley could coanchor the convention coverage with Murphy Brown, prime-time TV's toughest news interviewer, not from a booth, but down on the convention floor, laying bare a process that would even consider reelecting a president who didn't know until December 17th that the recession wasn't over. Sinéad O'Connor, the Geto Boys and Roseanne Arnold will do nightly commentary, maybe from the floor with working-stiff delegates. Spike Lee will air a series of documentaries on how race is being manipulated to win still another election, alternating with reports on how whites are getting screwed by the system, courtesy of Axl Rose, or perhaps an investigative special by Oliver Stone on how Ronald Reagan's election was the result of a conspiracy between the media, Hollywood filmmakers and jet-aircraft contractors.

"We are in danger of losing the central role the great newspapers have historically played in the functioning of our political system."

The Popular Media Debase American Politics

John Leo and Bill Moyers

John Leo is a syndicated columnist and a contributing editor for the national weekly newsmagazine *U.S. News & World Report*. In Part I of the following viewpoint, he disputes the argument that the entertainment media are adequate forums for the treatment of major news and social issues. In Part II of the viewpoint, Bill Moyers contends that the popular entertainment media reduce politics to verbal "mud wrestling" among special interest groups. He believes that the traditional American newspaper is essential for meaningful democratic debate. Moyers, an analyst for the Public Broadcasting System (PBS), is well known for his comprehensive interviews and documentaries, including *Joseph Campbell and the Power of Myth, World of Ideas,* and *The Secret Government*, a critique of the Central Intelligence Agency.

As you read, consider the following questions:

1. Why does an emphasis on visual stimuli harm the news, according to Leo?
2. According to Moyers, what does John Dewey call the "vital habits of democracy?"

I

The old argument was that print journalism is dead. The new argument is that Peter Jennings, Dan Rather, Tom Brokaw and perhaps CNN, too, are all terminal patients, due to be buried right along with newspapers and newsmagazines. This sounds unlikely, but the idea is floating around. Media critic Jon Katz, writing in *Rolling Stone*, says "the Old News"—balanced, moderate, objective, detached, fact-oriented, fair-minded—is "pooped, confused and broke." He explicitly makes this a generational issue: "The people watching and reading are aging and dying, and the young no longer take their place."

This decline has been on the minds of publishers for years, but the spotlight has focused on reading, or the lack thereof. Mr. Katz is right to remind us that the captains of TV news are in the same storm-tossed boat as publishers. The surveys show newspaper readership falling off dramatically among the young. They also show a similar decline in viewing patterns for television news, although the erosion is somewhat slower. It is not printed news that so many of the young reject, but news itself, or at least news as traditionally shaped and defined by the journalism industry. Not even the vividness and entertainment values built into TV news have been enough to hold the young.

The traditional, somewhat huffy, Old News explanation for this is that the entertainment industry has become such a juggernaut that it has eclipsed or suppressed the taste for serious news. Mr. Katz turns this argument on its head. He says the entertainment industry *is* the journalism industry of the young—"The New News is a heady concoction, part Hollywood film and TV movie, part pop music and pop art, mixed with popular culture and celebrity magazines, tabloid telecasts, cable and home video." What he means is that information, attitude, values and a grasp of social problems are reliably piped to the young through Guns N' Roses, Public Enemy, *The Simpsons, Roseanne* and Oliver Stone's "JFK," a New News product attacked, he says, for not being an Old News documentary.

A Blurred Line Between News and Entertainment

Before becoming appalled, let us admit that Mr. Katz is on to something here. The line between news and entertainment is hopelessly blurred now. But the crossover is in both directions. As traditional news takes on more and more of the trappings of entertainment (local TV newscasts now show live pictures of police car chases in progress, just like Burt Reynolds movies), show biz is becoming newsier. MTV has its own news department, which covered the New Hampshire primary (with background music, lest anyone fall asleep). It has a program, *Like We*

Care, that deals with issues such as privacy vs. safety in the use of metal detectors to check for weapons in schools.

Entertainment Weekly is evolving into a news mag for the fun-minded, dealing with the environment through a report on 20 celebrities begging President Bush to attend the Earth Summit in June 1992. Politicized celebs become a way of smuggling tidbits of actual news into magazines and TV shows aimed at the star-struck.

Beverly Hills, 90210 is watched by pre-teens as "news" about what their lives are soon to become, and rap is heard as news from the street, plus editorials. (Chuck D of Public Enemy calls rap the CNN of black America.) And TV producers have consciously turned up the dial on newsiness, not just in disease-of-the-week and victim-of-the-week movies, but also in regular weekly shows.

Newspapers: Indispensable Social Institutions

We all can recite the sad litany: Nearly everyone, especially the young, reads less; flashier media abound for both readers and advertisers; infotainment is overwhelming serious news; and the new tech-happy information age makes newspapers seem stale, dull and increasingly obsolete.

But wait. Instead of wallowing in the problem, perhaps the moment has come to consider what opportunities these changing times present. Not only are newspapers far from dead, they are being handed—if they will seize it—a historic chance to reclaim their status as indispensable social institutions. Awash as we are in a perplexing information age, never before have we so needed steady sources of news about the communities we inhabit. Never before have we so needed good newspapers. . . .

Despite difficult times, newspapers remain a national treasure, a lifeline of ideas and information. Inexpensive and readily available, they crisscross our culture with the effortless efficiency of electric power lines. They unify, connect, arouse and elevate us in ways so intimate that we take them for granted.

Carl Sessions Stepp, *American Journalism Review,* April 1993.

Recent Supreme Court rulings show up as crucial plot devices on *Law and Order*. Ethical and social problems are opened up on *Murphy Brown* and *L.A. Law*. And the industry's reaction time is getting shorter. *Designing Women* rushed through a quick program on Anita Hill and Clarence Thomas, and *L.A. Law* aired a stunning segment on an oblivious date-rapist athlete on the day of Mike Tyson's sentencing.

Fine. Thoughtful, topical entertainment is always better than escapist drivel. But it's hard for us Old Newsies to see fiction and song as a news delivery system, at least until we see a gripping made-for-TV movie about the budget deficit or a song about the inflation rate. Abstractions don't play well, but they count. A report on youth culture said: "We are a culture obsessed with visual stimuli." Alas, the future depends on each generation's responding to news and issues that don't easily fit into a visual framework, or that can't be jazzed up to boost ratings.

This tyranny of the visual and the exciting seems to be a problem for New News. Old News stories, Mr. Katz says, "are remote (from Yugoslavia, Nairobi, Beijing) or from institutions that feel as remote (Congress, Wall Street, the Supreme Court)." He is impatient with opposition to re-enacting news events as part of news presentations. ("The guardian crows of the old order shriek the innovators into submission.")

It is impossible to miss the extraordinary reliance on feelings and drama, both of which television is particularly good at producing. Mr. Katz says New News stresses passionate expression, hyperbole, and replaces objectivity with powerful, personal visions of truth. This is important, but these are the techniques of fiction and literature. Who's going to tell us straight—no personal visions, please—what happened yesterday?

II

Mine is the reporter's perspective—one small fish in that vast ocean we call the media. I want to put in a word for the craft, for reporting, the old-fashioned kind.

When I began working for *Harper's* in 1970, I thought I understood what the word "news" meant, where information stopped and entertainment began; what newspapers did that was different from television. Since then, we have witnessed a media explosion, the effect of which is like standing at ground zero seconds after the explosion of the atomic bomb. Walter Lippmann told us that journalism is a picture of reality people can act upon. What we see today is a society acting upon reality refracted a thousand different ways.

Reality or Insanity?

Where is America's mind today? It's in the organs, for one thing. Now folks can turn on a series called *Real Sex* and watch a home striptease class; its premiere was HBO's highest-rated documentary for the year. Or they can flip over to NBC News and get *I Witness Video*. There they can see a policeman's murder recorded in his cruiser's camcorder, watch it replayed and relived in interviews, complete with ominous music. Or they can see the video of a pregnant woman plunging from a blazing building's window, can see it several times, at least once in slow motion. Yeats was right: "We have fed the heart on fantasies, and the heart's grown brutal from the fare."

I wonder if *Real Sex* and *I Witness Video* take us deeper into reality or insanity? How does a reporter tell the difference anymore in a world where Oliver Stone can be praised for his "journalistic instincts" when he has Lyndon Johnson tell a cabal of generals and admirals: "Get me elected and I'll get you your war."

'Do you want to watch the news . . . news simulation . . . investigative news with docudrama or Geraldo opening someone's vault?'

Mike Peters. Reprinted with permission.

Rolling Stone dubs all this the "New News." Straight news—the Old News by *Rolling Stone*'s definition—is "pooped, confused, and broke." In its place a new culture of information is evolving— "a heady concoction, part Hollywood film and TV, part pop music and pop art, mixed with popular culture and celebrity magazines, tabloid telecasts, cable and home video." Increasingly, says the magazine, the New News is seizing the function of mainstream journalism, sparking conversation and setting the country's social and political agenda. So it is that we learn first from Bruce Springsteen that the jobs aren't coming back. So it is that inner-city parents who don't subscribe to daily newspapers are taking their children to see the movie *Juice* to educate them about the consequences of street violence; that young people think Bart Simpson's analysis of America more trenchant than many newspaper columnist's; that we learn just how violent, brutal and desperate society is, not from the establishment press, but from Spike Lee, Public Enemy, the Geto Boys and Guns N' Roses.

I don't want to seem a moralist. The public often knows what's news before we professionals do. But there's a problem: In this vast pounding ocean of media, newspapers are in danger of extinction. I don't mean that they're going to disappear altogether—but I do feel that we are in danger of losing the central role the great newspapers have historically played in the functioning of our political system.

Once newspapers drew people to the public square. They provided a culture of community conversation. The purpose of news was not just to represent and inform, "but to signal, tell a story and activate inquiry." When the press abandons that function, it no longer stimulates what the American philosopher John Dewey termed "the vital habits" of democracy—"the ability to follow an argument, grasp the point of view of another, expand the boundaries of understanding, debate the alternative purposes that might be pursued."

I know times have changed, and so must the newspapers. I know that while it's harder these days to be a reporter, it's also harder to be a publisher, caught between *Sesame Street* and Wall Street—between the entertainment imperatives that are nurtured in the cradle and survival economics that can send a good paper to the grave.

I sense we're approaching Gettysburg, the moment of truth, the decisive ground for this cultural war—for publishers especially. Americans say they no longer trust journalists to tell them the truth about their world. Young people have difficulty finding anything of relevance to their lives in the daily newspaper. Non-tabloid newspapers are viewed as increasingly elitist, self-important and corrupt on the one hand; on the other, they are increasingly lumped together with the tabloids as readers perceive the increasing desperation with which papers are now trying to reach "down-market" in order to replace the young readers who are not replacing their elders.

Verbal Mud Wrestling

Meanwhile, a study by the Kettering Foundation confirms that our political institutions are fast losing their legitimacy; that increasing numbers of Americans believe they are being dislodged from their rightful place in democracy by politicians, powerful lobbyists and the media—three groups they see as an autonomous political class impervious to the long-term interests of the country and manipulating the democratic discourse so that people are treated only as consumers to be entertained rather than citizens to be engaged.

That our system is failing to solve the bedrock problems we

face is beyond dispute. One reason is that our public discourse has become the verbal equivalent of mud wrestling. The anthropologist Marvin Harris says the attack against reason and objectivity in America today "is fast reaching the proportion of a crusade." America, he says, "urgently needs to reaffirm the principle that it is possible to carry out an analysis of social life that rational human beings will recognize as being true, regardless of whether they happen to be women or men, whites or blacks, straights or gays, Jews or born-again Christians." Lacking such an understanding of social life, "we will tear the United States apart in the name of our separate realities."

The Idiot Culture

For more than fifteen years we have been moving away from real journalism toward the creation of a sleazoid info-tainment culture in which the lines between Oprah and Phil and Geraldo and Diane and even Ted, between the *New York Post* and *Newsday*, are too often indistinguishable. . . .

We are in the process of creating, in sum, what deserves to be called the idiot culture. Not an idiot *sub*culture, which every society has bubbling beneath the surface and which can provide harmless fun; but the culture itself.

I do not mean to attack popular culture. Good journalism *is* popular culture, but popular culture that stretches and informs its consumers rather than that which appeals to the ever descending lowest common denominator. If, by popular culture, we mean expressions of thought or feeling that require no work of those who consume them, then decent popular journalism is finished. What is happening today, unfortunately, is that the lowest form of popular culture—lack of information, misinformation, disinformation, and a contempt for the truth or the reality of most people's lives—has overrun real journalism.

Carl Bernstein, *The New Republic*, June 8, 1992.

Taken together, these assumptions and developments foreshadow the catastrophe of social and political paralysis. But what's truly astonishing about this civic disease is that it exists in America just as a series of powerful democratic movements have been toppling autocratic regimes elsewhere in the world. While people around the globe are clamoring for self-government, millions of Americans are feeling as if they have been locked out of their homes and are unable to regain their rightful place in the operation of democracy. On the other hand, those same millions want to believe that it is still in their power to change America.

The Center for Citizen Politics at the University of Minnesota reports that beneath America's troubled view of politics "is a public that cares very deeply about public life. This concern is a strong foundation for building healthy democratic practices and new traditions of public participation in politics."

People want to know what is happening to them, and what they can do about it. Listening to America, you realize that millions of people are not apathetic; they want to signify; and they will respond to a press that stimulates the community without pandering to it; that inspires people to embrace their responsibilities without lecturing or hectoring them; and that engages their better natures without sugarcoating ugly realities or patronizing their foibles.

"New developments in cable and interactive television and in telepolling . . . [could] enable large numbers of people to have . . . active political participation."

Media Technology Can Improve Democracy

Amitai Etzioni

During the 1992 presidential election campaign, candidate H. Ross Perot proposed holding "electronic town meetings" in which citizens could use media technology—including the telephone—to directly express their opinions. In the following viewpoint, Amitai Etzioni argues that this idea, commonly referred to as "teledemocracy," could enhance democracy by giving individuals the opportunity to participate in the decision-making process. Etzioni is a professor at George Washington University in Washington, D.C., and the editor of the *Responsive Community*, a quarterly communitarian journal.

As you read, consider the following questions:

1. Why is a layered system of representation necessary in America, according to Etzioni? How do mandates function within that system?
2. Why does the author advocate allowing a day's delay between the introduction of an issue and the vote on it?
3. According to Etzioni, why is feedback important to political discussion?

The idea of technologically enhanced national "town meetings" has been around at least since Buckminster Fuller proposed it a generation ago. And it is not likely to go away. . . . The idea deserves serious examination, because if [Ross Perot and] the 1992 election campaign has taught us anything, it is that most Americans feel alienated from national politics as currently practiced, and there is a need to find ways to reinvolve them.

There are long-established precedents for the idea of adding some elements of direct democracy to our representative government. Twenty-three states currently grant their citizens the right to pass directly on items of legislation and even to modify state constitutions by putting amendments on a ballot. (California leads the pack.) In addition, numerous measures, such as school bonds and public-works funding, are regularly decided on by referenda of the electorate. Indeed, the number of initiatives and referenda has been increasing. A preponderance of the four hundred or so such measures introduced since the Progressives, in the first decades of this century, made them a hallmark of government reform have been introduced in the past twenty years, according to the political scientist Aaron Wildavsky.

To be sure, there is a big difference between adding some direct democracy to our representative system and replacing Congress with TV shows and push buttons. Electronic town meetings, though hardly a cure for all the ills of our democracy, could be arranged in ways that would avoid several of the pitfalls against which critics correctly warn. Or so I will argue.

Toward Active Participation

Twenty years ago I spent a third of a million dollars—a hefty sum in the early 1970s—of your (taxpayer) money, granted to me by the National Science Foundation, conducting experiments with electronic town meetings. Indeed, they are the subject of an article I published in *Policy Science* in 1972. I have good reason to believe that Ross Perot and his staff did not read my writings on the subject; their model lacked all of the features that I argued were needed to render electronic town meetings even approximately democratic.

To be frank, the NSF team started with the same simplistic notion that seemed to animate Perot: given new developments in cable and interactive television and in telepolling (which allowed incoming calls to be tallied automatically, without anybody's even answering the phone), we could engineer an electronic system that would enable large numbers of people to have the kind of active political participation that town meetings afforded the citizens of New England towns (and that, before them, the citizens of the Greek polis enjoyed). We sold a Columbia University professor of engineering, Stephen Unger, on the idea, and he joined the NSF team.

Having just outgrown the sixties and their notion of direct or participatory democracy, we were clear about one major principle: it would be undemocratic to replace elected representatives and legislatures with computerized voting or any other kind of electronic wizardry. One main reason, which became known by the NSF team as the Burke argument (after the political philosopher Edmund Burke), is that large groups need two or more layers of representation, rather than direct representation, in order to work out consensus-based public policies. History has proved that large groups are unable to agree on policies by means of the kind of dialogue possible in a town meeting, where fewer than two thousand people tend to be involved. In a layered system the voters grant their elected representatives "mandates," a kind of generalized guidance that reflects what the voters seek: Get us out of Vietnam. Focus on domestic issues. Do something about competitiveness. The voters neither feel compelled nor wish to be engaged in the specifics.

Perot the Rebel

The Ross Perot movement marked the strongest effort [of the 1992] American political season to close the gap between elitism and populism and embrace a commitment to the proposition that people can govern themselves. Perot himself merely demonstrated all the possibilities in the new communications technologies for end-running the old political parties and short-circuiting the old electoral processes. Perot understood what rebels around the world have long known: that coups are best accomplished by capturing radio and television stations, rather than legislative or government buildings.

Hazel Henderson, *New Perspectives Quarterly*, Fall 1992.

For the system to work at all, citizens must allow their representatives to engage in give-and-take, within the confines of their mandates, in order to find a shared public policy. If the various mandates have no overlap, no honest give-and-take is possible. Either a stalemate will occur until some parts of the electorate give in, or politicians will fudge, claiming that they are acting within the confines of their mandates while they are actually violating them. Each of these situations, in turn, will lead to policies that lack the support of the public and that contribute to its alienation. A case in point is the Maastricht Treaty, which provides for eventual political unification in Europe. The politicians signed the treaty without a mandate from their people. As a result, voters in Denmark rejected the treaty, and many others are grumbling.

Telepolling, like other forms of direct democracy en masse, provides only limited room for give-and-take. It can be made to work for a few isolated items that can be straightforwardly voted up or down (such as hospital bonds), but not for complex issues of the kind we typically face. Given such issues, direct democracy produces few if any opportunities to work out compromises that most people can feel comfortable ratifying.

For this reason, telepolling should be used to supplement the existing representative government. At the same time, if it was properly conducted, it could serve between elections as a continuous source of information to the legislature about the preferences of the populace.

Closer to Real Democracy

The National Science Foundation team experimented in New Jersey with a system both layered and containing mandates. Systems like it could be employed nationwide to bring teledemocracy a step closer to real democracy. Our experiment was conducted with the help of the League of Women Voters, which was attempting to decide, as it does once a year, which issues to give priority. We organized the league's members into groups of ten, and they conducted their "town meetings" by means of conference calls. Each group chose its own priorities and selected a representative to take that agenda to the next level for discussion. We then held conference calls with groups of ten representatives, who decided among themselves which views and preferences to carry to the third and final level, at which statewide policy decisions were made. A survey established that the members were highly satisfied with the results. Every member was able to participate in the decision-making process, and yet the elected representatives were free, within an area indicated by those who elected them, to work out a league-wide consensus.

Such a model could be applied to a nationwide audience, drawing on the magical power of exponential curves: if representatives were layered in the suggested manner, millions of participants could very quickly be included. Indeed, suppose that various experts addressed the country on Sunday from 10:00 to 11:00 A.M. about whether the United States should cut back the military by 50 percent over five years. The conference buzz would start with groups of fourteen citizens, each having an hour to discuss and vote. Each group would elect one representative to participate in conference-call discussions with thirteen representatives of other groups. Each group of representatives would in turn elect an individual to speak for them, and so on in a rising pyramid. If this process occurred seven times, by six o'clock in the evening 105 million adults could be reached, which is more than the 91 million who voted in the 1988 presidential election.

The technical problems we encountered in our experiments were minor. We discovered that it takes some practice to get used to a conference by telephone. For example, you have to find ways to let it be known that you wish to speak (raising your hand obviously will do little good). And it is not always easy to tell who is the chair, the person who facilitates the dialogue and must control those who hog time. We dealt with the first problem by making use of the fact that the receiver button can be briefly clicked without disconnecting the line. The resulting signal can be recorded on a panel attached to the chair's phone, showing that you are in the queue to speak. Costlier possibilities come to mind, but they might require that U.S. phone companies do what the government of France has already done: equip each citizen's phone with a small computer attachment. The second problem resolved itself, for during a short dry run most chairs quickly learned to assert themselves.

Discussion and Thought

Sesame Street teaches children about democratic elections in the following manner: You have three dollars to spend. Some people want crayons, others juice. You vote on what to buy. If the majority wants crayons, you get crayons. Such a simplistic explanation may do for young children, but adults who think of democracy as a voting machine miss an important feature of town meetings: such meetings expose people to conflicting arguments and make them think about their preferences before they vote.

The last thing a democracy needs is for people to vote their raw feelings, their first impulses, before they have had a chance to reflect on them and discuss them with others. Hence it is highly undesirable to expose people to a new idea, policy, or speech and ask them to vote on it immediately—which is precisely what most media polling currently does. A much more democratic model would result if at least a day's delay were required before the vote was taken, to enable people to discuss the matter with their families, neighbors, and co-workers.

We conducted such an experiment in three high-rise buildings in Queens, New York. These buildings, which contained about eleven hundred families, shared a cable system, and a studio in the basement of one of them enabled a person to address all the TV sets in the buildings. We provided the residents with questionnaires on which they marked their views on selected local issues. We then broadcast a panel discussion on TV. Next we created an opportunity for dialogue: residents were invited to walk over to the studio and address the community about the issues on the table. This was followed by a second brief question-naire. Unfortunately, owing to various technical difficulties, I cannot state unequivocally that the results were beneficial. The data suggest, however, that people moved from more extreme positions toward the middle, and that they moved either toward a consensus or, on one issue, toward two positions from a much wider, confused spread.

A minor but not trivial problem is that when citizens speak up in a live town meeting, they get immediate feedback on how their views are received. As a result, they continually adjust what they are saying, moderating their views (or expounding upon them) when faced with a negative reception and speaking more firmly (or more conciliatorily) if faced with a sea of heads nodding in approval. This feedback is largely lacking in confer-ence calls and other communication by electronic means. So the NSF team provided levers that participants in a lab could move on a continuum from "agree" to "disagree," thus affecting a small amber light that would shine brightly when a majority pulled their levers toward "agree," and would dim if many pulled in the opposite direction. This device provided speakers with some instant feedback. To provide a similar feature on a nationwide or community-wide basis, we would probably, again, have to move toward phone-system technology similar to that in France.

Faulty Criticisms

Once we put our minds to it, other shortcomings of the elec-tronic town meeting could be fixed. Take, for example, ballot-box stuffing. Even when much less than national policy is at stake, call-in polls have been grossly manipulated. Richard Morin, the polling director for *The Washington Post*, reports two such incidents. In one, *USA Today* asked its readers in June of 1990 if Donald Trump symbolized what was right or wrong with the United States. Eighty-one percent of the 6,406 people who called in said that he was great, 19 percent a skunk. It turned out that 72 percent of the calls came from two phone numbers. In another 1990 poll 21 percent of the callers on the issue of abortion voted at least twice.

This problem can be fixed. People could be required to punch in a Social Security number and two other identifying details, perhaps birth date and mother's maiden name. Computers could flag instances in which either the identifying information did not match the Social Security number or the same Social Security number was used more than once. And penalties like those now in place for election fraud could be extended to the electronic ballot box. The system would not be foolproof, but neither is the other system—as historians of the city of Chicago and biographers of Lyndon B. Johnson will tell you.

Those who complain that teledemocracy allows people to make only simple yes and no choices should note that the system can be as complicated as citizens wish. There are no technical obstacles to providing callers with three phone numbers instead of two (for "maybe" as well as "yes" and "no"), or with decision trees, in which, for example, they reach the "yes" line and are then offered a menu of choices, such as "only if the cost is less than $10 billion," or "less than $20 billion," and so on. Such a system would be at least as subtle as a vote that takes place on the electronic board of the House of Representatives or on a paper ballot loaded with local initiatives.

An Added Means of Public Expression

Several of the sharpest critics of teledemocracy focus on the fact that it is highly unrepresentative. James Fishkin, a political philosopher at the University of Texas, discussed this issue in the journal *The Responsive Community*, in an article about "America on the Line," a CBS program that aired after the 1992 State of the Union address. The network invited viewers to call in their reactions; seven million people tried to call, and three hundred thousand got through. When their reactions were compared with those of a scientific sample of public opinion taken at the same time, Fishkin reports, significant differences were noted. For instance, whereas 53 percent of the callers believed that America was worse off than it had been a year earlier, only 32 percent of the representative sample felt that way. Others have pointed out that those who are most likely to participate in a teledemocratic exchange are those who are educated, are politically active, or feel passionately about an issue.

All this would be a problem if one expected electronic town meetings to replace public-opinion polls and the ballot box. It is much less problematic, however, if teledemocracy is *added* to other means of public expression, each of which has its own defects—defects that can to some extent be compensated for by combining the various means. Take public-opinion polls, which play a major role in selecting candidates for office and affect policy between elections. Although the sampling methods used are accurate, and result in a cross-section of the public that is superior to anything to be hoped for in telepolling, the results can be deeply skewed by the phrasing of the questions. Even small changes in wording often lead to major changes in the public's response. Moreover, polltakers allow no time for deliberation or dialogue, and provide no information to those they query about the issues the pollsters are raising. Finally, those who show up at traditional ballot boxes do not themselves constitute a scientifically accurate cross-section of the public. They are more educated, more politically active, more affluent, and often more passionate about the issues than those who do not vote.

A key point is that actual voting allows citizens to have a say only once every two years at most. Present-day government, which directly affects numerous issues, from abortion to unemployment, from school busing to security of savings, requires ways to read the public mind between elections.

A Partial Solution

Electronic town meetings might reduce but would not expunge the deep sense of citizen disaffection, because they would address only part of the problem. The American political system suffers not only from a lack of opportunities to participate but also from the strong influence that special-interest groups wield upon national and state legislatures. Congress often knows quite well what the public prefers, but special-interest groups are a major source of the vast funds that members of Congress need for their election campaigns. Until this unholy alliance is severed, teledemocracy's primary contribution might well be to make it even clearer to the public that legislators often do not respond to the public will.

"The closer we get to direct democracy, the more we disempower the common man."

Media Technology Will Not Improve Democracy

Christopher Georges

Proponents of "teledemocracy" say it will make the American political system more democratic by letting people control government. In the following viewpoint, Christopher Georges disagrees, citing examples of this type of direct democracy at the state level to prove that teledemocracy will not eliminate the influence of money or special interests and will result in discriminatory policies. Furthermore, says Georges, it will eliminate argumentation, deliberation, and compromise, which are essential components of democracy. Georges is editor of the *Washington Monthly*, a political opinion magazine in Washington, D.C.

As you read, consider the following questions:

1. According to the author, what are the three forces contributing to the emergence of direct democracy?
2. According to the author, what are the negative consequences of the expensive campaigns waged over state initiative measures?
3. What two techniques does Georges say are used by special interests to influence voters?

By the time of the Major League All Star game in July 1992, Edgar Martinez was near the top of virtually every stack of numbers in the big leagues: third in the league in hitting (.319 average), 46 runs-batted-in, 14 home runs—and a standout third baseman. But come the big game, starting at third was not Martinez, but struggling Boston Red Sox Wade Boggs, whose ho-hum .268 average was 64th in the league, and who had 25 runs-batted-in and 6 home runs. So why did Boggs get the nod over Martinez? All Star starters aren't selected by experts, but by the fans in a popular vote. So while Seattle Mariner Martinez garnered 500,000 votes from the bleacher set—finishing *fifth* in the third base plebiscite—he wasn't even close to Boggs's 1.2 million. Were the fans duped—fooled perhaps by the cachet of the Boggs name? Or did they know Martinez was the best man, but still wanted to see the hobbling Fenway legend in one more All Star go-round?

Whatever the reason, Boggs's selection raises a broader question: The All Star selection process appeals to the fans, but does it produce the best team? The answer is relevant to more than just readers of *Baseball Digest*, because in a very different realm—the political one—we are creeping ever closer towards the kind of system that put Boggs in the All Star lineup: a direct, let-the-majority-decide democracy. That drift towards direct democracy, while certainly part of a larger movement, is currently led by Ross Perot. Problem is, the Prince of Populism's vaunted teledemocracy will not only give us more Boggses and fewer Martinezes, but rather than, as advertised, "taking America back," it may well hand it over to the special interests.

Populist Yearnings on the Rise

Of course, populist yearnings among the American people—from Thomas Jefferson to Robert LaFollette to Bill Clinton—have been as common as House scandals. But today, three forces have converged to make direct democracy a viable, even appealing, option. For one, the public's frustration with government—and with Congress in particular—has reached new heights: Eighty percent of those surveyed in a 1993 *Washington Post*/ABC News poll, for example, said that the "country needs to make major changes in the way government works." At the same time, the public is more eager than ever to give the government a piece of its mind. You don't have to be a talk show junkie to spot this trend; just ask the White House operators, who on a busy day during the Reagan years might have fielded 5,000 calls, but in 1993 were busy with 40,000 *a day*. Finally, factor in the most recent and significant development: the flourishing of technological tools that will allow anyone with a TV, a phone line, and a few minutes to spare to vote on any issue, any time.

The public apparently has few reservations about using [this technology]. More than two thirds of all Americans favor national binding referenda on major issues, according to a 1993 survey by the Americans Talk Issues Foundation. Gallup surveys have put the figure at nearly 70 percent. All of which helps explain the rise of a populist like Perot, who can preach with complete credibility, as he did during the [1992 presidential] campaign, that "we can show everybody in Congress what the voters want, and we'll be programming [Congress]. That's the way it's supposed to be."

To Empower the People?

What Perot's getting at—and what most advocates of teledemocracy preach—is that empowering the people with a direct vote in policy-making is the surest cure for the two great plagues of our representative system: It is strangled by special interests, and it moves at a glacial pace. Teledemocrats figure that if only we turned the levers of power over to the people, well, we'd fix all that. For one, the people, by going over the heads of Congress, could quickly eliminate the tiresome, time-consuming political haggling and, say, decide to outlaw fat cat political contributions tonight at 10, and, if we felt so inclined, approve stricter gun laws tomorrow at noon. And at the same time, in a single stroke, we'd wipe out the clout of the nasty special interests. That's because the people cannot be bought, making all the lobbying by the monied interests as relevant as eight-track tapes. "It's the best way I know," says Mike McManus, organizer of USA Vote, a Maryland-based group attempting to organize national televotes, "to empower the people against the special interests."

Or is it? As we take our first timid steps towards Perot's push-button utopia, it's worth pausing to consider what we might forfeit in the process. Despite the rhetoric of populists like McManus, the evidence is that the closer we get to direct democracy, the more we *disempower* the common man, and at the same time enhance—or at the very least keep intact—the muscle of the monied interests. And while teledemocracy, no doubt, can short-circuit the haggling that throttles Congress and jump start our chronically gridlocked process, that much maligned horse trading may, in fact, be more valuable than any legislation it holds up.

So what will it be? No doubt, James Madison and bookish fellow Framers were bright guys, but they weren't seers: Let's face it, America's no longer a nation of yeomen. Perhaps technology has made their experiment in government obsolete. Perhaps it's time to deposit those interminable *Federalist Papers* in the recycling bin and move our system of government into this century.

Should we, in short, stick with representarian Madison or turn to majoritarian Perot?. . .

"We go to the people on television," Perot told the nation during the campaign, "and explain an issue in great detail, and say: 'Here are the alternatives that we face. As owners of the country, what do you feel is best for the country?' The American people react . . . and we know what the people want." Just to make sure we knew he wasn't bluffing, citizen Perot gave his televote a dry run not long after his 19 percent Election Day showing, holding a "national referendum" on 16 issues which, although statistically dubious, was a referendum nonetheless. If you're un-American enough to believe Perot's gone a bit far, you're decisively in the minority. . . .

Toward Electronic Tyranny

Such an instant referendum [as advocated by Ross Perot] is exactly what the nation's founders feared. They believed that immediate and direct voting would encourage talented rabble-rousers to sway the electorate in a wave of emotion. Thus they created a representative system with two houses of Congress, an administrative and an executive branch, and an electoral college standing between voters and the final decision. Perot's system is a videocracy that would give the Leader direct access to the voters, and encourage a direct response. This could easily turn into electronic tyranny.

William F. Fore, *Christian Century*, December 2, 1992.

Most Americans will soon be hooked into our leadership through the already-under-construction data superhighway. In April 1993, the nation's largest cable company, Tele-Communications, Inc., sharply accelerated the race to link the nation by unveiling a $2 billion plan to lay fiber optic cable throughout 400 communities in three years. . . . Tele-Communications is not alone; the more than 60 firms scrambling to get a toehold in the interactive market come straight from the Fortune 500: Intel, Time Warner, Microsoft, General Instruments, NBC.

The cyberprize they're chasing is the edge in the two-way fiber optic cable communications market, which will not only allow users, through their TV sets, to respond instantly to commercials, order food, conduct bank transactions, play along with live sporting events, pay bills, or guess the outcome of "Murder She Wrote" (for cheesy prizes), but vote—or at least instantaneously voice an opinion. So when, say, President Perot gives us his pie chart lecture on the Social Security crisis, and then asks us for some insta-policy, you need only pick up your book-sized interactive box and let your fingers do the voting.

That's no hype dream. In fact, such a system is already in place in several cities and has been used for just that purpose. Interactive Network in Mountain View, California, for example, which has linked more than 3,000 homes, held instant votes immediately after both Clinton's 1993 State of the Union address (four minutes after the speech was completed, 71 percent of the viewers punched in that they supported the Clinton plan), as well as one of Perot's 30-minute infomercial[s]. Perot was so enamored of the results that he contacted Interactive regarding a more formal link between the two organizations, Interactive officials said.

And while televoting is just one of several two-way TV applications companies are pursuing, more than a half dozen for- and not-for-profit organizations are aiming to put the new fiber optic technology to use for national on-line voting. USA Vote, for example, plans to launch an interactive TV show that will feature 30 minutes of debate followed by an instant call-in vote on a major issue. Bruce Jaynes, president of Ohio-based Voter Systems Inc., who has spent eight years designing a system that will allow instant voting, is already attempting to negotiate a contract with a TV network to make his plan fly. And not-for-profits like the Markel Foundation and the Aspen Institute, as well as independent academics such as Amitai Etzioni and the University of Texas's James Fishkin, are examining ways to put the new technology to work. "The weird thing about all this," explains Gary Arlen, president of Arlen Communications Inc., a Bethesda research firm specializing in interactive media, "is that if you don't pay attention, you'll look up one day and it will all be here."

States Provide a Clue

What's not weird, however, is the larger question that the push-button technology brings: whether to push. If, as teledemocrats claim, majoritarian government is the magic bullet that will at long last make our government the true servant of the common man, why not?

Several decades of experience in direct democracy at the state level—namely state initiatives and referenda—provide a clue. California in particular offers a useful model, where citizens have voted on more ballot initiatives—more than 200 since 1912—than anywhere in the nation. In fact, no society since ancient Greece has sustained such a long history of direct democracy. But not even Homer could mythologize the success of majoritarian government in California and other states, especially with regard to the clout of the monied interests. Of course, there have been some notable reforms passed directly by the people over the years, such as campaign finance reforms, bottle bills, tobacco tax hikes, and term limits for state legislators. Even so, even Hill and Knowlton [a New York City public relations firm] couldn't put a happy face on the larger referendum picture.

More, not less, money is spent in direct democracy politics than in representative politics.

In California, in both 1988 and 1990, more money (about $125 million each year) was spent—through ad campaigns, ballot signing drives, and get-out-the-vote efforts—to influence California voters on initiative measures than was spent by all special interests to lobby California legislators on all other legislation (more than 1,000 bills). Spending on single initiatives there and in other states can run as high as tens of millions of dollars. The alcohol industry, for example, spent $38 million defeating a proposed alcohol tax in 1990. The truly bad news, however, is not so much that the people eventually end up paying for these massive industry-run campaigns in higher prices, but that to battle the well-oiled industries, the goo-goos have to raise equally huge sums. Alcohol tax proponents in California, for example, wasted $1.3 million on their losing effort and environmentalists there squandered more than $1 million in 1990 on a campaign to save the trees. Not only is coming up with that kind of cash a task in itself, but it saps valuable time and resources from other areas of the cause, such as, say, funding anti-drunk driving campaigns.

Money Talks

Not only is more money spent, but direct democracy does not diminish—and can even enhance—the wealthy interests' ability to affect legislation.

"Money is, all things being equal, the single most important factor determining direct legislation outcomes," concludes Colorado College political scientist Thomas Cronin, who authored perhaps the most comprehensive examination of direct democracy in the U.S. "Even proponents of direct democracy campaign reforms are pessimistic about solving the money problem." Study after study backs Cronin's claim: The Council on Economic Priorities found that in state initiatives the corporate-backed side almost always outspends its opponents, and wins about 80 percent of the time. And another examination that charted 72 ballot questions from 1976-82 similarly found that nearly 80 percent of the time the higher-spending side won.

And who has the most money to spend? Certainly not tree huggers nor mothers against drunk driving. Businesses in California kicked in more than 80 percent of the money for the 18 highest-spending initiatives since 1956, while grassroots organizations were able to raise just 3 percent of all funds spent. It's not unusual for monied interests to outspend their opponents by factors of 20-to-1. In 1980, for example, Chevron, Shell, ARCO and Mobil and friends made a more than $5 million investment, outspending their opponents by 100-to-1, to ensure the failure of a proposed California oil surtax. Not even OPEC [Organization of Petroleum Exporting Countries] could buy this kind of clout: Five months prior to the vote, 66 percent of the people favored the tax, but after the industry bludgeoned the public with TV ads and other propaganda, only 44 percent of the voters stuck with the humbled reformers. In 1990, a Los Angeles initiative to ban the use of a highly toxic chemical at a Torrance, California, refinery lost, thanks to Mobil Oil's $750,000 effort—a campaign that cost the company $53 per vote, or nearly 12 times what the ballots' proponents could muster. A few of the measures that big money helped defeat in recent years included bills that would have raised the alcohol tax, required greater oil and gas conservation, brought tougher insurance regulation, created smoking regulations, required stricter handgun control, promoted forest conservation, placed a surtax on oil profits, and limited state salaries.

Special Interest Cons

Voters are just as likely—and perhaps more likely—to be conned by special interests as representatives are to be bought by them.

Look at it this way: If you are a salesman trying to sell a car to an 80-year-old woman, would you rather deal with her, or her representative—her son the lawyer? For the monied interests, that's a no-brainer. One clever technique concocted by industry groups is wait to see what do-gooder initiatives qualify for the ballot, and then quickly draft counter measures—measures which have no hope of passing a plebiscite, but are intended instead merely to confuse voters; the monied interests are well aware of studies showing that voters are easily confused by conflicting initiatives and as a result tend to simply vote "no" on both of them. A 1990 California environmental reform package, for example, known as "Big Green," was matched by two corporate-backed initiatives, one of which was billed as a "pesticide safety policy," funded by Atlantic Richfield ($950,000), Chevron ($800,000), Shell ($600,000), and Phillip Morris ($125,000), among others. All three were voted down. Also in 1990, part of the $38 million outlay by the alcohol industry to kill a proposed liquor tax was spent pushing two counter measures: a bill proposing the industry's own version of a liquor alcohol tax as well as an anti-tax measure.

If the special interests don't baffle you with their counter measures, they'll probably get you with their deceptive advertising. One study of 25 initiatives concluded that the most successful initiative opposition campaigns have won in large part based on airing confusing messages through paid advertising. In fact, dubious initiative ad campaigns are more likely to confuse voters than negative or false advertising in candidate campaigns simply because issue initiatives fail to provide voters with the traditional political cues, such as party affiliation, to help voters decide. And while representatives are not immune to lies and deception, it's a lot easier, not to mention cheaper, for an environmental advocate to counter a dubious claim if he's only got to convince a few congressmen—as opposed to a few million otherwise-distracted citizens—that Exxon's pulling a con. . . .

What's also failed is direct democracy's ability to work in favor of racial and ethnic minorities. A few of the numerous examples where voters ganged up on those groups over the years include a 1964 California referendum in which citizens overturned by a 2-to-1 margin a law passed by the state legislature that prohibited racial discrimination by realtors. (In fact, of five referenda ever held in states to prohibit racial discrimination, not one has passed.) In 1992, voters in Colorado passed an anti-gay measure voiding any existing gay rights laws in Denver, Aspen, and Boulder. And if you think majority tyranny is limited just to ethnics, racial groups, and gays, talk to the children of Kalkaska, Michigan, where citizens earlier this year voted to close down the school system three months early instead of paying an extra $200-$400 each in taxes.

Popular Demands

Despite the evidence, let's assume the teledemocrats are *right*: Suppose that the people will take the time to be educated, and that the special interests will be persuaded or forced to refrain from false advertising and other deceptions. Suppose, in short, we *can* create a utopian system of majoritarian rule.

The good news for the Majoritarian Majority is that in some cases direct democracy will probably produce better results than representative government—say, in gun control laws. Which is precisely why the notion of push-button democracy plays so well in Perotville: It would be a wonderful world, indeed, if we could get the people together to vote on just those issues where we think the special interests are oppressing the rest of us.

But what about the rest of the issues, and especially those issues of belief, where fundamental rights come into play—issues such as the death penalty or gay rights. Do you want the majority deciding for you in those cases? One way to find out is by examining some examples of what the majority does believe. The majority of Americans would:

- sentence anyone who commits a murder to death
- send all occasional drug users to military style boot camps
- not allow any group to use a public building to hold a meet-

ing denouncing the government

- ban movies with foul language or nudity
- ban from libraries books that preach the overthrow of the U.S. government
- make it illegal to publish materials the government classifies as secret
- outlaw the use of obscene gestures towards public officials
- favor the government keeping lists of people who partake in protest demonstrations
- keep in custody, when the nation is at war, people suspected of disloyalty
- require the reading of the Lord's Prayer in schools
- make homosexual relations between consenting adults illegal
- have rejected the Marshall Plan, and every year since 1950 voted to have spent less on foreign aid, and currently oppose aid to Russia.

Of course, it is possible that the polls that produce such results were flawed; opinion can be distorted, after all, by the way questions are phrased. This is, in fact, the heart of the problem with majority rule through referendum. When the wording of an issue is frozen, and printed on the ballot, or even worse, flashed on the TV screen, there is no opportunity to do anything but take one side or the other—no chance, in other words, to see enough wisdom in the other person's arguments, or for him to see the point in yours, and for the wording to be amended accordingly.

In a representative government, legislators can, and do, deliberate and amend. These discussions can, of course, lead to imperfect compromise. But accommodation, however imperfect, may be essential to preserving the very fabric of democracy, especially when issues of morality and belief threaten to tear the nation apart. And the accommodation does not have to be imperfect. With deliberation, there is at least a chance that not only a better, but even the *right*, law will result. Teledemocracy will deprive us of that chance. And, if you're not convinced, we can always vote on it.

Periodical Bibliography

The following articles have been selected to supplement the diverse views presented in this chapter.

Terry Eastland	"The Dangers of a Talk Show Presidency," *The World & I*, March 1993. Available from 2800 New York Ave. NE, Washington, DC 20002.
Murray Edelman	"Constructing the Political Spectacle," *Kettering Review*, Winter 1992. Available from 200 Commons Rd., Dayton, OH 45459-2799.
William F. Fore	"Perot's Videocracy," *The Christian Century*, December 2, 1992.
Christopher Georges	"Mock the Vote: What's Wrong with MTV's Hot New Political Coverage," *The Washington Monthly*, May 1993.
Hazel Henderson	"Perfecting Democracy's Tools," *New Perspectives Quarterly*, Fall 1992.
William A. Henry III	"To 'Out' or Not to 'Out,'" *Time*, August 19, 1991.
Edward Herman	"Democratic Media," *Z Papers*, January/March 1992. Available from 150 W. Canton St., Boston, MA 02118.
Jon Katz	"The Plugged-In Voter: The New News Has Reconnected People and Politics," *Rolling Stone*, December 10-24, 1992.
Lewis H. Lapham	"Deus ex Machina," *Harper's*, November 1992.
Media & Values	"Rethinking Democracy: Citizenship in the Media Age," Spring 1992.
Elayne Rapping	"Television and Democracy," *The Progressive*, April 1993.
James C. Roberts	"The Power of Talk Radio," *The American Enterprise*, May/June 1991.
Michael Schudson	"Trout or Hamburger: Politics and Telemythology," *Tikkun*, March/April 1991.
Richard Zoglin	"Sitcom Politics," *Time*, September 21, 1992.

Is Advertising Harmful to Society?

Chapter Preface

A large portion of America's mass media communication is advertising. Every day, the American public is confronted with a nearly continuous barrage of words and images from billboards, radios, television sets, and even bumper stickers and clothing labels—all designed to incite the urge to buy. In the words of Deborah Baldwin, the editor of *Common Cause Magazine,* "The average American can't budge without hearing 'buy, buy' ten times." Many commentators note that children are often the deliberate targets of such messages.

Critics contend that advertisers exploit the vulnerability of children for profit. Education professors Nancy Carlsson-Paige and Diane E. Levin write that children are "easy prey for the sophisticated marketing practices aimed at them; they do not have cognitive skills to understand the purpose of advertising, much less consider its effects on them." Carlsson-Paige and Levin specifically condemn the toy industry's marketing technique of making toys that complement television programs so that toys and programs became advertisements for one another. They believe that corporations "have taken control of children's play" in order to sell toys. Commentator David Schatzky agrees, charging that advertisers exploit children's vulnerabilities by using fantasy in order to insinuate their products into children's fantasy lives. He concludes, "Advertisers will do anything to create customers for life. They don't mind hijacking the inner life of children for the purpose of profit."

While some believe advertising exploits children, others believe it is harmless, even beneficial. Jib Fowles, a professor of media studies, contends that "the gullibility of small viewers" is exaggerated by critics. Fowles contends that even very young children are able to distinguish between commercials and programs. Furthermore, as they mature, children develop a healthy skepticism and resistance toward advertising. Thus, says Fowles, commercials "do not shape capitalist stooges but rather highly sophisticated consumers." Fowles argues that advertising benefits both children and adults: "Many of the purchases [resulting from advertising] bring the youngster a great deal of pleasure, just as many adult purchases do. . . . For child as well as for parent, the relationship between producer and consumer is usually a reciprocal one, and beneficial to both parties."

Although commercials' effects on children are debatable, advertising is and will remain a central part of U.S. culture. The viewpoints in the following chapter debate the influence of advertising in American society.

Advertising Perpetuates Consumerism

Leo Bogart

America is a "commercial culture" in which the possession and consumption of material objects is an overriding preoccupation, according to Leo Bogart. In the following viewpoint, he argues that advertising, which dominates the country's mass media system, perpetuates this consumerism through deceitful messages promising health, beauty, comfort, and pleasure. Bogart is a public opinion specialist, a former advertising executive, and the author of *Polls and the Awareness of Public Opinion*, *Strategy in Advertising*, and *The Age of Television*.

As you read, consider the following questions:

1. How does the author define "commercial culture"?
2. According to the author, who are the primary clients of mass media enterprises? Of what importance are audiences?
3. How do advertisements arouse envy, according to Bogart?

From *The Amerian Media System and Its Commercial Culture* by Leo Bogart. Freedom Forum Media Center Occasional Paper no. 8, 1991. Reprinted by permission of the Freedom Forum Media Studies Center, Columbia University.

Our lives in contemporary America are dominated by financial transactions—anticipating them, engaging in them and consuming what we acquire from them. This requires a highly developed and productive economy, a universal and dense network of communications and a high level of literacy.

People exchange and consume goods and services in every society, but ours seems uniquely dedicated to that purpose. There are cultures in which sheer existence is so precarious that human beings find it hard to transcend the immediate tasks of obtaining food and shelter to survive. There are cultures whose members are primarily concerned with the integration of their individual existences into the pattern of nature and tradition; they are preoccupied with spirits, deities or ancestors. There are cultures that value time, indolence, the warmth of personal relationships and the cultivation, for mere pleasure, of skills that cannot be sold.

Commercial Culture

We are not immune to the appeal of non-material values in our own society. We practice the forms of religious worship, and find a place in our lives for affection, friendship, sport and the arts. But the satisfactions we obtain from these activities are embedded in the tissue of our lives as consumers. The practices of religion, sport and art acquire overtones of meaning from the social status of those with whom we engage in them and from the objects associated with them. Love is pursued in an automobile, at restaurants, at the movies. The zest for an active life requires running shoes or perhaps a private tennis court.

Culture may be defined as the whole body of beliefs, practices and material artifacts that a society uses. Our culture is commercial because of the central place material goods and reminders of material goods have in it. But the term "commercial culture" can be used in another sense as well, when applied to the flow of ideas and expressions that shape our national character and outlook. By this narrower definition, contemporary American culture is commercial because, overwhelmingly, it is produced for sale to meet marketing requirements. In this respect our culture differs from the cultures of other places and times, in which expression has either been valued as an end in itself or because of its ability to please a patron. Commercial culture assigns no value or meaning to communications apart from their market value, that is, the price that someone is willing to pay for them. . . .

Commercial culture, it is said, perpetuates the existing social and economic structure by making its principles the dominant and unquestioned ideology, suppressing any indications of its evils and impermanence, and lulling the masses of the population into a mindless acceptance of the status quo. It inhibits the ability of creative people to express themselves by subordinating their talents to the demands of the market. It favors vulgarity and the commonplace, and gives short shrift to experiment and innovation. It moves media content toward the lowest common denominator, suppressing variety in taste and opinion. . . .

The media system is driven primarily by advertising, and is itself part of a marketing system in which the production of goods is governed by manufacturers' perceptions of consumer demand. For advertisers, media are advertising media, not avenues of public enlightenment or cultural enhancement. Advertising is only one form of promotion, and promotion is used both to influence consumer demand directly and to insure that the necessary channels of distribution are kept open.

There are media like books, motion pictures, videocassettes, newsletters and comic books that are not generally thought of as channels of promotion, though advertising has actually intruded into all of them. But for most of the principal forms of mass communications, advertising is the main source of income. On-air broadcasting is totally dependent upon it and it provides four-fifths of newspaper and one-half of magazine revenues.

This means that the people who manage most media enterprises have, for many years, regarded advertisers, rather than the public, as their primary clients. To be sure, they work hard to generate audiences. They do so not as an end in itself but because audiences are the commodity they sell to their real customers. The structure and content of the media system is profoundly affected, if not actively controlled, by the judgments and practices of advertisers whose interest in media structure and content is entirely instrumental and pragmatic. Advertisers have no functional concern with the meaning or consequences of mass communication except insofar as it provides a mechanism for the delivery of their messages to prospective customers. . . .

The Presence of Advertising

Advertising is a powerful presence. It fills about 60 percent of newspaper space, 52 percent of magazine pages, 18 percent of radio time, 17 percent of network television prime time and Saturday morning children's time (including the occasional public service commercials and promotional commercials for programs), 27 percent of network programming other than prime time, and an additional 10 percent of all broadcast time on local television stations over and above the network feed. This does not mean that advertising occupies an equivalent proportion of the communications to which people are attentive or responsive. Reading is an extremely selective process, and readers can rapidly and efficiently screen out unwanted advertising, along

252

with unwanted information of other kinds. With broadcast commercials, some members of the audience leave the room, while others let their attention wander.

With due allowance for inattention, the sheer volume of advertising messages received and retained unquestionably makes a substantial impact upon the American psyche. These messages tell us, as critics of advertising have long pointed out, to consume, and to consume now, right away. They represent a continuing advocacy for hedonism, for making our lives easier, more enjoyable. They urge us on to accumulate more possessions and new experiences. They tantalize us with visions of pleasures beyond our capacities to taste and often beyond our ability to afford. Advertising teaches us to take pride in our outer appearances and in the way we present ourselves to others. It reinforces traditional conventions and values that contrast with the moral anarchy that suffuses the surrounding news and entertainment programming.

© Jeff Reid. Reprinted by permission.

Is advertising imagery and symbolism different from that of other media content? In some respects the casts of characters are similar, though on television women play a more significant role in commercials than they do in drama. The human relations depicted in advertisements, unlike those in drama, are upbeat and positive, with conflict shown only in the most playful form. There is an emphasis on comparisons, establishing superiority, pricing, quality, performance and service. Novelty is highly praised; to be new is to be improved. There is a strong veneration of inanimate objects: they are endowed with the ability to arouse levels of emotional affect that most human beings normally feel only toward each other. And broadcast messages move at a much more rapid pace than programs do, because there is so little time to say what has to be said.

Taken together, advertisements represent an enormous affirmation of the importance and value of the material comforts of life that are available in a wealthy industrial society. Along with this constant reassurance of how lucky we are, advertisements also offer constant reminders of the possessions that we don't have and of the envied privileges of those who do have them. Quite apart from any of the specific products they promote, they exert a persistent pressure to acquire more things and therefore, on most of us, a pressure to work harder, to achieve more so that we too can acquire them. On people who feel personally inadequate for this achievement, advertisements may have a different effect, creating illegitimate notions of entitlement—fostering the idea that possessions are so important that they must be acquired by any means. (How does the constant display of goods on television affect the moral judgments of normally law-abiding poor people who loot—whether in Panama City or in Detroit? How did commercials on West German television assist in the political education of the East Germans?)

Advertising conveys many other meanings besides its exhortations to buy whatever it is overtly selling. These meanings, it must be noted, are different in different media. Newspaper ads, which are overwhelmingly retail and classified, tend to be nuts and bolts, price-oriented, descriptive, factual; they are short on the depiction of human faces and figures and relatively devoid of emotional overtones. National brand advertising in magazines emphasizes products more than people, unlike commercials on TV. Models used in print ads have always been abstract idealizations, just as the women who once illustrated magazine fiction were always lithe and lovely, the men trim and firm-jawed.

False Sentiments and Discontinuities

The people and scenes of TV commercials resemble those of TV drama; they are better looking than the reality they represent. The latent messages seem to be highly subordinate to the primary message of persuading viewers to buy a particular brand of merchandise; they are a continuing affirmation of mainstream, middle-class values; they preach the value of physical beauty, health and well-being. Advertisements are not part of the world of violence, anger, depression and offbeat sex that fills the columns of the press and the prime-time hours of television. Theirs is a world of pure romance and warm feelings of fellowship, of strongly knit, secure family relationships, of individuals untroubled except by the fleeting, easily curable distress of bad breath or clogged drains. While television entertainment depicts a society with strong elements of tension and pain, the world of commercials is upbeat and uplifting in its mood, oozing false sentiment and simpering pseudo-humor. Its characters are loving, caring, friendly and supportive of each other. It is a world dominated by the euphoria of youth, with its people in a state of perpetual motion, a kinetic, almost frenzied world that moves to the beat of rock music.

Shorter commercials, with their agitated fast-cuts, have run in greatly increased quantities since the Federal Trade Commission (FTC) forced the abandonment of the National Association of Broadcasters' Code in 1982. They represent merely one aspect of another important effect of advertising's mere presence—the interruption of communication. Our reading of a book is interrupted when we put it down between sessions; our reading of a magazine or newspaper pauses when we flip from the start of a story to its continuation on another page, or when our gaze shifts from one story to something else on the spread. But we don't put down a novel for the night in the middle of a gripping episode, and we don't move to to an ad from an article unless the ad holds greater interest. Interruptions in reading are qualitatively different from the sharp discontinuities that occur when a commercial "pod" interrupts a television program.

The public is indeed resigned to broadcast interruptions; they are generally regarded as the necessary price that must be paid to assure a variety of programming choices. Moreover, the growing use of remote controls for television encourages the viewers to sample other alternatives as soon as their attention to a program wanes. When communication takes on such a scattered, fragmented form, its meaning changes; it is inherently less compelling and the experience is trivialized. Whether we deplore this development or say with a sigh that it's just the way things are, this is a significant by-product of advertising's substantial presence in our daily lives.

"The social aspects of consumption do not depend on advertising."

Advertising Does Not Perpetuate Consumerism

Michael Schudson

Critics have often blamed advertising for perpetuating consumerism. In the following viewpoint, however, Michael Schudson argues that such critiques reveal America's historical aversion to materialism, not the power of advertising. Schudson contends that because it is a symbolic medium, advertising is far less influential in shaping behavior than institutions such as the family, the church, the schools, and the workplace. He concludes that while advertising can have negative effects, it is a positive presence to the extent that it promotes a belief in choice, variety, pluralism, and democracy. Schudson is a professor of communication and sociology at the University of California, San Diego, and the author of *Advertising: The Uneasy Persuasion*.

As you read, consider the following questions:

1. According to Schudson, what sustains America's "consumer culture"?
2. What is the true purpose of advertising, according to the author?
3. Why does Schudson question the criticisms of "consumer culture"?

Boris Yeltsin, president of the Russian Republic, returned from a nine-day American tour in the fall of 1989 effusive about the extraordinary wealth of American life: "Their supermarkets have 30,000 food items," he told supporters in his first public appearance back home. "You can't imagine it. It makes the people feel secure.". . .

While resembling the simple immigrant's astonishment at American abundance, Yeltsin's comments reveal something more. Abundance and choice, he is saying, provide a feeling of security, social and even spiritual comfort. This celebratory attitude toward American materialism is far from the skepticism shared by home grown American journalists and intellectuals. The native American view of materialism draws on the anti-capitalism of the left, anti-bourgeois attitudes redolent of aristocratic values, and most of all a distaste for consumerism at the very heart of the American tradition. Jimmy Carter, in his famous 1978 "malaise" speech on America's spiritual crisis, had no trouble finding in his own evangelical Protestantism the anxiety that "too many of us now worship self-indulgence and consumption" and the affirmation that "owning things and consuming things does not satisfy our longing for meaning."

Getting It Wrong

Contemporary social critics may imagine their critiques of consumer culture to be deeply radical and subversive, but they are generally only versions of a critique that American culture itself has long nurtured. And confused versions, at that. Take, for example, criticism of advertising, often attacked as the most egregious emblem of materialism, even as its cause. In fact, America was materialist, consumerist, and enterprising, as Alexis de Tocqueville [a French historian and philosopher who studied America in the early 1800s] observed, long before advertising held much visibility or importance in American cultural life. Yet advertising is today the chief symbol, if not the chief engine, of consumer culture.

As the chief symbol of consumer culture, advertising has also been a chief subject of analysis for critics looking for the hidden springs of American life. David Potter, a widely respected American historian, got it wrong forty years ago in his classic study of consumer culture, *People of Plenty* (1954), and much American thinking about advertising and culture has yet to recover from the error he expressed more directly and clearly than anyone else. Potter held that a society that moves from a producer orientation to a consumer orientation must develop a culture to correspond to it. Advertising responds to "the need to stimulate desire for the goods which an abundant economy has to offer and which a scarcity economy would never have produced."

For Potter, advertising was one of a very few institutions that can "properly be called instruments of social control." And what is an institution of social control? It is one that guides a person "by conceiving of him in a distinctive way and encouraging him to conform as far as possible to the concept." Potter used as examples the church, which conceives of a person as having an immortal soul; the schools, conceiving of the person as a reasonable creature; and the free-enterprise economy, conceiving of the person as a useful producer. Advertising, in contrast, "conceives of man as a consumer."

Commercials Convey Information

Commercials can convey various kinds of information relevant to the act of purchasing. Television specializes in the promotion of new products, so the very fact that something is being offered in the marketplace which wasn't there before can be informative. Whether old or new, the product is usually shown, along with its packaging, so that Americans can get an image of it. Frequently its intended uses are illustrated—the bowl of cereal is being eaten, the recreational vehicle is bounding over hillsides, the hottest new shoes are worn by the well-known athlete. Distinctive features will be mentioned, even if it's only an unintelligible but extra ingredient, or a particular color.

Jib Fowles, *Why Viewers Watch: A Reappraisal of Television's Effects*, 1992.

The trouble with Potter's argument is that advertising is not at all like church, school, and workplace, the institutions he lists as archetypal institutions of social control. (The sociologist would be more likely to list the church, school, and family.) Having recently watched my five-year-old go off to kindergarten, I have no illusion that the kind of control advertising exercises is half as determinative, controlling, influential, or potentially as destructive as that exerted by the institution of schooling. Even if children were to spend as much time watching commercial television as they do in school (and they do not—television is turned on in the average American household seven hours a day but no individual member of the family watches it for that length of time), children would be able to exercise freedoms in front of the television that they instantly lose in the classroom. Before the television, they can come and go as they like; they can choose to attend or not to attend without fear of the punishing glance, voice, or raised eyebrows of the advertiser responding immediately to their inattention; they can like or dislike, scowl or smile as they wish, without the fear that thirty others will be examining and taking cues from their behavior. In short, the television advertisement can offer no social punishment, no social reward, no social reference group.

Potter, like many others, fails to distinguish the social control exercised by schools and churches from the cultural influence exercised by the mass media. Social control always has a cultural or symbolic dimension; symbols are one of the media through which schools, churches, families, and workplaces operate. These institutions use not only threats, coercion through measures such as confinement, and even physical violence, but more ordinarily symbolic inducements and enticements. The symbolic dimensions are so important that, mistakenly, we may even identify churches with their doctrines and schools with their curricula. But religions are defined as much—if not more— by their social practices as by their doctrine. Similarly, the schools inculcate patterns of behavior in children through a "hidden curriculum" of social control, as sociologists have described it in many studies since the 1950s.

But while social control always has a cultural dimension, the reverse is not true. A cultural or symbolic medium, like advertising, does not necessarily have a social dimension. Or, to put it another way, the social aspects of consumption do not depend on advertising. For example, when we feel good and think we look smart wearing a cashmere coat, we may be reflecting some influence of advertising. But we are just as likely reflecting the practices of other people in the social set to which we belong or aspire. Big houses give a feeling of privacy, space, and security; advertising does not induce that sensation. Owning a book rather than borrowing it, or owning a washer and dryer rather than using the neighborhood laundromat, gives a pleasure of possession, convenience, and self-possession that ads for Stephen King blockbusters or laundry detergents have no part in. If the things we buy did not satisfy or seduce, the images conjured up by advertising would ordinarily fade. The consumer culture is sustained socially not by manufactured images but by the goods themselves as they are used.

People Want More

Potter's analysis seems to suggest, as did other analyses of the 1950s that still guide our thought on this matter, that people need to be instructed in the emotions as well as the arts of consumption. People have to learn to desire more goods. That was the argument made by liberals like Potter and John Kenneth Galbraith and by the social critic Vance Packard. It was the point argued by Marxists Paul Baran and Paul Sweezy and taken up later by Stuart Ewen. It is also a notion pushed by the people responsible for selling propaganda to business—that is, by advertising agencies themselves.

Curiously, both the critics of advertising and its spokesmen seem to share the peculiar premise that material goods require force feeding. But is consuming so unpleasant? Is wanting more so unnatural? Is aping the neighbors or seeking to be fashionable so unheard of that a multibillion dollar enterprise is required to coax us into it? Is desire for possessions so rare? Is pleasure in goods so unusual a joy?

I do not claim that wanting more is universal. I certainly do not claim any universality for the peculiar features of the Protestant ethic that Max Weber identified as leading our culture to value hard work aimed at accumulating riches. But I do claim that in America—which in the person of Benjamin Franklin best exemplified for Weber the spirit of capitalism—no multibillion dollar industry was needed to make people want more and more or to breed in them a dissatisfaction that they could quell only in the marketplace.

In this society, as I read it, an insistent ideological campaign promoted self-discipline and self-denial. The assumption was that people would naturally want to consume more and that an elaborate ideological system had to keep desire in check. This Puritan superstructure aimed at constraining old Adam was in the nineteenth century increasingly directed at working-class and immigrant communities, as it still is in the class-skewed movement now against tobacco and alcohol use.

Put this way, the underlying assumption in Potter and company seems preposterous. But, then, what is advertising for if not to turn us into desiring consumers? And why should people as smart as David Potter have tried to explain advertising as the instigator of desire for goods if this is so absurd a proposition?

An Information System

The first question is easily answered. Large outcomes, like the rise of advertising, do not require large causes. Slight ecological advantage may cause large institutional change. Men and women share all chromosomes but one; that little one-forty-sixth of the genetic makeup makes all the difference. Advertising is a complex, wasteful, often distasteful informational system for a consumer economy of competitive businesses and competitive, otherwise unsubsidized mass media. It is an important signaling system between business and business, business and consumer, wholesaler and retailer, consumer and consumer.

But it isn't more important than that. Along with films and novels, advertising provides the iconography, but not the engine, for abundance. Its emergence was not a response to a need to educate consumers' desires and tastes but a response to specific problems and opportunities in production and marketing in certain late nineteenth-century industries—an adjustment by a range of manufacturers and retailers to a new urban life with central business districts, public transportation, and mass circulation newspapers.

The second question—why smart people should accept a notion with neither evidence nor logic to support it—has to do with the availability, almost the inescapability, of long-standing intellectual traditions of distrust of material goods. Criticism of consumer culture has deep roots in America. Indeed, criticism of what today we call consumer culture originated before anything very closely resembling consumer culture had emerged— certainly before advertising as the central institutional expression of abundance took root.

This criticism emerged not so much from a single tradition as from a set of traditions [Puritan and Quaker, among others] that have become intermingled in contemporary criticism of consumer culture. . . .

An Ideology of Choice

Advertising at times seems to be materialism at its worst, the sizzle without the steak, the idolatry of goods divorced from the utility and enjoyment goods provide, but even this is too simple a view. It recognizes neither the aesthetic appeal of some advertising that touches us nor the plain wrapping, anti-magical character of most advertising. The most common advertising is, in a sense, Quaker itself—it points to price and so helps keep in mind economy as a chief criterion in buying. Or it is Puritan—recommending a product not because it provides moral or social or theological salvation but because it serves certain banal purposes well. It cleans your sink. It gets you to New York in time for your business meeting. It provides high-fidelity sound recording.

True, advertising is rarely republican—it does not focus on the needs of public life. And it often takes a stance toward the public life that may not be healthy. If views of the person and the society can be ranged along a continuum between those that emphasize the moral embeddedness of the individual in a community and those that emphasize the isolation of the autonomous individual, then advertising typically falls near the latter end of the continuum.

Advertising offers and is expressive of an ideology of choice. It unifies us around a belief in difference, variety, abundance, pluralism, choice, democracy. Consumer culture and advertising, along with elections, are the most important institutions that promote an ideology of choice. Yet while elections and advertising do present real choices, they also distract us from the structure of choosing, the hidden choices behind the choices. We become fascinated with the agenda and forget who sets it. And perhaps we come to believe, at bottom, that popular sovereignty governs both politics and economic life. So if the politician is corrupt, we learn to say that "we get what we deserve." And if the product fails, we learn to say that "you get what you pay for." We learn to dissent by exit rather than by voice. We are instructed in choice but not in living with or against the choices we make.

In the past generation, people have listened to one set of voices from the East and have borrowed notions of a simple life, a life of self-discipline and self-denial, from Buddhist traditions of Asia. Now we are listening to a different set of voices from a different East—the voices of Yeltsins and the unashamed emulation of economic abundance. Eastern European nations, as symbol and substance of their legitimacy on a world stage, are seeking to partake in the kind of consumer affluence the West has enjoyed for two generations.

We see this and it should stir us to question our received criticisms of consumer culture. At the same time, we have growing concerns about environmental and ecological catastrophe and the distribution of consumption not only among rich and poor within a society but among rich and poor nations within a world system. We should not learn the lessons of Eastern Europe so well as to deny ourselves the right to criticize consumerism. But it must be a new critique. Freeing ourselves from Biblical or republican or Marxist moralisms and recognizing a certain dignity and rationality in the desire for material goods, we should seek to reconstruct an understanding of our moral and political view of consumption that we and others can live with.

> *"Ad media purposely utilize symbolism [a subliminal technique] to sell products, ideas, and personalities."*

Subliminal Persuasion Is a Threat

Wilson Bryan Key

Wilson Bryan Key is the author of several books on subliminal persuasion—the theory that human behavior can be controlled by messages that bypass conscious perception and operate directly on the unconscious mind. He is best known for his assertion that violent, gruesome, and sexual images appealing to unconscious impulses are commonly embedded in the ice cubes of alcoholic beverage ads. In the following viewpoint, he discusses the subliminal use of archetypal symbols in advertising. Key's books include *Subliminal Seduction*, *The Clam-Plate Orgy*, *Media Sexploitation*, and *The Age of Manipulation*, from which the following viewpoint is excerpted.

As you read, consider the following questions:

1. How do symbols affect people, according to Key?
2. According to the author, what are the three most important human experiences? What are their symbolic meanings?
3. Why are ads that contain symbols of male genitalia directed at men, and those that display symbols of female genitalia aimed at women, according to Key?

A*rchetypal* literally means "the original form." There have been numerous theories that archetypal symbolic meanings are innate, inherited aspects of genetic heritage. They are found in sight and sound, and in smell, taste, and touch. Archetypal symbols were first discussed in the writings of third-century scholar-priest Saint Augustine. He discovered religious symbols with similar meanings in cultures that had had no known contact over long time periods. Saint Augustine attributed archetypal symbolism to "the hand of God."

Archetypal symbols of one sort or another are common to all cultures and peoples. Symbolic meanings generally involve unconscious perceptual mechanisms and underlie conscious definitions. Humans label consciously, but symbolic significance remains at an unconscious level. Archetypal symbols usually involve the two polarities of human existence—the beginning (reproduction, birth, rebirth) and the end (death, actual or symbolic). These two polarities of human experience have been the major preoccupations of philosophy, literature, art, and religious thought for thousands of years. . . .

Symbols circumvent conscious thought and logic. They evoke vague, unspecific feelings. Symbolism constitutes a subliminal technique of communication. Sophisticated, carefully researched, and powerful symbolic communication is basic to commercial manipulation. Symbols directly affect perception, feelings, and behavior. They do not depend upon conscious definitions or explanations. . . .

Birth, Reproduction, and Death

In his *Letter IV*, Saint Augustine explained that "teaching accomplished with symbols feeds and stirs the fires of love which help humans excel and surpass themselves." Archetypal symbols appear as rich and varied as do life situations. Repetition of certain life events over thousands of years may have engraved these into human predispositions or memory. The most important experiences are, of course, birth, reproduction, and death. These are the basic subjects around which most of the world's religions, philosophies, literatures, arts, and other deeply meaningful experiences focus. Even with modern pretensions to scientific objectivity, these fundamental experiences are still perceived as magical, their specific details and implications usually repressed from conscious awareness. These three fundamental human experiences still carry near universal ritualistic, spiritual, religious, and superstitious significance. . . . The symbolic significance of these three events appears vital to individual and social human survival. Every known religion, state, and social group has sought to control and utilize these three common human experiences for power or profit. Symbolic values related to these experiences powerfully affect behavior, while conscious awareness of these effects remains repressed.

As an archetypal symbol, birth has little to do with biological sex or reproduction. Unconsciously, birth symbolically relates to such human enigmas as *where did I come from, what was the beginning of existence, feeling, knowing,* and *why do I exist?* The human body and its functions, early in life, become the primary unconsciously perceived reality. Symbolic separation and independence from the mother also appears a basic, universal human dilemma.

Subliminal Hostility

If you define subliminal ads as those that appeal on an unconscious level as well as a conscious one, then subliminals surely exist. The best example is Newport's long-running and immensely successful "Alive With Pleasure!" campaign. The photos always show outdoorsy yuppies horsing around. But amid all this jollity, there is a strong undercurrent of sexual hostility, usually directed at women. . . . Women are about to be clanged by a pair of cymbals, carried off on a pole, pulled along in a horse collar, or slam-dunked in the face by a basketball-wielding male.

John Leo, *U.S. News & World Report,* July 15, 1991.

Sexual reproduction unconsciously symbolizes, on one hand, a threat to independence and autonomy. On the other hand, however, are the deep symbolic implications of love, bonding, intimacy, search for identity, creativity, eternal life through reproduction, transference, and purification. The unconscious significance of sex within the human psyche extends far deeper than the silly banalities of ad media's pornographic, kick-trip-oriented manipulations.

The most fearsome, private event is death, both in reality and in symbolic terms. Death symbolizes the conclusion of human existence, the ultimate tragedy, the end of feeling, aspiration, expectation, the entrance into the truly great unknown, and—as alluded to in Genesis—"the return to dust.". . .

Manipulating Symbols of Reproduction

Ad media purposely utilize symbolism to sell products, ideas, and personalities. The most intensely exploited, visible area of symbolic manipulation surrounds human reproduction. Sexuality is clearly the area of human experience most vulnerable to manipulation, exploitation, and the eventual development of neurotic and psychotic behaviors. This appears especially true in the acquisitive value systems of Western societies, but probably all humans share a similar vulnerability.

One Oscar Mayer sliced meat ad is typical of archetypal symbolism applied to merchandising and consumer manipulation. The ad was widely and expensively published in national men's magazines such as *Esquire* and *Gentleman's Quarterly* (*GQ*). The Italian-style beef slices on the left are styled to form a male genital, the cracked black pepper ham slices on the right form a somewhat smaller genital, though perhaps, as the copy explains, "more sharp and peppery." Remember, these symbols were directed at male unconscious perception. The female genital is symbolically represented in the center by smoked chicken breast slices. A recessive area has been subtly painted on the roasted chicken, suggesting female genitalia around the visceral cavity opening. Few macho males could resist the expectational fantasy of two men and a woman intermixing their genitalia. The Oscar Mayer ménage à trois reflects a sexual extravaganza, with male homosexual implications.

Symbolic imagery circumvents conscious, critical thought. It involves not only pictures but also words and numbers. The three symbolic representations in "Select Slices" unconsciously convey spiritual synthesis, childbirth, conflict resolution, harmony, and unity—all associated with heaven or the Trinity. Had the artist utilized a two-, four-, or five-part arrangement, unconscious meanings would have changed. The "select" consumer who unconsciously identifies with the Oscar Mayer ad never consciously considers the expensive artwork significant.

The simple ad layout effectively optimizes the return on Oscar Mayer's media investment. The genital symbolism, in addition, is enhanced by the copy, which tells us that each meat is 95% fat-free. It would be far more medically important if the prospective consumers were 95% fat-free. U.S. readers have been trained to mindlessly accept, trust, and consciously ignore media. Any critical evaluation would quickly reduce the ad's effectiveness.

Phallic and Vaginal Symbols

Almost any erect, long, stiff object can be deliberately engineered into a phallic symbol adaptable to mass-communication media. Audiences are rarely aware of what is going on. Awareness, of course, immediately puts the audience back into control, cancels or at least diminishes the ad's potential to modify behavior. For symbols to motivate sales, they must be consciously perceived as functional or logical. In ad media, phallic symbols are regularly developed from walking sticks, broom handles, fish, neckties, bananas, candles, flagpoles, skyscrapers, lampposts, whales, trees, obelisks, towers, lighthouses, space rockets, weapons, chimneys, cannons, elephant trunks, birds, swords, lances, spears, ejaculating champagne bottles, keys, cigarettes, cigars, automobiles, airplanes, electric guitars, microphones, thumbs and fingers—the list is endless.

Vaginal symbols are as rich in variety as the phallic. Female genitalia can be insinuated by almost any elliptical opening—a skin crevice under an arm, knee, elbow, or the rim of a glass or cup. In one Chivas Regal ad, the phallic bottle penetrates the elliptical rim of the whiskey glass. Similarly, the rim on the dip cup in one McDonald's ad has been penetrated by the symbolic seminal fluid dripping from the Chicken McNugget. . . .

Casual examination of ads reveals an imaginative assortment of deliberate genital symbols. Curiously, the male genitalia ads appear directed at male consumers, the female genitalia ads at females. Through trial and error, advertisers became convinced ads sell far better via this seeming contradiction. Psychological explanations are tentative. Arguments have been made that such ads appeal to latent homosexuality in both men and women, and that by increasing the taboo nature of the stimuli, consumers become more involved, responsive, and vulnerable. To the ad huckster, it really doesn't matter as long as the ad sells.

A Powerful Mind Massage

In a thirty-second TV ad for Wishbone salad dressing, subliminal techniques and symbolism combine into a powerful mind massage. The brand label "Wishbone" alludes to magic, belief in resurrection, and, in Hebrew tradition, an indestructible tree and its inner, hidden, inviolable heart. Subliminal meanings are often hidden in video superimpositions—one scene fades as a new scene emerges. Subliminals are easily concealed in this transition. Unless the transition is taped and viewed one frame at a time, the flimflam remains hidden from consciousness. The Wishbone TV ad is a technological masterpiece.

The transition begins with a voluptuous model swimming in a tropical lagoon. As she shoots up from the water, arms and legs apart, the scene transfers to a head of lettuce held by two female hands. The thumbs holding the lettuce appear to press on the model's genital area. As the swimsuit model fades, the lettuce is split in half, symbolically as though a birth had occurred. Emerging from the V-split lettuce head, now appears the symbolic Wishbone bottle. The bottle design includes a male phallic upper portion and an elliptical female bottom—the symbolic unity of male and female in a romantic tropical setting. The scene changes to a head shot of the model, who appears to be licking the female portion of the bottle. As the bottle fades, the model's tongue appears as a tomato in her mouth. The four transitions occur sequentially in less than ten symbolically powerful seconds. Every detail records perceptually at unconscious levels. Tomatoes (also called love apples) and lettuce are symbolic of birth, spring, resurrection, abundance, fertility, fecundity, and regeneration of life. Tomatoes symbolize love; lettuce symbolizes spring and a renewal of life.

Birth, reproduction, and finally death provide strong, underlying archetypal themes for numerous ads. The Seagram's Crown Royal broken bottle is an example of a subliminal death appeal, inviting the drinker to self-immolate and destruct. Castration is another archetypal death symbol. The death wish is one of the most well-articulated theories in psychological literature—an innate compulsion to seek death, either actually or symbolically.

Numerous ads for alcohol and tobacco were illustrated in earlier studies of subliminal perception. A castrated penis, skulls, and nightmare monster faces appeared in a Johnny Walker ad. The word *cancer* was embedded in a two-page Benson and Hedges cigarette ad. Bizarre skulls, scorpions, dead birds, and sharks were embedded in Bacardi and Calvert ads. All these expensively manufactured images are archetypal symbols, personifications of death and self-destruction. They were expensively engineered, tested, and applied as marketing techniques. They sell, or are believed by the advertisers to sell. They have made a great deal of money for advertisers. What the ads accomplished for defenseless consumers can be perceived in public-health statistics. . . .

No one has, as yet, made serious long-term investigations into the eventual effects of ad-media flimflam upon human personality, mental health, behavior, and survival. The U.S. blindly allows the commercial establishment to inflict avaricious self-interest upon the entire population. Virtually no one appears to hear the faint ticking of our time running out.

> *"Now is the time to lay the myth of subliminal sorcery to rest."*

Subliminal Persuasion Is a Myth

Anthony R. Pratkanis

Many people believe in the power of subliminal persuasion—the theory that human behavior can be controlled with messages that bypass conscious perception and operate directly on the unconscious mind. In the following viewpoint, Anthony R. Pratkanis argues that while evidence exists that proves messages can reach the mind subliminally—that is, other than through conscious perception—little evidence supports the assumption that these messages can control human behavior. Pratkanis contends that people believe in subliminal persuasion, in spite of the lack of scientific credibility, because it confirms whatever life philosophy they subscribe to. Pratkanis is an associate professor of psychology at the University of California, Santa Cruz, and a coauthor of the book *Age of Propaganda*.

As you read, consider the following questions:

1. According to the author, what is a "cargo-cult science"?
2. How should science teachers respond to Wilson Bryan Key's assertions, according to Pratkanis?
3. According to the author, what is the cost of society's belief in subliminal persuasion?

From "The Cargo-Cult Science of Subliminal Persuasion" by Anthony R. Pratkanis, *Skeptical Inquirer*, Spring 1992. Reprinted by permission of the Committee for the Scientific Investigation of Claims of the Paranormal.

Imagine that it is the late 1950s—a time just after the Korean War, when terms like *brainwashing* and *mind control* were on the public's mind and films like the *Manchurian Candidate* depicted the irresistible influence of hypnotic trances. You and your friend are off to see *Picnic*, one of the more popular films of the day. However, the movie theater, located in Fort Lee, New Jersey, is unlike any you have been in before. Unbeknownst to you, the projectors have been equipped with a special device capable of flashing short phrases onto the movie screen at such a rapid speed that you are unaware that any messages have been presented. During the film, you lean over to your companion and whisper, "Gee, I'd love a tub of buttered popcorn and a Coke right now." To which he replies, "You're always hungry and thirsty at movies, shhhhh." But after a few moments he says, "You know, some Coke and popcorn might not be a bad idea."

A short time later you hear that you and your friend weren't the only ones desiring popcorn and Coke at the theater that day. According to reports in newspapers and magazines, James Vicary, an advertising expert, had secretly flashed, at a third of a millisecond, the words "Eat Popcorn" and "Drink Coke" onto the movie screen. His studies, lasting six weeks, involved thousands of moviegoing subjects who received a subliminal message every five seconds during the film. Vicary claimed an increase in Coke sales of 18 percent and a rise in popcorn sales of almost 58 percent. Upon reading their newspapers, most people were outraged and frightened by a technique so devilish that it could bypass their conscious intellect and beam *subliminal* commands directly to their subconscious.

A Smudge on America's Consciousness

In an article titled "Smudging the Subconscious," Norman Cousins captured similar feelings as he pondered the true meaning of such a device. As he put it, "If the device is successful for putting over popcorn, why not politicians or anything else?" He wondered about the character of people who would dream up a machine to "break into the deepest and most private parts of the human mind and leave all sorts of scratchmarks." Cousins concluded that the best course of action would be "to take this invention and everything connected to it and attach it to the center of the next nuclear explosive scheduled for testing."

Cousins's warnings were taken to heart. The Federal Communications Commission immediately investigated the Vicary study and ruled that the use of subliminal messages could result in the loss of a broadcast license. The National Association of Broadcasters prohibited the use of subliminal advertising by its members. Australia and Britain banned subliminal advertising. A Nevada judge ruled that subliminal communications are not protected as free speech.

The Vicary study also left an enduring smudge on Americans' consciousness—if not their *sub*conscious. As a teacher of social psychology and a persuasion researcher, one of the questions I am most frequently asked is, "Do you know about the 'Eat Popcorn/Drink Coke' study that *they* did?" At cocktail parties, I am often pulled aside and, in hushed tones, told about the "Eat Popcorn/Drink Coke" study. Indeed, my original interest in subliminal persuasion was motivated by an attempt to know how to respond to such questions.

Three public-opinion polls indicate that the American public shares my students' fascination with subliminal influence. By 1958, just nine months after the Vicary subliminal story first broke, 41 percent of survey respondents had heard of subliminal advertising. This figure climbed to 81 percent in the early 1980s, with more than 68 percent of those aware of the term believing that it was effective in selling products. Most striking, the surveys also revealed that many people learn about subliminal influence through the mass media and through courses in high school and college.

But there is a seamier side to the "Eat Popcorn/Drink Coke" study—one that is rarely brought to public attention. In a 1962 interview with *Advertising Age*, James Vicary announced that the original study was a fabrication intended to increase customers for his failing marketing business. The circumstantial evidence suggests that this time Vicary was telling the truth. . . .

Little Evidence

The "Eat Popcorn/Drink Coke" affair is not an isolated incident. The topic of subliminal persuasion has attracted the interest of Americans on at least four separate occasions: at the turn of the century, in the 1950s, in the 1970s, and in the late 1980s and early 1990s. Each of these four flourishings of subliminal persuasion show a similar course of events. First, someone claims to find an effect; next, others attempt to replicate that effect and fail; the original finding is then criticized on methodological grounds; nevertheless the original claim is publicized and gains acceptance in lay audiences and the popular imagination. Today we have reached a point where one false effect from a previous era is used to validate a false claim from another. For example, I recently had the occasion to ask a manufacturer of subliminal self-help audiotapes for evidence of his claim that his tapes had therapeutic value. His reply: "You are a psychologist. Don't you know about the study they did where they flashed 'Eat Popcorn and Drink Coke' on the movie screen?"

During the past few years, I have been collecting published articles on subliminal processes—research that goes back over a hundred years and includes more than a hundred articles from the mass media and more than two hundred academic papers on the topic. In none of these papers is there clear evidence in support of the proposition that subliminal messages influence behavior. Many of the studies fail to find an effect, and those that do either cannot be reproduced or are fatally flawed on one or more methodological grounds, including: the failure to control for subject expectancy and experimenter bias effects, selective reporting of positive over negative findings, lack of appropriate control treatments, internally inconsistent results, unreliable dependent measures, presentation of stimuli in a manner that is not truly subliminal, and multiple experimental confounds specific to each study. As T.E. Moore points out, there is considerable evidence for subliminal perception or the detection of information outside of self-reports of awareness. However, subliminal perception should *not* be confused with subliminal persuasion or influence—motivating or changing behavior—for which there is little good evidence.

No Reliable Evidence

One hundred ninety nine professors of advertising from journalism, communication and marketing settings responded to a questionnaire involving subliminal advertising. These academics had an average of 13 years teaching and 9 years of trade experience. Less than three percent felt that subliminal advertising was used "always" or "often." Another eight percent felt it was used "sometimes.". . . In sum, although it is impossible to completely disprove the existence of the use of subliminal advertising, there is no reliable evidence that the technique is commonly employed.

Eric J. Zanot, *Advertising and Popular Culture: Studies in Variety and Versatility*, 1992.

It seems to me that our fascination with subliminal persuasion is yet another example of what Richard Feynman called "cargo-cult science." For Feynman, a cargo-cult science is one that has all the trappings of science—the illusion of objectivity, the appearance of careful study, and the motions of an experiment—but lacks one important ingredient: skepticism, or a leaning over backward to see if one might be mistaken. The essence of science is to doubt your own interpretations and theories so that you may improve upon them. This skepticism is often missing in the interpretation of studies claiming to find subliminal influence. Our theories and wishes for what we would like to think the human mind is capable of doing interferes with our ability to see what it actually does.

272

The cargo-cult nature of subliminal research can be seen in some of the first studies on the topic done at the turn of the century. In 1900, K. Dunlap reported a subliminal Müller-Lyer illusion—a well-known illusion in which a line is made to appear shorter or longer depending on the direction of angles placed at its ends. Dunlap flashed an "imperceptible shadow" or line to subliminally create this illusion. He claimed that his subjects' judgment of length was influenced by the imperceptible shadows. However, Dunlap's results could not be immediately replicated by either E.B. Titchener and W.H. Pyle (1907) or by H.M. Manro and M.F. Washburn (1908). Nevertheless, this inconsistency of findings did not stop H.L. Hollingworth (1913) from discussing the subliminal Müller-Lyer illusion in his advertising textbook or from drawing the conclusion that subliminal influence is a powerful tool available to the advertiser. . . .

Key's Legacy

In the early 1970s, during the third wave of popular interest in subliminal persuasion, the best-selling author Wilson Bryan Key advanced the cargo-cult science of subliminal seduction in two ways. First, Key argued that subliminal techniques were not just limited to television and movies. Cleverly hidden messages aimed at inducing sexual arousal are claimed to be embedded in the photographs of print advertisements. Key found the word *sex* printed on everything from Ritz crackers to the ice cubes in a Gilbey Gin ad. Second, Key was successful in linking the concept of subliminal persuasion to the issues of his day. The 1970s were a period of distrust by Americans of their government, businesses, and institutions. Key claimed that big advertisers and big government are in a conspiracy to control our minds using subliminal implants.

The legacy of Key's cargo-cult science is yet with us. I often ask my students at the University of California, Santa Cruz, if they have heard of the term *subliminal persuasion* and, if so, where. Almost all have heard of the term and about half report finding out about it in high school. Many received an assignment from their teachers to go to the library and look through magazine ads for subliminal implants.

These teachers miss an opportunity to teach science instead of cargo-cult science. Key reports a study where more than a thousand subjects were shown the Gilbey Gin ad that supposedly contained the word sex embedded in ice cubes. Sixty-two percent of the subjects reported feeling "aroused," "romantic," "sensuous." Instead of assuming that Key was right and sending students out to find subliminals, a science educator would encourage a student to ask, "But where is the control group in the Gilbey Gin ad study?" Perhaps an even higher percentage would report feeling sexy if the subliminal "sex" was removed—perhaps the same, perhaps less. One just doesn't know. . . .

Ill-Directed Faith

The history of the subliminal controversy teaches us much about persuasion—but not the subliminal kind. If there is so little scientific evidence of the effectiveness of subliminal influence, why then do so many Americans believe it works? In a nutshell, I must conclude, with Feynman, that despite enjoying the fruits of science, we are not a scientific culture, but one of ill-directed faith as defined in Hebrews 11:1 (KJV): "Now faith is the substance of things hoped for, the evidence of things not seen."

We can see the workings of this faulty faith, not science, in the more than a hundred popular press articles on the topic of subliminal persuasion. Many of the articles (36 percent) deal with ethical and regulatory concerns of subliminal practices—assuming them to be effective. Only 18 percent of the articles declare flatly that subliminal influence is ineffective, with the remaining either claiming that it works or suggesting a big "maybe" to prompt readers' concern. In general, popular press articles fail to rely on scientific evidence and method to critically evaluate subliminal findings. Positive findings are emphasized and null results rarely reported. Problems with positive subliminal findings, such as lack of control groups, expectancy effects, setting subliminal thresholds, and so on, are rarely mentioned. If negative information is given, it is often presented at the end of the article, giving the reader the impression that, at best, the claims for subliminal effectiveness are somewhat controversial. Recent coverage of subliminal self-help tapes, however, have been less supportive of subliminal claims—but this may reflect more of an attack on big business than an embrace of science.

The "Witch Test"

Instead of the scientific method, those accused of subliminal persuasion (mostly advertisers) are subjected to what can be termed the "witch test." During the Middle Ages, one common test of witchcraft was to tie and bind the accused and throw her into a pond. If she floats, she is a witch. If she drowns, then her innocence is affirmed. Protestations by the accused were taken as further signs of guilt.

How do we know that subliminals work and that advertisers use them? As Key notes, advertisers spend a considerable amount of money on communications that contain subliminal messages. Why would they spend such vast sums if subliminal persuasion is ineffective? The fact that these subliminal messages cannot be readily identified or seen and that the advertisers deny their use further demonstrates the craftiness of the advertiser. After all, witches are a wiley lot, carefully covering their tracks. It appears that the only way that advertisers can prove their innocence, by the logic of the witch test, is to go out of business at the bottom of the pond, thereby showing that they do not possess the arts of subliminal sorcery. In contrast, just as the motives of the Inquisition for power and fortune went unquestioned, so too the motives of the proponents of subliminal seduction, who frequently profit by the sale of more newspapers, books, or audiotapes, are rarely (or have only recently been) questioned.

The Benefits of Belief

The proponents of subliminal persuasion make use of our most sacred expectations, hopes, and fears. Each manifestation of interest in subliminal influence has been linked to the important philosophies and thinking of the day—New Thought [the belief that the mind possesses an unlimited but hidden power] in the 1900s, brainwashing in the 1950s, the corruption of big governments in the 1970s, and New Age philosophy today.

But the belief in subliminal persuasion provides much more for the individual. We live in an age of propaganda; the average American will see approximately seven million advertisements in a lifetime. We provide our citizens with very little education concerning the nature of these persuasive processes. The result is that many may feel confused and bewildered by basic social processes. The negative side of subliminal persuasion is presented as an irrational force outside the control of the message recipient. As such, it takes on a supernatural "devil made me do it" quality capable of justifying and explaining why Americans are often persuaded and can seemingly engage in irrational behavior. Why then did I buy this worthless product at such a high price? Subliminal sorcery. On the positive side, a belief in subliminal persuasion imbues the human spirit at least with the possibility of overcoming the limitations of being human and of living a mundane existence. We can be like the gods—healing ourselves, finding enjoyment in everything we do, working for the benefit of humankind by tapping our own self potentials. Perhaps our theories of what should be or what we would like to be have caused us to be a little less critical of the claims for the power of subliminal influence.

Lay the Myth to Rest

But belief in subliminal persuasion is not without its cost. Perhaps the saddest aspect of the subliminal affair is that it distracts our attention from more substantive issues. By looking for subliminal influences, we may ignore more powerful, blatant influence tactics employed by advertisers and sales agents. We may ignore other, more successful ways—such as science—for reaching our human potentials.

Consider the tragic suicide deaths of teenagers Ray Belknap and James Vance that were brought to light in the recent trial of Judas Priest. They lived troubled lives—lives of drug and alcohol abuse, run-ins with the law, learning disabilities, family violence, and chronic unemployment. What issues did the trial and the subsequent mass-media coverage emphasize? Certainly not the need for drug treatment centers; there was no evaluation of the pros and cons of America's juvenile justice system, no investigation of the schools, no inquiry into how to prevent family violence, no discussion of the effects of unemployment on a family. Instead, our attention was mesmerized by an attempt to count the number of subliminal demons that can dance on the end of a record needle.

In this trial, Judge Jerry Carr Whitehead (*Vance & Belknap* v. *Judas Priest & CBS Records* 1990) ruled in favor of Judas Priest, stating: "The scientific research presented does not establish that subliminal stimuli, even if perceived, may precipitate conduct of this magnitude. There exist other factors which explain the conduct of the deceased independent of the subliminal stimuli." Perhaps now is the time to lay the myth of subliminal sorcery to rest and direct our attention to other, more scientifically documented ways of understanding the causes of human behavior and improving our condition.

"A total ban on both cigarette advertising and promotion is necessary."

Cigarette Advertisements Should Be Banned

Larry C. White

In the following viewpoint, Larry C. White argues that cigarette advertisements should be banned because they are deceitful and they threaten the health of Americans. Furthermore, a ban on cigarette ads would not violate the First Amendment, says White, because—unlike "noncommercial" speech, which cannot be censored—advertisements are examples of "commercial" speech, which is subject to governmental regulation. White is a lawyer and the author of *Merchants of Death: The American Tobacco Industry*.

As you read, consider the following questions:

1. What are the four criteria used to determine whether commercial speech warrants protection, according to White?
2. According to the author, why is a ban on cigarette advertisements not an overly extensive measure?

"Is Cigarette Advertising Protected by the First Amendment?" by Larry C. White, *Priorities*, Summer 1993. Reprinted by permission of the American Council on Science and Health.

A few years ago Philip Morris (PM) made a deal with the National Archives. For $600,000, PM was given the right to associate itself with the Bill of Rights. At least one person I know thought that the world's largest cigarette maker had bought the original document (actually there are several originals). But what PM wanted was not the old parchment—it wanted to buy the living substance of the First Amendment and pervert it to protect cigarette advertising.

Using First Amendment sentiments, the tobacco people say: "Where do you draw the line? If you start banning cigarette advertising where will you stop? What disfavored product will be hit next?"

This argument very cleverly echoes civil libertarian themes. Our nation was founded by disestablishmentarians. There was to be no official orthodoxy. In practice this meant that the government was not to persecute unpopular religions and beliefs.

Since tobacco has become unpopular with the majority of Americans, the tobacco people have tried to identify themselves as a potentially persecuted minority. We all know that it is bad to take rights away from a group merely because they are in disfavor. The dismal history of the twentieth century in much of the world demonstrates how taking the rights away from one group often leads to widening circles of repression. (Nazi Germany is the classic case—first Jews, then Gypsies, homosexuals, the retarded. . . .)

Commercial vs. Noncommercial Speech

But wait a minute. Can a commercial product, whatever its characteristics, be in the same constitutional category as a minority of people? Does it make sense to worry that discrimination against cigarettes might lead to discrimination against toothpaste or that banning cigarette advertising could embolden government to censor Coke commercials? Let's get real. Regulation of advertising is part of the government's obligation to police the marketplace. Snake oil ads are forbidden; mineral oil ads are not.

Regulation of commercial "speech" is fundamentally different from noncommercial speech. Just look at this basic First Amendment principle: government may not inquire into whether protected speech is true or false. In regulating such speech, the government must be content neutral. The government cannot decide that one viewpoint or idea may be heard while another will be censored.

Obviously, this principle does not apply to commercial speech. Government inquires into the truth of claims made in ads all the time and may ban those that are false. The Supreme Court declared the following in 1976 in the first case that gave commercial speech some limited protection *[Virginia Board of Pharmacy v. Virginia Citizens' Council]*:

> The First Amendment as we construe it today does not prohibit the state from insuring that the stream of commercial information flows cleanly as well as freely.

Contrast this with noncommercial speech. Government may not censor even the worst racist Nazis—no matter how hate-filled and "dirty" their speech.

Luring Young People to Cigarettes

Although cigarettes are no longer advertised on television, cigarette marketing is a thriving business. Through a staggering variety of activities and distribution of goods, it keeps its appeal to youth going strong—in the form of youth-oriented events, displays at sporting events and distribution of promotional items such as T-shirts, posters, and caps. These items are typical of such marketing schemes around the country.

After all, the tobacco industry must replenish the half million smokers who die each year from smoking-related disease and the one million who quit!

I am deeply concerned that many young people are lured to start smoking and using tobacco by these aggressive marketing ploys.

Antonia C. Novello, speech delivered at the Center for Substance Abuse Prevention, Washington, D.C., February 8, 1993.

The simple fact is that government does regulate (and ban) numerous types of commercial "speech." Insurance companies are forbidden by law to publish "scare" advertising or to advertise certain products to older people. Federal regulations define within very narrow limits what can be said by those who sell securities. Statutes regarding insider trading forbid speech that might lead to abuse—even certain casual remarks on the golf course; antitrust warnings are read aloud to participants in intra-industry meetings to warn them not to say certain things to each other.

Since 1976, the Supreme Court has struggled with the limits of "commercial free speech." Finally, in the 1980 decision of *Central Hudson Gas and Electric Corp. v. Public Service Commission*, the Court developed a four part analysis to decide whether any particular type of commercial expression was protected by the First Amendment:

1. Does the "speech" in question concern lawful activity and is it not misleading?

2. Is the government interest in suppressing it "substantial"?

If both questions can be answered in the affirmative, then:

3. Does the particular type of regulation directly advance the asserted government interest?

4. Is the regulation not more extensive than necessary to serve that interest?

Let's subject cigarette advertising to this test. Oops!—It fails the very first point. While smoking is legal, cigarette advertising clearly is misleading. Smoking is the number one cause of premature, preventable death and disease in our society. The whole purpose of cigarette advertising is to make people forget that central fact. If that is not misleading, I'm the Marlboro Man.

True, cigarette advertising makes no health claims anymore, but its images convey youth, vitality, fun—in short, health. Also, the medium is the message. It's hard for young people, in particular, to believe that government would allow unlimited advertising of a product that kills 450,000 Americans each year and is more addictive than heroin.

But, just for fun, let's say that cigarette advertising is not the conspiracy of deception that it really is and proceed down the Court's analytical list. Is the governmental interest in suppressing cigarette advertising "substantial"? That interest is protecting the health of young people, let's say. Any court would say that is a substantial state interest.

Would a ban on cigarette advertising directly advance the government's interest in protecting the health of young people? Consider Joe Camel. He's the cartoon figure pictured in airplanes and submarines and at beach parties on the pages of magazines read by teens and pre-teens. Does he make smoking attractive to kids? You can be sure that R.J. Reynolds wouldn't spend hundreds of millions of dollars to put his ugly mug everywhere if he didn't.

Would a ban on cigarette advertising be more extensive than necessary to promote the health of America's young people? Well, we've had warning labels on cigarette packs and advertising for twenty years now and there are still fifty million smokers. The rate of smoking among young women may be on the rise. Camels are increasing their share of the cigarette market, especially with youthful smokers—a real advertising success story. The existence of cigarette advertising as well as its content effectively negates health warnings of all types.

A Total Ban

Actually, a total ban on both cigarette advertising and promotion is necessary. Otherwise, the tobacco companies will simply transfer their vast resources to whatever type of promotion is permitted. Foreign experience shows that partial bans have little effect on consumption. Total bans, such as that in Norway, have made significant inroads against smoking, particularly among the young.

Would a ban on cigarette promotion erode the principle of free speech? Let's not forget that this principle, when applied to advertising, was invented in 1976, not 1776. "Commercial free speech" will probably go the way of a theory such as "economic due process" (which forbade the regulation of child labor). The product of a fleeting Supreme Court majority, it was untenable as a guiding principle of constitutional law. Can anyone seriously believe that the First Amendment was intended to protect the right of a powerful industry to use highly sophisticated methods of mass persuasion to sell a deadly and addictive product?

> "The antidote for allegedly harmful speech is not government-imposed censorship, but more speech from more sources."

Cigarette Advertisements Should Not Be Banned

Michael G. Gartner

In the following viewpoint, Michael G. Gartner argues that cigarette ads should not be banned. He contests the common charge that cigarette ads lead to increased smoking among young people. Although he concedes that cigarettes are a national health threat, he concludes that more speech, rather than restrictions on speech, will provide the public with the information it needs to make informed decisions. Gartner is a lawyer and the author of *Advertising and the First Amendment*, from which this viewpoint is excerpted. After completing this book, he went on to become president of NBC News.

As you read, consider the following questions:

1. Many people contend that cigarette advertisements harm children. What does Gartner mean when he calls this a "backdoor approach to fiddling with freedom of expression"?
2. According to Dr. Scott Ward, whom the author quotes, what influences young people to smoke?

In these health-conscious days, it has become fashionable for commentators on all sides to join the ban-the-cigarette-ad campaign, usually out of sincere belief that smoking is deadly. It is, of course, but so is tampering with freedom. Liberals back the ban in the interests of social reform. Conservatives back it in the guise of paternalistic concern for the weak of will. And the weakest, these commentators argue, are our children.

Consider the position of George Will, the conservative columnist, television commentator, friend of first ladies, and Chicago Cubs fan: "Examine the average cigarette advertisement—toothsome young people frolicking in surf, a picture of a mountain meadow, slogans such as 'Get a taste of it' or 'Come to where the flavor is.' Try to measure the information content. Cigarette advertisements are not seminars; they are inducements. . . ." These inducements, he says, are especially effective on young people. "The evidence from the nations with the severest limits on cigarette advertising is that after such advertising is limited, adult smokers continue but fewer young people start." Therefore, says Will, the government should protect the young by limiting what they hear.

As for the First Amendment, Will dismisses it as "an amendment to a political document. Its primary protection is for speech related to the process by which we govern ourselves— the working of representative government and the cultural activities that nourish a free society."

A Slippery Slope

Shouldn't we go further, then, and protect the young from hearing about things other than the social joys of smoking? Shouldn't we protect them from hearing about the pleasures of sex? Why not ban advertising for explicit books and movies and even suggestive clothes? Liquor kills, just as cigarettes do. Sex, through AIDS, kills. And what about the sun? Should we allow Florida to advertise the joys of sunshine now that we know that the sun causes cancer?

Will is not far from banning Bogie. But tobacco is unique, argue those who favor banning cigarette ads. The Toronto *Globe and Mail*, announcing in 1986 that it would no longer run tobacco ads, offered this explanation: "Why single out tobacco? Because unlike even alcohol, whose abuse can destroy the lives of drinkers and create other victims, tobacco is unsafe when used *precisely the way the manufacturer intends* [emphasis in original]." Ban proponents always argue that a tobacco ad ban would not lead down the slippery slope to prohibiting other forms of advertising as well. "Tobacco is a unique danger," asserts a 1986 New York State Bar Association report by lawyer Henry C. Miller. "To say we cannot distinguish between tobacco and other products is absurd. It's the difference between the bubonic plague and the common cold."

The slippery slope argument, ban proponents say, wrongly assumes that legislators and judges do not know how to draw distinctions. As evidence, they note that the broadcast ban on tobacco ads has been in effect for more than fifteen years without spreading to other products.

In fact, every time commercial speech is singled out for censorship—gambling ads, ads for lawyers or doctors—advocates always argue that the speech is somehow "unique" and that the regulation would not be extended.

Too Much Power for the Government

A complete ban on tobacco advertising would give the government an opportunity to censor nonmisleading speech about a legal product, without leaving open alternative channels of communication. Nowhere in modern First Amendment law has the government ever been regarded as having such power.

Robert S. Peck, *Priorities*, Summer 1993.

Will and others focus on the effect of cigarette advertising on minors. Some witnesses at congressional hearings have contended that cigarette advertising actually is targeted at minors; since cigarette sales to minors are illegal in all but six states, they argue, all cigarette advertising itself should be illegal. After 1987 hearings on the ad-ban proposals [Rep. Mike Synar's "Health Protection Act of 1986"], Wally Snyder, a senior vice president of the American Advertising Federation, said the emphasis on minors represented a new way to justify a ban on otherwise-protected speech. It is a backdoor approach to fiddling with freedom of expression.

"Rep. Synar acknowledged that establishing a link between tobacco ads and minors might help overcome the First Amendment problems that hinder other congressmen from jumping onto the ad-ban wagon," *Advertising Age*, the trade publication, reported.

But this line of reasoning seems weak. In the 1950s, the Supreme Court ruled that it was wrong to "reduce the adult population . . . to reading only what is fit for children." Hollywood can make movies that cater to adults. Publishers can print books that are suitable mainly for adults. Editors can edit magazines with adult audiences in mind. It stands to reason that manufacturers can make products intended for use by adults and advertise those products, even if impressionable youngsters might see—and be enticed by—those advertisements.

Guy L. Smith IV, publisher of *Philip Morris* magazine, put a somewhat finer edge on this same point in 1987 in a guest column in *Adweek*. "There is simply no way to make an ad disappear should a child view it—no way other than censorship. But . . . limiting all information to that which is palatable to a child is unacceptable. The same logic would strip the libraries of great literature, the museums of great art and the media of any information that is remotely reflective of reality in today's troubled world."

Advertising Not to Blame

Apart from all this, there is evidence that advertising is not a significant influence on the decision by young people to smoke. On the contrary, say some experts, advertising is one of the least significant factors influencing smoking by teenagers. Dr. Scott Ward, author and professor of marketing at the University of Pennsylvania's Wharton School, maintains that those who favor banning tobacco advertising wrongly assert that such advertising causes children and teenagers to decide to smoke. Ward testified at a House subcommittee hearing that "the available evidence indicates that advertising is among the least influential factors involved—certainly not influential enough to warrant an advertising ban, even if we agreed that it is proper for the government to try to manipulate consumer behavior by suppressing information."

Ward testified that the most forceful determinants of smoking are parents and peers, both of whom "are much more important determinants of children's developing consumer behavior patterns than advertising." He concluded: "Most teenagers choose not to smoke, responding to the positive and negative influences in a manner that should satisfy antitobacco advocates. My own study of over 600 children and their parents demonstrated that even young children can and do develop skills to evaluate advertising."

So the idea of shielding children from advertising in order to protect them from the evils of smoking seems ill-advised.

It has no ground in the law.

It has no ground in marketing.

It has no ground in psychology.

The best way to convince your children not to smoke is simply to quit smoking yourself.

The worst way to teach them about democracy is to allow their freedoms to be chipped away. . . .

More Speech

The experts are split on the likely effects of an advertising ban. But even if the experts could agree that a ban would reduce domestic consumption, it would still be a bad idea. It is not the government's responsibility to reduce cigarette consumption. It is the government's responsibility to assure that people have all the information they need to make an informed personal decision about smoking.

Government should not be permitted to impose ignorance as a means of changing people's behavior. As John Seigenthaler, president of the American Society of Newspaper Editors and editor of the *Nashville Tennessean*, told the House subcommittee considering the Synar bill in 1987, "We always have protected our citizens from allegedly offensive or harmful information by providing more, not less information. Our Founding Fathers were clear and correct in their belief that the antidote for allegedly harmful speech is not government-imposed censorship, but more speech from more sources, calculated to permit the individual to make free, informed choices."

There is no question that smoking poses the greatest threat to our national health. Consider the evidence:

• The surgeon general has identified cigarette smoking as irrefutably the single most preventable cause of death in America.

• More than 350,000 Americans die from cigarette smoking each year. . . .

• Exposure to tobacco smoke increases the incidence of lung cancer in nonsmokers.

• Smoking is responsible for one-quarter of all deaths caused by fire.

• Smoking during pregnancy increases the risk of premature birth, spontaneous abortion, and stillbirth.

• The federal government spends more than $4 billion annually to treat smoking-related illnesses.

But should America do anything to curb tobacco advertising in the face of this devastation? No.

The premise of the First Amendment is that if the antismoking interests and the tobacco industry are left to compete in the marketplace of ideas, the truth about smoking will prevail. The experience of the antismoking ads in the 1960s bears this out. The right answer is to use all available information to persuade people not to smoke. The wrong answer is to stifle speech about smoking.

Periodical Bibliography

The following articles have been selected to supplement the diverse views presented in this chapter.

Nell Bernstein	"Selling the Cause: Advertising in the Public Interest," *Nuclear Times*, Spring 1992.
Bryce J. Christensen	"Sell Out: Advertising's Assault on the Family," *The Family in America*, February 1990. Available from 934 N. Main St., Rockford, IL 61103.
Peter F. Eder	"The Future of Advertising," *The Futurist*, July/August 1993.
Danny R. Johnson	"Tobacco Stains: Cigarette Firms Buy into African-American Groups," *The Progressive*, December 1992.
George F. Kennan	"American Addictions," *New Oxford Review*, June 1993. Available from 1069 Kains Ave., Berkeley, CA 94706.
Konstantin Kolenda	"Honesty in Advertising," *The Humanist*, November/December 1991.
John Leo	"Hostility Among the Ice Cubes," *U.S. News & World Report*, July 15, 1991.
Morton Mintz	"Marketing Tobacco to Children," *The Nation*, May 6, 1991.
Timothy E. Moore	"Subliminal Perception: Facts and Fallacies," *The Skeptical Inquirer*, Spring 1992.
Roger Neill	"The Vital Role of Advertising in Successful Economies," *Vital Speeches of the Day*, March 15, 1992.
Antonia C. Novello	"Alcohol and Tobacco Advertising: Prevention Indeed Works," *Vital Speeches of the Day*, May 15, 1993.
Robert Peck	"Is Advertising Protected by the First Amendment?" *Priorities*, Summer 1993. Available from 1995 Broadway, 2nd Fl., New York, NY 10023-5860.
Samantha Sanderson	"'You've Come a Long Way, Baby'—or Have You? The Way Advertisers View Women," *USA Today*, November 1990.
Jacob Sullum	"'Toons Out," *Reason*, May 1992.
Utne Reader	"Commercial Break," January/February 1992.

For Further Discussion

Chapter 1

1. Steven Allen enumerates seven methods to detect media bias in order to prove his contention that the American news media favor liberal views over conservative opinions. Michael Parenti, on the other hand, examines the spectrum of political talk shows and the press treatment of popular demonstrations to illustrate what he perceives to be a conservative bias in the media. Which approach is more convincing? Do you believe the news media reflect a liberal bias, a conservative bias, or a balanced view of events? Why?

2. Conservatives such as David Horowitz contend that the documentaries produced by the Public Broadcasting System (PBS) endorse left-wing political opinions. How does Eric Konigsberg counter this charge? What evidence does Konigsberg cite to substantiate his assertion that PBS supports a corporate ideology?

Chapter 2

1. Michael Medved cites various public opinion polls to support his assertion that the media do not reflect the values of most Americans. Douglas Davis, on the other hand, describes long-term social changes to substantiate his argument that the media reflect social realities. Which approach do you find more convincing? Why?

2. Susan Faludi relies on her own interpretive abilities to illustrate that American films reflect a societal backlash against feminism. Stanley Rothman, Stephen Powers, and David Rothman base their opposite conclusion that American films support feminism on a "systematic analysis." Based on the description of their method, do you believe their findings are reliable? Why or why not? Which viewpoint do you find more convincing? Explain.

3. J. Fred MacDonald cites the argument that television depictions of middle-class and upper-middle-class black families (such as that presented on *The Cosby Show*) are harmful because they gloss over the harsh realities of black life in America. Bishetta Merritt and Carolyn A. Stroman, on the other hand, argue that black family life as depicted on *The*

Cosby Show is beneficial because it encourages positive attitudes among black children. Do you agree with MacDonald or Merritt and Stroman? Why?

Chapter 3

1. David S. Barry argues that viewing violence in the media causes violent behavior. Examine the role of the mass media in your life. Do you believe the media have the power to influence your behavior? Explain.

2. Larry Woiwode contends that because it relies on images, television erodes analytical and verbal skills. Do you watch television? If so, do you believe that it affects your thinking and language skills for the better, for the worse, or not at all? Why?

Chapter 4

1. Patrick D. Maines and Danny Goldberg believe that government regulation of television violence would violate the television industry's freedom of speech. Newton N. Minow, Craig L. LaMay, and Megan Rosenfeld argue that the violent programming produced by the television industry is morally irresponsible and does not deserve First Amendment protection. Do you believe television violence constitutes free speech? Why or why not?

2. Do you believe that the execution of condemned criminals should be televised? Why or why not?

Chapter 5

1. Kathleen Hall Jamieson discusses the 1988 presidential campaign to illustrate her point that the media have reduced political discourse to sound bites. Samuel L. Popkin does not isolate any particular campaign to make his argument that media campaigns enhance voter knowledge. Which approach do you find more compelling? Why?

2. Jon Katz is the media critic for *Rolling Stone*, a popular entertainment magazine. Bill Moyers is a reporter and an analyst for the Public Broadcasting System (PBS). John Leo is a syndicated columnist and a contributing editor for *U.S. News & World Report*, a national weekly newsmagazine. How might their respective careers account for their differing assessments of the traditional news media? Explain your reasoning.

3. Although Amitai Etzioni believes that telephone voting should be used to supplement America's representative form of government, he cites the "Burke argument" to show why pure direct democracy would not benefit America. What is the Burke argument? Do you agree with it? Why or why not?

Chapter 6

1. Leo Bogart writes that advertising encourages consumerism, while Michael Schudson maintains that social institutions such as the family, the church, and the school have a greater influence on human behavior. Do you believe that advertising influences you to buy particular products? Or do you think social factors—including peer pressure—control your buying habits? Explain.

2. Leo Bogart states that "advertising conveys many other meanings besides its exhortations to buy whatever it is overtly selling," including "mainstream middle-class values" and "the value of physical beauty, health and well-being." Describe two or three advertisements you have recently observed. What meanings did they convey? Did they sell values and lifestyles as well as products?

3. Describe two or three recent purchases that were important to you. Why were they important? Were the products you purchased featured in any advertisements that you can remember seeing? If so, describe the advertisements and try to determine what values they promoted.

Organizations to Contact

The editors have compiled the following list of organizations concerned with the issues debated in this book. The descriptions are derived from materials provided by the organizations. All have publications or information available for interested readers. The list was compiled on the data of publication of the present volume; names, addresses, and phone numbers may change. Be aware that many organizations take several weeks or longer to respond to inquiries, so allow as much time as possible.

Accuracy in Media (AIM)
1275 K St. NW, Suite 1150
Washington, DC 20005
(202) 371-6710
fax: (202) 371-9054

AIM is a conservative media watchdog organization. It researches public complaints on errors of fact made by the news media and requests that such errors be corrected publicly. It publishes the semimonthly *AIM Report* and a weekly syndicated newspaper column.

Adbusters Media Foundation
1243 W. 7th Ave.
Vancouver, BC V6H 1B7
(604) 736-9401

The foundation is a media watchdog organization that criticizes the influence of the advertising industry on society. It publishes the quarterly *Adbusters*, which includes *Big Noise*, a supplement for high school students.

American Advertising Federation (AAF)
1400 K St. NW, Suite 1000
Washington, DC 20005
(202) 898-0089
fax: (202) 898-0159

The federation promotes advertising through education and public relations. It favors self-regulation rather than governmental intervention in the advertising industry. It publishes the quarterly *American Advertising*.

American Society of Newspaper Editors (ASNE)
PO Box 4090
Reston, VA 22090-1700
(703) 648-1144
fax: (703) 620-4557

The society consists of editors in charge of major policy decisions on American daily newspapers. It publishes the *American Society of Newspaper Editors—Bulletin* nine times a year and various research reports, manuals, handbooks, and brochures.

Center for Investigative Reporting (CIR)

530 Howard St., 2d Floor
San Francisco, CA 94105-3007
(415) 543-1200
fax: (415) 543-8311

The center is a group of investigative journalists who cover economic, environmental, social justice, public policy, and constitutional government issues. It produces investigative reports, offers consulting services to news and special interest organizations, and conducts workshops and seminars for investigative journalists. It publishes the periodic *Muckraker: Journal of the Center for Investigative Reporting*.

Center for Media and Public Affairs (CMPA)

2101 L St. NW, Suite 405
Washington, DC 20037
(202) 223-2942
fax: (202) 872-4014

The center is a research organization that studies the media treatment of social and political affairs. It uses surveys to measure the media's influence on public opinion. It publishes the monthly *Media Monitor*, the monograph *A Day of Television Violence*, and various other books, articles, and monographs.

Center for Media and Values

1962 S. Shenandoah
Los Angeles, CA 90034
(310) 559-2944

The center is a media education organization. It seeks to give the public power over the media by fostering media literacy. It publishes the quarterly *Media & Values*.

Fairness and Accuracy in Reporting (FAIR)

130 W. 25th St.
New York, NY 10001
(212) 633-6700
fax: (212) 727-7668

FAIR is a liberal media watchdog organization. It believes that the media are controlled by, and support, corporate and government interests, and that they are insensitive to women, labor, minorities, and other special interest groups. It publishes the periodical *EXTRA!* and the books *Unreliable Sources* and *Adventures in Medialand* and produces the nationally syndicated radio show "CounterSpin."

Freedom Forum Media Studies Center

2950 Broadway
New York, NY 10027-7004
(212) 280-8392

The center is a research organization dedicated to the study of mass communications. It strives to educate the public about the media, to increase media professionalism, and to analyze the effects of the media on society. It publishes numerous conference reports and papers, including *Radio: The Forgotten Medium* and *The Media and Women.*

Media Alliance (MA)

Ft. Mason Center, Bldg. D
San Francisco, CA 94123
(415) 441-2557

The alliance consists of progressive writers, photographers, editors, broadcasters, and public relations workers. It seeks to achieve cooperation among the various practitioners in the media professions. It publishes the bimonthly newsletter *MediaFile* and the quarterly *Propaganda Review.*

Media Network (MN)

39 W. 14th St., Suite 403
New York, NY 10011
(212) 929-2663

The network consists of filmmakers, teachers, students, social workers, community organizers, special-cause activists, and other groups and individuals. It seeks to initiate social change by educating the public about the influence of the media in their lives and by presenting alternative, progressive views not offered by mainstream media outlets. It publishes the quarterly *Immediate Impact.*

Media Research Center

113 S. West St.
Alexandria, VA 22314
(703) 683-9733
fax: (703) 683-9736

The center is a conservative media watchdog organization that documents what it perceives as liberal bias in the news and entertainment media. It publishes the monthly newsletters *Media Watch,* which focuses on the news media, and *TV, Etc.,* which examines the Hollywood entertainment media.

Morality in Media (MIM)

475 Riverside Dr.
New York, NY 10115
(212) 870-3222

MIM is a group that opposes what it considers to be indecency in broadcasting—especially pornography. It works to educate and organize the public in support of strict indecency laws, and it has launched an annual "turn off TV day" to protest offensive television programming. It publishes the *Morality in Media Newsletter* and the handbook *TV: The World's Greatest Mind-Bender.*

National Association of Black Journalists (NABJ)
11600 Sunrise Valley Dr.
Reston, VA 22091
(703) 648-1270
fax: (703) 476-6245

NABJ is an organization of news media employees that seeks to increase the role of blacks in the news media, to point out the "institutionalized racism" in the news industry, and to improve the quality of reporting on the black community. It publishes the *NABJ Journal* ten times a year.

National Coalition Against Censorship (NCAC)
275 7th Ave.
New York, NY 10001
(212) 807-NCAC
fax: (212) 807-6245

NCAC is an alliance of organizations committed to defending freedom of thought, inquiry, and expression by engaging in public education advocacy on national and local levels. It believes that censorship of violent materials is dangerous because it represses intellectual and artistic freedom. Its publications include *Censorship News* and *Report on Book Censorship Litigation in Public Schools*.

National Coalition on Television Violence (NCTV)
PO Box 2157
Champaign, IL 61825
(217) 384-1920

NCTV is a research and education association dedicated to reducing the violence in films and television programming. It distributes ratings, reviews, and violence research. It publishes the quarterly *NCTV News* and the bimonthly *Research Press Release*.

National Council of Teachers of English (NCTE)
Committee on Public Doublespeak
1111 Kenyon Rd.
Urbana, IL 61801
(217) 328-3870
fax: (217) 328-9645

The committee consists of English, rhetoric, and semantics teachers critical of "doublespeak" ("language used to lie or mislead while pretending to tell the truth") in the media. The committee monitors public discourse in the media for examples of such language. It publishes the *Quarterly Review of Doublespeak*.

Society for the Eradication of Television (SET)
PO Box 10491
Oakland, CA 94610-0491
(415) 763-8712

The society consists of households devoid of a working television set. It believes that television is an addictive presence that harms people's inner lives, disrupts human relations, and wastes time. It publishes *SET Free: The Newsletter Against Television* and various pamphlets, manuals, and leaflets.

Student Press Law Center (SPLC)
1735 Eye St. NW, Suite 504
Washington, DC 20006
(202) 466-5242
fax: (202) 466-6326

The center seeks to ensure the First Amendment rights of high school and college journalists. It offers information and legal advice concerning censorship to students and teachers. It publishes the newsletter *Student Press Law Center—Report*, the booklets *Rights, Restrictions and Responsibilities* and *Access to Campus Crime Reports*, and the book *Law of the Student Press*.

Women's Institute for Freedom of the Press (WIFP)
3306 Ross Pl. NW
Washington, DC 20008
(202) 966-7783

WIFP is a network of women concerned with freedom of the press and democracy in the world's communications systems. It advocates restructuring communications systems in order to allow women the opportunity to speak for themselves. The institute publishes the booklets *Media Without Democracy, and What to Do About It* and *The Source of Power for Women: A Strategy to Equalize Media Outreach*, and other publications.

Bibliography of Books

Kiku Adatto	*Picture Perfect: The Art and Artifice of Public Image Making.* New York: Basic Books, 1993.
Donna Allen	*Media Without Democracy: And What to Do About It.* Washington, DC: Women's Institute for Freedom of the Press, 1991.
Ken Auletta	*Three Blind Mice: How the TV Networks Lost Their Way.* New York: Random House, 1991.
Robert K. Avery and David Eason, eds.	*Critical Perspectives on Media and Society.* New York: Guilford Press, 1991.
Ben H. Bagdikian	*The Media Monopoly.* 4th ed. Boston: Beacon Press, 1992.
David Bianculli	*Teleliteracy: Taking Television Seriously.* New York: Continuum Publishing, 1992.
L. Brent Bozell III and Brent H. Baker, eds.	*And That's the Way It Is(n't): A Reference Guide to Media Bias.* Alexandria, VA: Media Research Center, 1990.
Noam Chomsky	*Necessary Illusions: Thought Control in Democratic Societies.* Boston: South End Press, 1989.
George Comstock	*Television and the American Child.* San Diego, CA: Academic Press, Inc., 1991.
Sammy R. Danna, ed.	*Advertising and Popular Culture: Studies in Variety and Versatility.* Bowling Green, OH: Bowling Green State University Popular Press, 1992.
Jannette L. Dates and William Barlow, eds.	*Split Image: African Americans in the Mass Media.* Washington, DC: Howard University Press, 1990.
Douglas Davis	*The Five Myths of Television Power: Or Why the Medium Is Not the Message.* New York: Simon & Schuster, 1993.
Murray Edelman	*Constructing the Political Spectacle.* Chicago: University of Chicago Press, 1988.
Jib Fowles	*Why Viewers Watch: A Reappraisal of Television's Effects.* Rev. ed. of *Television Viewers vs. Media Snobs.* Newbury Park, CA: Sage Publications, 1992.
Michael G. Gartner	*Advertising and the First Amendment.* New York: Priority Press, 1989.
George Gilder	*Life After Television: The Coming Transformation of Media and American Life.* New York: W.W. Norton, 1990.

296

Doris A. Graber	*Mass Media and American Politics*. 4th ed. Washington, DC: Congressional Quarterly Inc., 1993.
Mike Gunderloy and Cari Goldberg Janice	*The World of Zines*. New York: Penguin, 1992.
Edward S. Herman	*Beyond Hypocrisy: Decoding the News in an Age of Propaganda, with a Doublespeak Dictionary for the 1990s*. Boston: South End Press, 1992.
Alan Hirsch	*Talking Heads: Television's Political Talk Shows and Pundits*. New York: St. Martin's Press, 1991.
Aletha C. Huston et al.	*Big World, Small Screen: The Role of Television in American Society*. Lincoln: University of Nebraska Press, 1992.
Shanto Iyengar	*Is Anyone Responsible? How Television Frames Political Issues*. Chicago: University of Chicago Press, 1991.
Kathleen Hall Jamieson	*Dirty Politics: Deception, Distraction, and Democracy*. New York: Oxford University Press, 1992.
Kathleen Hall Jamieson	*Packaging the President: A History and Criticism of Presidential Campaign Advertising*. 2d ed. New York: Oxford University Press, 1992.
Sut Jhally and Justin Lewis	*Enlightened Racism:* The Cosby Show, *Audiences, and the Myth of the American Dream*. Boulder, CO: Westview Press, 1992.
Douglas Kellner	*Television and the Crisis of Democracy*. Boulder, CO: Westview Press, 1990.
Wilson Bryan Key	*The Age of Manipulation: The Con in Confidence, the Sin in Sincerity*. New York: Henry Holt and Company, 1989.
Wilson Bryan Key	*Subliminal Seduction*. New York: Prentice-Hall, 1973.
Howard Kurtz	*Media Circus: The Trouble with America's Newspapers*. New York: Times Books, 1993.
Martin A. Lee and Norman Solomon	*Unreliable Sources*. New York: Carol Publishing Group, 1990.
Judith Lichtenberg, ed.	*Democracy and the Mass Media: A Collection of Essays*. New York: Cambridge University Press, 1990.
S. Robert Lichter, Linda S. Lichter, and Stanley Rothman	*Watching America: What Television Tells Us About Our Lives*. New York: Prentice Hall Press, 1991.
S. Robert Lichter, Stanley Rothman, and Linda S. Lichter	*The Media Elite: America's New Powerbrokers*. New York: Hastings House, 1990.

John R. MacArthur	*Second Front: Censorship and Propaganda in the Gulf War.* New York: Hill and Wang, 1992.
Mathew D. McCubbins, ed.	*Under the Watchful Eye: Managing Presidential Campaigns in the Television Era.* Washington, DC: Congressional Quarterly Inc., 1992.
Bill McKibben	*The Age of Missing Information.* New York: Random House, 1993.
Lloyd J. Matthews, ed.	*Newsmen and National Defense: Is Conflict Inevitable?* McLean, VA: Brassey's (US), 1991.
Michael Medved	*Hollywood vs. America: Popular Culture and the War on Traditional Values.* New York: HarperCollins, 1992.
Jill Nelson	*Volunteer Slavery: My Authentic Negro Experience.* Chicago: Noble Press, 1993.
Joyce Nelson	*The Perfect Machine: Television and the Bomb.* Philadelphia: New Society Publishers, 1992.
W. Russell Neuman, Marion R. Just, and Ann N. Crigler	*Common Knowledge: News and the Construction of Political Meaning.* Chicago: University of Chicago Press, 1992.
Michael Parenti	*Inventing Reality: The Politics of the News Media.* 2d ed. New York: St. Martin's Press, 1993.
Anthony R. Pratkanis and Elliot Aronson	*Age of Propaganda: The Everyday Use and Abuse of Persuasion.* New York: W.H. Freeman and Company, 1992.
Andrea L. Press	*Women Watching Television: Gender, Class, and Generation in the American Television Experience.* Philadelphia: University of Pennsylvania Press, 1991.
Jay Rosen and Paul Taylor	*The New News v. the Old News: The Press and Politics in the 1990s.* New York: Twentieth Century Fund, 1992.
Tom Rosenstiel	*Strange Bedfellows: How Television and the Presidential Candidates Changed American Politics, 1992.* New York: Hyperion, 1993.
Charlotte Ryan	*Prime Time Activism: Media Strategies for Grassroots Organizing.* Boston: South End Press, 1991.
Larry J. Sabato	*Feeding Frenzy: How Attack Journalism Has Transformed American Politics.* New York: The Free Press, 1991.
Herbert Schiller	*Culture, Inc.: The Corporate Takeover of Public Expression.* New York: Oxford University Press, 1989.

Michael Schudson	*Advertising, the Uneasy Persuasion.* New York: Basic Books, 1984.
Michelangelo Signorile	*Queer in America: Sex, the Media, and the Closets of Power.* New York: Random House, 1993.
Christa Daryl Slaton	*Televote: Expanding Citizen Participation in the Quantum Age.* New York: Praeger, 1992.
Anthony Smith	*The Age of Behemoths: The Globalization of Mass Media Firms.* New York: Twentieth Century Fund, 1991.
Lawrence C. Soley	*The News Shapers: The Sources Who Explain the News.* New York: Praeger, 1992.
James D. Squires	*Read All About It! The Corporate Takeover of America's Newspapers.* New York: Times Books, 1993.
Doug Underwood	*When MBAs Rule the Newsroom: What the Marketers and the Managers Are Doing to Today's Newspapers.* New York: Columbia University Press, 1993.

Index

women
actresses, during 1930s, 89
advertising messages about, 265
African-American, 118
employed, 85, 99
film portrayals of
are more positive than men's
103-104
as capable, 103-105
as seeking marriage, 99-101
as unhappy in careers, 93-94
as villains, 90, 104, 105
during 1970s, 89-91
have broadened, 101-102
reflect social changes, 213-217
journalists, 47, 50-51
TV's portrayal of, 81, 82, 118

Zanot, Eric J., 272